BEYOND

— THE —

PETTUS

BRIDGE

Trish Dolasinski, Ed.D.

Publishing Services provided by Paper Raven Books LLC

Printed in the United States of America

First Printing, 2022

Hardback ISBN: 979-8-9855060-1-3
Paperback ISBN: 979-8-9855060-0-6

PRAISE FOR
BEYOND THE PETTUS BRIDGE

"An effective story of the courage and sisterhood that helped blur stark racial lines in 1960s America. Readers will close Beyond the Pettus Bridge *with an appreciation for how far the nation has come and renewed hope for an even better future."*

-Jessica McCann, award-winning author of
All Different Kinds of Free and Peculiar Savage Beauty

*"*Beyond the Pettus Bridge *by Trish Dolasinski is an exploration of several relatable themes: racial relations, transitions, sacrifice, sisterhood, loss, and reconciliation. Dolasinski expertly navigates the terrain of these complicated topics with characters that linger in the reader's mind. Ultimately, the novel gives shape to what it means to hope in an uncertain landscape."*

-Rudri Bhatt Patel, Writer and Co-Founder/Co-Editor of *The Sunlight Press*

"When Northern teacher Claire Zuretski attempts to bridge the racial and social divides in her new hometown of Selma, Alabama, she encounters dangerous intimidation and fear for her life while striving to adjust to life in the South. An emotionally gripping story with twists and turns, Beyond the Pettis Bridge, *presents an honest, compelling portrayal of the racially charged atmosphere of 1969 Selma, exposing layers of social injustice and prejudice that set Claire on a journey toward reconciliation and healing that she never dreamed she would take.*

-Anita Bunkley , Author of *The Twisted Crown* and award-winning author of over 30 novels in the historical context from the Afro-centric perspective

"Congratulations to Trish Dolasinski for bringing this story to the public. It is encouraging to know Southern white women worked to end racism in the south when it was a dangerous path to follow. Black and white need to know and remember these stories of the brave men and women of both races who worked for equality for all."

-Gloria Markette Ed. D., Assistant Professor Retired, Bethune Cookman University

"In 1969, a young white teacher from the North, Claire Zuretski, finds herself unexpectedly embroiled in the local politics of Selma, Alabama, when she takes a job in an all-Black school. Refusing to bend to social pressures to quit her job, she befriends women of all races who are working quietly behind the scenes to unite the community. Ultimately, she learns that the solidarity of sisterhood can be a powerful force for change in the face of deep-rooted prejudice and discrimination. I loved this story of hope and found myself rooting for Claire as she summoned the courage to speak out for justice and equality—a message still needed in America today."

-Susan Pohlman, Author *Halfway to Each Other* and *A Time to Seek*

"A young, white, Northern transplant—a newlywed, and new teacher— finds herself caught up in civil rights history in this engrossing novel by Trish Dolasinski. From the beginning, the author draws us into the Southern landscape with all of its charm and all of its ugliness. Dolasinski gives the reader a genuine heroine, Claire, who doesn't move to Selma with an agenda to fight racial injustice. She's not trying to fix anyone; she's simply trying to do the right thing. This is a story, not often told, from a point of view not often represented, and here it's done with sensitivity and fairness."

-Dana Johnson, retired educator, and avid reader

Photo courtesy of Roma Swenson

ACKNOWLEDGMENTS

Living the foundation of this story fifty years ago, I had no idea I'd ever write a book about the extraordinary experience my husband, Frank, and I had during the late 1960s—newly married, just out of college, and expecting our first child. The times were tumultuous with civil unrest in Detroit and Los Angeles and a war far away in Vietnam. As the years have flown by and much of a fulfilling and happy life has transpired, the memories remained and begged to be shared from the voice of this *Yankee* teacher, wife, and mother... now, grandmother! Perhaps at this time more than ever we need to be reminded of the value of hope in humanity and to see the outcome of Dr. King's words: *I have a dream...*

What is particularly extraordinary and outstanding, is my fortuitous encounter with Elizabeth L. Bostick, Ph.D., Alabama resident, university professor, and a believer of what can be if people work together, with underlying loving hearts. Her research and willingness to share her discovery of the underground sisterhood with me provided the main theme of this fictional portrayal of the times. I am eternally grateful to Dr. Bostick who generously offered her knowledge, her thesis, and her encouragement.

Writing is a solitary endeavor, while the completion of this novel has been the result of much guidance, expertise, and support throughout this eleven-year journey to the finish line. It would take pages for me to recognize all the people who have inspired me, taught me, critiqued my drafts, and supported my work in completing *Beyond the Pettus Bridge*. Traveling back to Selma with Frank in 2011, I was able to talk to many citizens who lived in the city during the 1960s, as well as those who were younger. These wonderful people openly and willingly shared their memories and experiences surrounding life in the Deep South. In addition, I was honored and humbled to have a chance to learn through conversations with residents who were both black and white, including educators, and senior citizens who lived in Selma prior to Civil Rights legislation, as well as business and municipal leaders. Thank you!

I am grateful for the mentorship of Susan Pohlman, Windy Lynn Harris, Rudri Patel, Betty Webb, and Carol Test. Stuart Horwitz guided me in novel structure, while the careful perusal of copy editor Nancy Prenzno fine-tuned my manuscript. How fortunate I was to meet author Anita Bunkley at an Arizona State University writer's conference. Anita writes African American historical fiction and was a thoughtful and generous developmental editor who guided my references and phrasing surrounding both storyline and racial reference. Dana Johnson, African American English teacher, and a voracious reader was invaluable in her review and encouragement of my novel. Thanks so much to the team at Paper Raven Books, especially Karen Furr my resourceful project manager—they made the professional and practical matter of how to get a novel published flow so smoothly!

Thank you to all the writer friends who have offered feedback and have encouraged me toward the completion of the novel. You have played a huge role in motivating my writing, and I am grateful for your support and your endearing friendship. Lastly, I am eternally grateful to my family for their belief in me. My husband of over fifty years is my rock and has been behind me 100% of the way! His keen pragmatic nature has also given me perspective and clarity. We lived this story together, and he willingly relived the memories through my writing. My children, Brian (and wife, Michelle) and Debbie (and husband, Tom), have been my cheerleaders and my sounding boards—I am blessed to have you. Finally, my cherished grandchildren who wanted Mimi to finish this novel: George, Nicholas, Ted, Jacob, David, Annie, Maya, and Jane. I love you all.

"Once you choose hope, anything's possible."

Christopher Reeves

CHAPTER 1

My husband of eighty-five days tightened his grip on the steering wheel as we slipped past the WELCOME TO *SWEET* SELMA, ALABAMA sign. The skinny envelope that set this journey in motion had accidentally gotten stuck between the pages of my recent *Glamour* magazine. I recalled how it spilled onto the new orange shag rug in our flat back home, and it felt like someone had kicked me in the gut.

Noting his furrowed brow and pursed lips, I grunted and said, "If only I'd ripped that draft board summons into shreds and flushed it down the toilet, maybe they would have forgotten about you. Forgotten about us."

"Hah. Fat chance, babe," Bruce feigned a grin at my attempt at humor.

A metallic thud punctuated his outburst. "What's that?" Instinctively, I grabbed at my belly to protect a baby that was no longer there. The scraping sound from beneath the car intensified, and Bruce slackened our speed to a crawl.

"Don't know, but it doesn't sound good." He grimaced, glaring straight ahead.

As our '64 Ford Custom 500 scuttled along the highway, we got a closer look at the shanties that hugged the fringes of the road. Strewn about the landscape, the dwellings flapped a sorrowful assortment of loose shingles, with plywood porches leaning into the dirt. The windows opened to darkness—dull eyes void of hope.

With raised eyebrows, Bruce lowered the volume on the

radio as the newscaster announced this historical day "… *Today, March 25, heralds the fourth anniversary of the march from Selma to Montgomery. On this day, Dr. Martin Luther King…*" I clearly recalled that ominous day as I watched the event on television at the Tri Zeta sorority house, two thousand miles away. I missed college life. Hanging out. Being cool. Debating what to wear was a major morning dilemma. Military life wasn't part of my plan. Nor was living in the Deep South.

Bruce's voice brought me back to our current reality. "Here's hopin' we can find a gas station before whatever it is, gets worse," he said. His wish was throttled as the engine sputtered loudly and steam escaped in puffs from beneath the hood. Bruce snatched a rag from under the seat and leaped from the car, dropping to his knees to peer under the frame.

As I hopped out of the car to see what I could do, a white pickup navigated toward us. Expecting the men inside would stop and offer a hand or give us a lift to a gas station sent a glimmer of hope. Yet, without a second glance, the driver gunned the engine and drove on, kicking up dust in his wake.

Bruce jumped to his feet and shouted, "What the hell! Trying to kill us? Damn jerks!"

I rushed to his side and stretched my arm around his waist, gently offering, "They are sure in a big hurry for something."

Bruce closed his eyes and wiped his brow with his shirt sleeve. "Let's give it another try. Hop in, honey."

After a few key rotations, the engine growled and kicked into gear.

"Buckle up! Let's go for it," he said.

Embraced by his confidence and protective words, including joyful trepidation, I complied. An only child raised by his grandmother, Bruce was an instinctive caregiver. He was also a promising architect who received two coveted awards at graduation. In search of the nearest mechanic, we crept along the highway toward a densely wooded area. Still the only car on the road.

"Looks like there's life here." I pointed toward clotheslines with colorful dresses hanging by the shoulders, threadbare towels. Off-white sheets flapped gently, as a row of diapers and baby sleepers tugged their weight on another line. A clothespin holding one pink cotton sleeper snapped, with the second barely holding the other shoulder on the line. The sight made my empty womb ache. Other baby clothes hung proudly on the line, so still in their stance.

Dabbing at the wells pooling in the corners of my eyes, I saw two young women clutching opposite handles of a large metal bucket, laundry spilling over the sides. The older of the two wore a red bandanna and looked about my age. Giggling and bending over, she snatched the apron strings of the smaller girl who tumbled to the ground. In barely blinking time, she was back on her feet and reached her lanky arm toward the taller girl's bandanna. She missed. The chase began. They headed toward an empty clothesline hidden behind two giant oak trees. Rather oblivious of the female activity surrounding him, a young boy sat with his back against one of the massive trunks. Horn-rimmed glasses consumed his face as he pored over the pages of a book held close to his nose. A few more shabby, thatched dwellings stood tucked in among trees and shrubs.

We turned away from the wooded area and glided into the driveway of a weathered building with dangling peels of paint and a faded sign that read GAS. We looked at each other in semi-relief, but with the same unspoken "what-choice-do-we-have" question, and hopped out of the car.

Bruce poked a thumb in the direction of three white pickups parked off the side of the road. "Looks like our race-track truck driver likely reached his destination."

"And he has lots of company," I added, raising my eyebrows and scanning the scene for signs of life.

Soon a thin, aging man sauntered up from behind the building, hands jammed in overall pockets.

He snatched the dangling cigarette from his mouth and said, "Fill 'er up, sir?" The attendant grinned hopefully, revealing the few yellowed teeth he had left.

Bruce described the noisy sound, and the mechanic examined the underside of the Ford. Diagnosing a broken clamp, he explained how it likely caused the exhaust pipe to drop. Noting the heat on the hood, he said the engine also needed to be checked. Leaving the passenger seat, I stood limply next to the two men wondering what this hiccup meant to our plans. We didn't know much about car mechanics, but it sounded like the station guy did.

"Shouldn't take more than an hour or so to fix. Y'all make yourselves at home," he said with an assured glance in our direction. With a slight nod and a cap adjustment, he turned away. The only available seats were at a splintered picnic table perched alongside the road.

After a few steps and as if he'd forgotten to say something, the mechanic placed five grime-filled nail beds on his bony hip. He peered at our Michigan license plate.

"What on earth are y'all doin' out here in the sticks? All the way from up North. I'll be danged." His gaze shifted beyond us as if looking for someone. His friendly inquiry didn't match his body language.

"I'm in the Air Force. Got a draft notice. The Air Force offered the possibility for entrance into Officer Training School, so here I am at Craig Air Force Base."

"Oh, yeah. Gotta work your way up the ladder, son." He flashed a smile as he turned his eyes toward Bruce.

"Although this stint may not have been our choice, it is

much better than being an army grunt and slogging through rice paddies," said Bruce. "Although a lot of good men are doing just that right now," he added in a more somber tone.

I knew Bruce loved our country. Military life just wasn't part of our plan. He wouldn't think of taking off for Canada to dodge the draft like many guys were doing.

Lightening up the mood, I chimed in, "We've only been married a few months, too." Warmth filled my cheeks as a proud smile crept across my face.

The mechanic looked more thoughtful for the moment and nodded with exaggerated respect. "Mighty fine. Yup. Sure are lots of folks down here at the base, with Vietnam and all."

He stood rubbing his jaw as he chewed harder and glanced about the wooded space. Noticing the parked pickups, he suddenly startled with a jerk and lowered his voice as if he had a secret to share.

"Things just ain't the same as they used to be." His voice trailed off, then he seemed to collect himself and stood a little taller. "You just need to be careful in these parts. 'Specially with this pretty young lady here." With a wink in my direction, he spun around and went to get his toolbox.

Bruce shrugged and took my hand. "Don't know what he's talking about. Shall we saunter as we wait, *pretty young lady*?" He brushed a dangling curl from my forehead.

"Why not?" I replied with a tilt of my head and looking up into his sometimes-blue, sometimes-green eyes. Fingers interlaced, we walked up the nearby dirt road that led into a sanctuary of trees.

The drive from Shepard Air Force Base in Texas where Bruce was assigned after basic training had been tiring and tedious. In Texas, we lived in a trailer for a month—not exactly fancy digs. My parents would have been appalled, and I recalled exaggerating the truth when I spoke to my mother on the phone.

"We've got lovely temporary housing here in Texas, Mother. So fun to travel around the country," I had chimed. *Information and enthusiasm. Check.*

She had hesitated for a moment, then spoke, "Well, I'm glad to hear it." Immediately she continued with a refresher about how she and Dad had gotten the deposit returned when we canceled our wedding date.

"Cancelling your wedding reception with a formal sit-down dinner for 350 wedding guests was nothing to ignore, my dear. Good thing your father knows people in the business, and we were able to reschedule for the earlier date you both wanted—with no added cost," she had said.

For at least the fiftieth time, I voiced appreciation for all my parents had done for us and apologized. Mother didn't probe further about our living arrangements. *What would I soon need to say about our home in Selma?*

My angst subsided as we ambled among the swaying veils of weeping willows and Spanish moss. Bruce's intertwined fingers tightened around mine. Fresh air brought a wave of freedom, regardless of the military orders that interfered with the late summer wedding date. Truth be told, the main reason for moving the date forward was my pregnancy. *My parents never knew that part.*

"Bruce, did you notice the two girls carrying a laundry basket back near the edge of the forest? They looked like sisters having fun together." The scene felt like a movie set.

"No. Too busy praying for a miracle to save the Ford." He looked down at the ground as he ran his fingers through spikes of his hair still growing in after boot camp. With a sudden awareness, he continued, "Maybe those girls made you think about when you and Lucy were little."

"Not much these days," I grunted. "But there was a time before our pup Trixie died. Lucy tried to teach Trixie to fetch tennis balls, with me as her assistant." I winced. "Those times were before Dad became president of the electric company and Mother became his social attaché." I rolled my eyes. I didn't add how Lucy, the ambitious labor lawyer, and five and a half years my senior, fit neatly into the mold my mother had envisioned. *Little Claire did not.*

A sudden rustling intruded upon the silence. An eerie sensation prickled the fine hair on my arms. The engulfing solitude of the forest became a delusion as the rustling intensified. I tugged a chunk of black hair behind my ear and looked skyward. My husband stood an inch taller and tugged at his jeans.

"You look like you've seen a ghost. Let's get back to the station." He clasped my hand.

As I trekked behind him, a pungent whiff of burnt leaves assaulted my nostrils. "Do you smell that?" I asked covering my nose.

Before Bruce could respond, crackling sparks danced among the trees and the visible intermittent shanties in the woods. Our eyes bounced from one flicker to another, each an ominous sparkle, competing for attention. A shriek sliced through the air. The mingling of burning wood and fusty odors hung over us like a sour washrag. Instantly a gush of flames burst skyward, swallowing branches and devouring limbs. Dozens of people emerged from nowhere, including the two girls I had seen. With clenched hands, they darted through the depths of the forest. The young boy following behind them tripped and scrambled about the leaves and branches.

"There they are. The two sisters and that little boy. Look, he fell. Bet he dropped his book too." The girls didn't seem to notice the boy had fallen. Releasing my fingers from his grip, I leaped over a rock and charged past the billowy arms of a weeping willow. The boy pulled and tugged at fallen limbs on the ground. With a couple of strides, Bruce reached for my arm, pinching my skin.

"Ouch!"

"Stop, Claire! Are you crazy?"

I glared at him. "The little boy doesn't see very well, Bruce. The fire is raging. He could burn, for God's sake."

Jerking from his grip, I stumbled toward the trees. As I looked back toward Bruce, I saw him trip, then catch himself before hitting the ground. Sweat from his brow dripped into thick eyebrows, knitted painfully together. With torn emotions, I rushed back toward my husband.

He struggled to his feet and gripped my shoulders. "Claire, we need to get back to the station, now. We'll call the fire department and let them do their job."

Paralyzed with indecision in the wake of his tone, I turned toward the little boy. A distinguished, older gentleman helped him up to his feet, a book with faded ribbons dangling beneath pages tightly tucked under his arm. I watched the older man raise his eyes toward the heavens, parting his lips gently. His manner offered a sense of tranquility, and Bruce pulled me close. I felt the pounding of his heart as it thumped against my chest.

"I bet that man is a preacher," I said.

"One is certainly needed," Bruce whispered as he buried his head into my hair and asked God to intervene. I thought how it would take a miracle to help these people.

Arms about each other, we hurried toward the path where we saw several men emerge from the trees. They sprinted across the road toward white pickups, a couple of station wagons, and a bright red Corvette. On their heels, a speeding fire truck and an ambulance whirled up to the scene. Firemen quickly emerged, tugging at hoses as they hurried toward the spiraling flames.

"Thank God!" I coughed from the smoke that now surrounded us. Bruce handed me his handkerchief. A faint scent of Old Spice lingered but offered little solace. His grip tightened around my elbow as he steered us away from the blaze.

Tripping over the twine-like underbrush, I saw the medical crew maneuver a stretcher toward the ambulance with a clear view of the victim. He was a large man, feet dangling beyond the edge of the stretcher with yards of bloodstained fabric tossed over his moaning body. The cuts on his face did not hide his skin color. He was white. So was the robe he was wearing.

CHAPTER 2

Winded, we approached the station. The sole mechanic sat on our front bumper, cigarette dangling from one hand while he dabbed a yellowed rag across his wrinkled brow with his other. "Sure glad to see those big red trucks."

He tugged a drag from the Camel as if seeking strength to go on. "A few more minutes, my station and your car wudda been history."

He stood up, eyes bulging toward us and absent-mindedly scrubbed at the back of his thin neck.

"Glad we're all safe!" Bruce spoke more to himself than anyone else as he yanked out his wallet from a hip pocket, eager to pay and leave.

"How did it start? Did a camper forget to put out a fire, maybe?" I asked.

No one in my family would ever consider camping in the woods, but everybody knew about Smokey Bear and careless campers. These seemingly innocent questions camouflaged a painful memory from a previous historic summer evening in Detroit. It was also the evening Bruce proposed.

In July of 1967, the city was under a curfew due to civil disorder. Blocks of stores and houses were destroyed by fire overnight. Vigilant members of the black community were outraged with living conditions and the available job opportunities. White flight to the suburbs had reduced the flourishing economy in many inner-city traditional, old money neighborhoods.

"Told y'all 'bout bein' careful." The pitched voice and single raised eyebrow of the mechanic jabbed shards across my back. As if his face had been smacked, he glared in my direction midway through counting dollar bills into my husband's palm. With a purposeful turn, while giving Bruce his change, he stood as erect as his thin frame would allow.

Bruce jangled his keys as he came to my defense. "It seems odd that there was…well, quite a mix of people hidden in those woods."

Reinforced, I continued, "Yeah, lots of colored folks running to escape. We also saw some white men, and one was hurt. Took him away on a stretcher. Hope he's okay."

Nodding his head, the mechanic concurred, "Yes'm. Likely some sort of men's meetin' in them woods. Yup. It's all quite a ceremony." Slower nod. "They're always careful, 'course." His demeanor had shifted, and he even chuckled, like it was not unusual for the group to be in the woods. "As fer the fire, probably got started by one of those nigras hopped up on liquor and smokin' a pipe." With a grimace, he shook his head from side to side. Disgusted.

"Anaway, I'm sure it'll be fine." He nodded glancing at us flashing a pasted, vulpine smile that took over his entire face. "Well, you folks take care now, ya hear?" He gave another brief nod, indicating that the transaction was over.

"Let's go, honey," said Bruce. "We need to get something to eat before we go out to see the housing units. Thank you, sir. Much obliged."

The mechanic flashed the same big, yellow-toothed grin. "By the by, if y'all are lookin' for some good eatin', Dottie's Place is the best in town. All home cooked. Order the biscuits and gravy. Pure manna from heaven." He smacked a kiss on his fingers and tossed the gesture heavenward.

"Thanks, again," said Bruce. "We've got an appointment to see some housing near the base. But will sure keep Dottie's Place in mind." He took my hand and moved toward the Ford.

I felt steel-gray eyes rivet our backs. When we got to the car, I turned to look out of the rear window. The mechanic had disappeared into the station. Through the grimy window, I saw him on the phone, a cigarette dangling from a side of his lip, head nodding. As Bruce turned the key in the ignition, the mechanic looked up. Our eyes connected, sending menacing sensations that left a raw queasiness in my gut.

Bruce revved the engine and kicked up dust as we took off.

"Why did you drill him like that, honey? This is not any of our business. We're not on a mission to save the world here."

"Okay, Bruce. So, we're supposed to act as if nothing happened and go merrily on our way?" My heart was racing. "Just bet those white guys we saw were up to no good. Maybe they even wanted to kill all those colored people. And to listen to the mechanic, you'd think it was the people that lived in the forest who were to blame."

"Oh, come on, that's ridiculous. You've been reading too many novels. You're letting your imagination get the upper hand over your reasoning."

I glanced at Bruce's profile, with his prominent forehead and square chin. "I think we should report what we saw to the police."

"Please stop it, Claire." He clutched the steering wheel and shot me a dismissive look. "Don't we have enough to handle right now?"

I sighed and glanced out the passenger window. "Yes, something bigger and uglier and more troubling. But how could we simply ignore it?"

"Look, babe, let's not make our lives more complicated by sticking our noses into something that is bigger than both of us," Bruce said.

Bruce maneuvered the car toward town. As we turned onto Main Street, the blinking neon letters on the restaurant, DOTTIE'S PLACE, beckoned. Neither of us was very hungry, even though we hadn't eaten since morning.

"Do you want to stop?" Bruce asked. Before I could answer, he continued, "I'd like to get to the base and check out the housing situation."

"Right. Let's go see about housing," I said with a reluctant shrug. We needed to get settled.

Bruce sped slightly to make up for the lost time, eager to get to the Family Housing Office before it closed. Maneuvering through traffic, however, we got stuck behind a parade of pickups.

"I've never seen so many pickup trucks in one place in my whole life. Especially with rifles mounted in the rear windows."

"That's because you are a Northern city girl who has been protected from redneck culture," said Bruce as he waved a *what-da-ya expect* hand in the air.

Bruce liked to jibe about my rich family as if it was an award-winning life trophy. Not sure if he really understood what it was like to live in the shadow of *Miss Perfect Lucy*—the class valedictorian, the homecoming queen, the first call for *Big Man on Campus* dates. Plus, Lucy did every proper thing Mother expected. She would never get pregnant before she was married. *Of course not.* I wrinkled my nose. But I had *the* handsome husband. A smile, then it faded with the remembrance that we had lost our baby. My chin cupped within the palms of my hands, I stared straight ahead, mixed emotions churning beneath the surface. No one would know the truth about our baby's pre-nuptial conception.

The paved highway made the drive easy. It was even pleasant with weeping willows drenched in remnants of a spring rainstorm from the night before. A grimy old truck swerved onto the highway from an intersecting dirt road and tossed chunks of mud in every direction.

"Ugh!" Bruce coughed. We could smell the dank, musty mildew.

"At least the pasture manure that dragged along on our ride from Texas is gone," I said shaking my head.

A cluster of charred shanties dotted the highway, a blatant reminder of what we had seen in the woods upon our entry into Selma. I adjusted the volume on the radio.

"Let's remember to get a newspaper tomorrow and see what's reported about the fire."

"So, what will you do if the article doesn't appear or isn't written as you expected?" Bruce spoke each word of his question with exaggerated precision.

I stammered, "Well, I'd like to see how the people are doing and maybe how it started. Something. Wouldn't you?" Considering his comment, I spun my head, eyes wide.

He raised his brows and glared into my eyes as he spoke, "Honestly, I just want to get us settled right now."

Practical Bruce. Always thinking about our well-being. I appreciated his answer and reached over to rub his shoulder. "I know this tour of enlisted duty is for four years. But it could be a year or less if you are admitted to Officer Training School like the recruiter said could happen."

"Yeah. Let's hope someone notices my degree and I get an offer." He pursed his lips.

I peered into the gray Alabama River as we drove across a bridge. Lazy, murky waves ruffled below us, while a couple of colored teens tossed and tugged their fishing poles along the shoreline. The sign over the bridge read: EDMUND PETTUS BRIDGE. I thought about the stories the bridge could tell if it could speak.

"Wow! Martin Luther King's famous march started right here on this exact bridge," I said.

Bruce snarled, "That march was ugly. All those cops and guard dogs and fire hoses. It wasn't very peaceful, or non-violent."

The scene Bruce described was visible to the world through the wonders of television, making all of us witnesses to history. I wondered what Edmund Pettus would think of the bridge that was his namesake. I planned to look up Mr. Pettus and learn more.

"Lots of people paid a big price for freedom," Bruce almost whispered. I didn't think Bruce heard what I had said about Mr. Pettus. I wondered if he was now thinking more about the Vietnam War than the civil rights movement.

"Seems like civil rights haven't changed much here, though," I continued to pursue the topic.

"Let's forget about the world's problems," said Bruce. He reached up and grabbed hold of my waving fingers and planted a *hang-in-there-baby* smooch across my wedding band.

"Hmm." I sighed and closed my eyes.

"Hey, that finger looks swollen. Maybe you should take the band off, hon."

"Naw. I hate to do that. I just got it." I grinned. *So there, Lucy!* "It's probably due to the heat and some weight gain. Pretty normal." ... *for better or for worse, for richer, for poorer.* The ring would stay, and I anticipated *for richer* when Bruce became an officer.

Nagging lyrics of the popular *Harper Valley PTA* tune twanged over the scratchy radio waves until we stopped at a traffic light. Along with the Southern music tune, the sudden rich aromas of gardenia and jasmine that wafted into the car reminded me of where we were. The mixture of scents was like the bouquet of my mother's perfume drawer—melding, with each competing for individual attention.

"Lovin' the sweet smell of those flowers." With a dreamy stretch, I opened the passenger window. It wouldn't budge. Bruce reached over and rolled the window down.

He smiled and nodded as if in presentation. "All of your favorites."

A panorama of hot pinks, flaming reds, and fuchsia purples complimented the floral scents. Tinges of white and coffee-colored cream mingled amidst the rainbow before us. I basked in the aura of the Selma springtime, glad to be away from the ice storms of late March and April in Detroit. The climate differences hijacked my senses. Spring bore down heavy, like the logs soaking in rain-filled marshes along the Louisiana highways we had passed a day earlier.

Looking at the floating clouds, I mulled over the last phone conversation with my mother.

"At least if Bruce had a military appointment as a commissioned officer, you'd have more of a social life. Friends who were more like you," said Mother. "You know what I mean."

Her meaning was clear, and it stung. "Bruce will be in Officer Training School by Christmas, Mother." We would make do until we were in a better place. She wouldn't understand that.

Bruce interrupted my reverie and asked if the wind was too much. He knew how I detested having my hair messed.

I crooked my head in his direction and smiled. "I'm fine." Afflicted with a twinge of guilt for entertaining my mother's comments, I squeezed his arm. This situation wasn't his fault. Yet, the words of the parish priest did resonate. "Why not wait for Bruce to return from the service before you marry?" Incensed by the suggestion at the time, it now brought renewed anguish. The pregnancy had cinched my decision.

As we approached the garage-style family housing duplexes on the base, I was struck by the contrast to what we had left back home. The guard saluted us as we drove through the entrance. Before us were rows of trim, red brick units. All the same. They reminded me of tiny summer vacation rentals lining the Lake St. Claire shoreline as my father drove to our summer cottage in northern Michigan. However, the dwellings before us were like garages, minus a lake. We approached the first unit where an airman with a single embroidered bar on each sleeve stiffly greeted us. As he opened the door and we entered, the sudden splash of daylight sent a couple of roaches, big enough to barbeque, scurrying into the nooks and crannies. I turned around and fled toward the car.

From inside the unit, I heard Bruce utter, "My wife isn't feeling well. Long trip. We'll visit another time. Thank you."

When we were both back in the car, I breathed deeply and said, "Do people actually *live there?*"

"Housing in this town is hard to come by. 'Specially during these times. Little is available for married enlisted men like me. Like us. We don't have many choices." His tone was stern.

I felt tears welling and slumped down into the seat as blood rushed into my cheeks.

"Where will we live?"

Bruce squeezed my thigh. "We'll find something. Maybe this unit was just an older one and not kept up by the previous tenants."

CHAPTER 3

We checked in at a motel, collapsed from exhaustion, and didn't wake up until the sun beamed through curtains we had forgotten to close. The first to awaken, I nudged Bruce's toe.

"I'm starved."

Sleepily, he wrapped his arms around me and kissed my lips. "Hmm. Me too." I knew what he was thinking and snuggled closer. We put aside the rest of our lives for a little longer.

When we finally got up, Bruce said, "Let's go eat at that Dottie's Place."

We dressed, hopped in the Ford, and headed toward the diner. Overpowered by soggy odors of pervading mold and fungus from lush plant life, I jolted forward as Bruce slammed on the brakes. Two ladies wearing identical red bandannas, one petite with creamy caramel skin, the other darker-skinned and a bit heftier, hopped off the curb right in front of us.

"They didn't even look," said Bruce in a louder tone.

The tiny one braced a small child on her hip and was also pregnant. I cringed. The other lady wore heavy glasses and held the arm of the first.

"Those girls look like the ones we saw running from the fire, Bruce. You know, the ones I thought were sisters."

"You sure? How can you tell?"

"You mean how can you tell they might be sisters?" I asked.

"Well that too. But how can you recognize colored people? I sure can't."

My automatic response surprised me. "Stop acting like every person with black skin looks alike."

Bruce glanced hesitatingly in my direction. "Jeez, I just said it's hard for me to recognize differences, that's all."

I decided not to say more. The girls were in a big hurry to cross over to the other side of the street where the people moving along the sidewalk were all colored folks. On the same side where the girls were crossing, a large sign dangled from a nail off the single-story building behind them. It read: COLORED.

I pointed toward the sign. "You'd never see a sign like that back home."

"You mean you'd never see a *written* sign." Bruce peered at me over the rim of his sunglasses.

"What's that supposed to mean?"

"Come on. Lots of signs separated the whites and the blacks. They just aren't as obvious as that one." Emphasis on *obvious*.

Nonplussed by his patronizing tone, I encompassed the surroundings and waved my arms into the air. "Martin Luther King walked these streets."

Bruce nodded. "And he was eventually murdered in Memphis because of it."

The neon sign, DOTTIE'S PLACE, beckoned ahead. We walked toward the diner with arms entwined and entered. Ahead of us were two other young couples. By the twang of their conversation, they sounded like natives.

"If my maid hadn't helped my gramama, I swear, she'd be out the door. She's jis' so lazy these days," said the taller of the two women as she dabbed powder on her tiny nose in the mirror of her compact. She flipped the ends of her auburn hair as we approached, glanced at Bruce, and batted her long lashes.

"As y'all know, all this rebellion has come about since that dang march. Everything was fine until King decided to take up his cause for the coloreds," said the man standing next to her.

"Well, it's a good thing we have strong Southern gentlemen to take care of such reckless behavior. We just ain't gonna put up with it, friends," said the second man. He nodded at the others.

"Oh, just stop this borin' talk, y'all. We're out to dine. Let's have some fun." One of the women brushed her hand along the back of the second man. His face was red, without restraining a grin.

Fortunately, we were next in line. The cheery, Southern charm of a voluptuous hostess, with a pencil woven throughout her platinum beehive, eased my febrile nerves.

"Would y'all like a booth or a table?" She smiled broadly at Bruce who grinned back. I couldn't take my eyes off her full lips, slathered with red lipstick, as she seated us in a booth and handed us menus. Bruce thanked the hostess as I inhaled the smoky scent of fried bacon that wafted throughout the restaurant.

"Let's see what looks good," said Bruce.

Snuggling closer, I said, "You do."

He poked away a reckless curl on my forehead. "You look better," he said, as he reached down to plant a kiss on my cheek. *The touch on my knee was nice.* The stubble on his chin that tickled the bridge of my nose was almost the same length as the hair on his head. I thought how handsome he was, even without his mane of thick black hair that had been shaved as per Basic Training regulations.

An assortment of unfamiliar breakfast options appeared on the menu, including grits offered in multiple presentations. We decided to forego the recommended biscuits and gravy and settled instead on hamburgers and fries. Familiar.

Our order arrived quickly. As I sipped my pop, I tucked a chunk of hair behind my ear, then dragged a couple of thick, succulent fries through a glob of catsup.

"What do you think about what we heard between those couples waiting to be seated ahead of us?"

"They do have their opinions about the whites and blacks in Selma." He lunged into the grilled burger.

"Yeah. Did you see how red the guy's face was getting as he spoke? Wonder if he's connected with the men who started that fire. He bragged about the 'strong Southern gentlemen.'"

"Whoa!" Bruce mumbled through his food. "That's a leap. We really don't know that the fire in the woods was started on purpose. You heard the mechanic—ceremonial meetings in wooded areas, candles, chants, the whole hoopla." Coughing, he took a swig of pop and cleared his throat. "A careless cigarette can easily go astray. An accident."

"Hope so," I said, picking at a couple more fries. "A lot of poor families live in those shanties. Just not right to take reckless chances that threaten lives."

With a burger in hand, I added, "And, those couples ahead of us certainly had their biases. Can't see why people have to be so divided."

Bruce chewed a little more slowly, then laid his half-eaten hamburger on his plate.

"You've never known anyone who didn't have white skin. There were lots of colored kids in my neighborhood. They didn't go to Catholic school, but they lived close by." He raised his eyebrows and rested his chin on a clenched fist propped up by his elbow perched next to his plate.

"Did you play with them? Football or baseball?" I never thought much about Bruce's neighborhood growing up and had only been to visit his grandmother a few times. He was always at my house.

"Not really." He took a breath, picked up the mustard, and drizzled a few more drops on the bun.

"How come?"

He placed the back of his head against the vinyl seat and stared at the checkered tablecloth. "When I was about ten, the day after summer vacation started, I rode my new bike to my buddy's house. Five older colored kids came from nowhere. One said, 'Hey kid, nice bike. Can I ride it?' Before I could say 'no,' the biggest kid said, 'Get him!' I raced like mad toward my grandmother's candy store and charged through the door, bike and all. I tracked mud onto the white marble floors. She was mad as hell. Well, for two minutes." He grinned, winked at me, and took a big chunk out of the burger.

I thought of Bruce's grandma. "*Baci* could never be angry at you." We both laughed, glad to break the tension the surroundings had posed. A sudden warmth rushed through me. His Polish grandmother loved kids, candy, and stuffed cabbage. Growing up, I hardly ever saw my own grandmother. She was always off on some cruise or trip somewhere. I had dozens of dolls in native folk costumes from all over the world. She always mailed them.

"Yeah. It's different here." The lingering thought of the couples we overheard at the diner entrance along with the fire in the forest had turned my belly into a battleground.

Bruce stopped smiling, blinked purposefully, then locked his eyes on mine. "What we've experienced is dismal, but we're from a different place and we need to be careful. Just keep our heads down and stay away from trouble." He took a final swallow of cola.

Not able to ignore the twinges in my belly, I left the rest of my food on the plate.

As we approached the cashier, the hostess who greeted us thrust her chest forward and leaned over for optimum exposure of her cleavage. Tucking her chewing gum somewhere into the back crannies of her mouth, she flashed her toothy smile.

"Hope y'all enjoyed your meal. Come back, ya' hear." She fixed her gaze on Bruce.

He thanked her and counted out bills to pay. While the

lady tallied our change, Bruce asked about a flyer advertising an apartment that was posted on the bulletin board behind her.

She snatched it from the corkboard. "Y'all can keep it. We've plenty more."

He scanned the flyer and asked, "Where is this Rohns Manor?"

"Over yonder. Just outside of town, sir. Mrs. Sylvia Rohns Bader is the owner. I hear she's rentin' out rooms to military folks. Ain't many places to live here in town." Her last comment was more of a grunt than a sales pitch.

CHAPTER 4

The Confederate flag lay neatly folded inside a glass case mounted above a Victorian table covered with a lacy doily. A vase of freshly snipped yellow roses filled the space. The sterling silver tag spread across the lower edge of the glass frame read: IN RECOGNITION OF GENERAL WILLIAM J. ROHNS FOR VALOR IN THE WAR OF NORTHERN AGGRESSION. It was signed SELMA LADIES LEAGUE.

"Looks like it belongs in a museum," I whispered and quirked an eyebrow. The possibility of living in this historical mansion tempted my imagination. *Our life might be looking up after all.*

As we stood staring at the shrine of the yellowed rebel flag, Sylvia Rohns Bader limped through one of the framed glass doors. As if presenting the Queen of England, a colored maid, dressed in black from head to toe, with a starched white apron covering most of her slender middle, held the door open for Mrs. Bader. A large bronze-colored cat skulked alongside the woman's ankles.

"Thank ya', Mamiza."

The maid nodded, bending from the waist. "Yes'm."

"I do believe y'all are taken with our grand ole Southern cross. Here in Alabama, we are mighty proud of her." The matron struggled to elevate her frail frame as she spoke. She fanned her wrinkled forehead with a lace handkerchief and steadied an onyx cane clenched in her other fist as she navigated toward us. The thud of each step ended in front of Bruce. Mrs. Bader extended her perfectly manicured nails toward him. I noticed the diamond ring on her boney white finger. It was three times the size of mine.

The matron introduced herself and mispronounced our name. "Howdy-do, Lieutenant Zoosky. I'm Sylvia Rohns Bader. Welcome to Rohns Manor." Bluish-tinted curls fell onto her forehead as she bowed her head in greeting.

Bruce did command an official presence, even though he hadn't donned the crisp new uniform I had starched and ironed. He gently took her palm.

"My name is Bruce Zuretski, ma'am, and I'm Airman Zuretski. This is my wife, Claire." As an afterthought, he said, "She's a teacher." A proud smile crossed his face.

I almost added, "and a writer," since my college double major was in journalism and English but decided to check further comments. It was important for this Southern matriarch to like me — like us. The airman part made me unconsciously flinch, however. The sacrifice of leaving Detroit to build a married life in Selma, Alabama, gnawed continuously. *How would I ever get used to what wartime had dealt us?* With a demure smile, I shook her hand as well.

"You have a lovely home, Mrs. Bader. We've been admiring it." We exchanged affirming nods.

"Why thank you, my dear." Her tone softened. "I suspect y'all would like to see my first-floor apartment." Without awaiting a response, she tugged a ring of keys from the pocket of her sweater coat and headed toward the door. "That other lieutenant got shipped over to Vietnam. Sure do hope y'all will be here a while." She smiled and spoke casually over her shoulder as she wriggled to turn her body toward us. With wide-eyed expressions, Bruce and I exchanged glances.

In five minutes, Mrs. Bader had touched two of my most vulnerable spots: Bruce's rank and the Vietnam War. Just because Bruce was an enlisted man didn't mean we weren't educated. We were college graduates, and Bruce enlisted in the service because of, well, bad luck! *Honest.* I flinched at my own resentment, reminding myself of how much we loved our country. I struggled to stay grounded and felt like a buoy off the Michigan shoreline.

Mrs. Bader opened another thick door that led to the downstairs apartment adjacent to the main foyer. The same oak floors that led to the second floor extended into a parlor strewn with thick oriental rugs. The ceiling height was twice that of our duplex back home and the windows vaulted from the floor halfway up the wall. The lacy, draped window curtains framed a floral cornucopia of color that stretched forever outside the windows. The overstuffed upholstered floral brocade furniture complemented the scene.

"This looks so, so comfy." I grinned as I walked past the two formal Queen Anne style chairs perched triumphantly off to the side. Seeing no television, I was glad we brought ours.

As if she had read my thoughts, Mrs. Bader said, "Y'all can hook up your television set by the window over yonder." Her quick mind contrasted with her fragile demeanor.

She walked toward the fireplace trimmed with tiny blue and white square tiles. The hearth housed a giant space heater in the spot where fire logs had flared a hundred years earlier.

It was an artifact of an era when the master needed to heat the rooms of the plantation.

"Our nights get a bit chilly. 'Specially in the winter. Y'all might have to turn on the heater." She tossed a nod toward the unit.

I noticed the ornate mahogany dining table in a corner of the large room. Mother would say how perfect it would be for dinner parties. She'd be right about that. I hoped we'd have friends to invite. Bruce noticed me admiring the table and flashed a quick grin in my direction.

Daunted by the splendor of this space and beckoned by Mrs. Bader, we filed through the narrow hallway leading into the immense, and only, bedroom. This huge room mirrored the one we had just left, with another fireplace and another space heater. The house obviously had no central heating.

"Of course, y'all pay for the electricity. I take care of the water." Mrs. Bader smiled, showing a row of straight, white teeth that were likely not originals.

"I understand." As Bruce spoke, he raised his eyes toward the sky-high ceilings, likely calculating electricity costs.

Down a hallway toward the kitchen, I poked my head into a large bathroom complete with adorned, period design fixtures. A massive tub was supported by curly feet that resembled bumpy gargoyle faces. With a hand to my mouth, I resisted a giggle. The late morning sun glistened through the frosted windowpane, a contrast to the heavier, ornate spaces in other parts of the apartment. However, the mold dotting the bottom hem of the shower curtain didn't escape my eye. It was fixable.

As I caught up with Bruce and Mrs. Bader, she spoke in the tone of a proud realtor who had just cinched a sale, "Here's your kitchen, my dears."

Bruce's stare held no emotion. A tiny stove and a refrigerator sat like guards on a wall next to the sink. If we left the hallway door ajar, we both might be able to sit at the kitchen table. Not likely that guests-to-be would be in the kitchen anyway.

The two of us exchanged glances. Bruce cleared his throat and spoke, "What is the monthly rent, Mrs. Bader?"

Mrs. Bader raised her chin into the air. "The rent is one hundred and fifty dollars a month. I require an additional first month's rent as a deposit."

I swallowed hard and felt blood rush to my face as Mrs. Bader turned away to cough into a handkerchief. Bruce looked at me and raised his eyebrows, raising the unspoken question.

With a meek grin, I nodded assuredly. My stomach grumbled thinking about the monthly living allowance of $115 from the Air Force.

Bruce finalized the deal. "When can we move in?"

"Anytime would be just fine, Lieutenant."

"Okay. How about tomorrow?" With hands in the air, Bruce smiled with polite deference and reinforced who he — we, both were. "And please call me Bruce. Bruce and Claire." He nodded extra hard in my direction as if he wanted to make our names clear.

Mrs. Bader stood triumphant and an inch taller. "Good. Hope y'all will be happy here."

She continued to tell us more, "It's a quiet place 'cept for the school groups who visit on history tours to see real antebellum architecture. The Selma Ladies League sets it up, but they always call me ahead of time."

This story didn't excite me, but it gave me the chance I'd been waiting for. "Oh, Bruce has a degree in architecture." With chin lifted, I beamed toward him.

"I'm not an expert," Bruce said. "But Selma has many nationally recognized historic buildings. The plantation styles in the entire Black Belt region are reminiscent of a Greek revival style. In fact, this entire region is also renowned for its rich soil, fertile for growing crops and cultivating cotton. The land and those monumental plantations were maintained through hardworking slaves." He grinned and nodded as he addressed the facts he had studied.

Mrs. Bader smiled and held her gaze upon us in stone-cold silence for what seemed like an eon. Finally, she spoke, "Well, Bruce, I am mighty impressed with your knowledge of my land. We do have our fields. Not as many as in the past when I was a girl, of course."

Still smiling, she blinked her eyes and humbly bowed her head. Gentile Southern charm.

Proud of Bruce's explanation, dampness seeped under my arms as our landlady raised her head, eyelids narrowed. Lifting her chin barely an inch higher, she spoke in a clear, measured tone, "We love our nigras, sir. They have been a part of our family service for generations. We take good care of them folks." Taut lips punctuated her words with a summative smile that brought the conversation to a halt.

With moist palms, I resisted the urge to wipe them against my shift. Her words and her actions, a mismatch.

Mrs. Bader suddenly turned toward the window and pulled out the lace handkerchief she had tucked under a sleeve. She dabbed at the corner of an eye and enunciated each syllable as if her next sentence was of great importance, "Do pardon me."

Still crunched together in the tiny room, we followed her gaze out the kitchen window and watched a man step with vigor from a red Corvette. Mrs. Bader scurried toward the back door. With only dirt on the surrounding grounds, I thought how we'd likely be tracking mud and debris from our shoes whenever we came through the back door.

"Yoo-hoo, Billy Chas. I'm over here, honah." Mrs. Bader pushed open the screen door with her cane and waved the handkerchief. She turned to us with a glint in her eyes and said, "My son."

The man adjusted his tweed beret and walked with casual aplomb around the rose bushes, heading toward the house. He navigated each of the four wooden porch steps as if he didn't want to scuff his designer wingtips and entered the kitchen. His cologne filled the space, competing with his towering frame, while introducing a welcome reprieve from the musty odor of the kitchen. Handsome, with a slight scar across the bridge of his nose. A bandage was pasted above a thick eyebrow.

"My lands, this is a surprise," said Mrs. Bader. "Come in and meet my new tenants."

He pulled off his cap, revealing thick, blondish hair with comb marks, much like a rake pulled through the beach sand.

He turned devoutly toward his mother and pecked at her left pink cheek.

"What on earth happened to your forehead, Billy?"

"Just a little nick from a kitchen cabinet door, Mama. I'm fine."

Mrs. Bader cleared her throat. "Bruce is an architect by trade and an airman over at Craig Air Force Base. This is Claire, his wife. She's a teacher." Her tone implied personal credit for our credentials.

Bruce greeted Billy Chas as he gripped my husband's hand, grinning as he pumped it firmly. He bowed deeply in my direction. "Pleased to meet y'all."

He turned toward me and spoke in a soft tone, "Ma'am, I'm on the Dallas County Board of Education and know all the principals at the white schools in Selma. Glad to talk with them about getting you a fine job." With a slight bow of his head, he continued, "That is, of course, if you're interested in teachin' while you're here."

"Thank you, but I'm not sure whether I'll be working. At least not right now." I looked hesitatingly at Bruce. With the pregnancy, we hadn't discussed my teaching. Although, taking a job might help us to meet others. People like us. It would help with our finances as well.

Bruce interjected, "Appreciate the thought. Right now, we just need to get settled in."

"I see. Of course," said Billy Chas, bobbing his head up and down, as he ran his eyes over my husband. "It takes time to settle in. 'Specially these days here in our beautiful Selma. Our fine city does have its dark side, though. Lots of unrest, demonstrations, fights, even fires."

"Fires?" I blurted at the mention, but Bruce's glance stopped me from saying more.

Bruce jumped in. "With all of the trees and forestry in this beautiful city, a fire could be a serious threat." He nodded with a realistic appraisal, ignoring the elephant in the room.

A stern façade overcame Billy Chas's demeanor, but only briefly. He continued in a more wistful tone, "Things just aren't the same as when I was a kid. But I guess they never are, right?" He laughed at his own cliché. "Do I detect a Yankee accent?" Billy Chas teased a smile.

"Yes, sir," said Bruce. "Claire and I were born and raised in Detroit. Still would be there if it wasn't for the draft board." His response was a manly harrumph. An effort to mask the bitterness.

"Well, we do things a little different down here, for sure."

With an abrupt movement, he turned toward Mrs. Bader. "See ya' in the house, Mama. I'll git Mamiza to make me a sandwich. It was nice meetin' y'all." He nodded toward us and left.

Three sets of eyes followed Billy Chas as he walked with familiarity through the apartment to the main part of the manor. Sylvia Rohns Bader broke the tension as she cleared her throat and spoke, "Well, now. Welcome to Rohns Manor."

Aware of the slightly icy cloud that remained in her son's wake, I was sure she was eager to close the deal. For me, the chill remained. Something about the way he carried himself looked familiar. I couldn't swear to it, but he looked like one of the men heading out of the forest fire toward the pickup. *Was the nick on his forehead really from a run-in with a cabinet door?* I folded my arms and crunched them against my ribs. *Maybe Bruce was right about my imagination.*

Bruce opened the checkbook and wrote out the deposit to our new Southern landlady.

We knew he had to get a part-time job—and fast.

CHAPTER 5

"Did you notice how Billy Chas Bader emphasized the danger of the fires in Selma?" I asked as we climbed into the Ford to head to our motel.

"He was just making conversation," said Bruce. "Everybody knows this city has had its problems with post-civil rights stuff. Cuts right to the chase, baby." Bruce raised a punctuated fist into the air.

"That's putting it mildly. If you ask me, this city has more than a problem with post-civil rights stuff." I resisted the urge to note my husband's cavalier attitude and played along with his drama.

"I thought he had a lot of *Suthon* charm," I teased a twang, and I rolled my eyes.

As Bruce started the car, I noticed a wisp of lacy curtain drop over a pane of glass in a third-floor turret window. Probably just the maid, Mamiza, doing some house cleaning. Her silhouetted figure cast a foreboding shadow against the bright light. The admonitions by Mrs. Bader's son about the dark side of Selma fit with the forest fire that greeted our entry into the city. It felt like we were being warned and watched by the guys we'd met so far.

"I wonder why Billy Chas Bader isn't serving in the military." I changed the subject before allowing instincts to carry me too far into my suspicions.

"He's older than us by eight, maybe ten years. Probably did his time. Not everyone's a draft dodger. Even though the draft board seemed to think I was one of those guys." Bruce pursed his lips and tightened his jaw.

"Wish you wouldn't say that." I slumped. Even though this venture wasn't planned, that didn't make us criminals. "The quotas that were in place for the military draft were created in Detroit during World War II. You were placed in a district that had been cleared through urban renewal and nobody bothered to update the population numbers. It's the pits." I reached over and rubbed the back of his neck. "We'll survive, honey," I spoke the words with conviction but doubted it would be easy.

A smile crept across his face before he fell back into his anger. "That's all true. Those goons were out to get me after my bosses and even Congressman Dingell tried to negotiate a critical skill deferment for me. The other planners all got deferred because of our federally funded urban renewal work. But not me."

"Right. The whole thing isn't fair," I said.

"No, it's not fair. In fact, it's downright devious. Those SOBs delayed the pleas from the politicians. My *plea was under advisement*—ha! My ass it was. They knew the Selective Service was about to change the draft procedures, which basically would remove the appeal process at the state level and give the local draft board final status authority. They just chose to sit on it until the revision went through. Gave 'em a good excuse to legitimately deny my deferment request."

"Bruce, whatever happens, you did the right thing. You would not want to turn your back on your country."

"Of course not. I just wanted to serve where the help was most needed—which was working on the urban renewal project in Detroit." He looked out the opposite window, agitatedly. "Fair treatment in this entire scenario would have been appreciated too."

His disappointment hovered in the space around us like a cloud waiting to pour torrents of rain. We had been through this conversation a dozen times. He just needed to vent, again. A few more minutes and we would be at the motel.

Wincing, I wondered if this Selma assignment was another fateful twist of misfortune. We had left the remnants of civil disturbance and the explosion of civil riots in Detroit. The city was still reeling from the siege and the looting. Resting my head back against the vinyl seat, the red-tape disaster droned on inside me. The first Uncle Sam letter arrived only two days after we had returned from our honeymoon. The announcement in bold print stated Bruce had been listed as 1-A and draft eligible.

The memory still had me searching for restitution.

"Just think, in nine months you'll be in officer training. Nine months will go by fast."

"Or, we could be stuck in this enlisted status for the full four years," Bruce had said.

Really? Another knot in my stomach.

The roller-coaster ride of the past months ricocheted through my head over and over. Bruce had been accepted to the Navy Officer Candidate School. He applied right after he received the 1-A status, which meant he couldn't be drafted and deployed immediately to Vietnam. While we awaited his naval orders, the draft board had reclassified his status, again. He was no longer considered 1-A. City officials along with the Congressman requested his release from the Navy this time to allow him to work on rebuilding the besieged city of Detroit. The Navy granted the request and Bruce was safe from military clutches. Or so we thought.

Within weeks, we received another unexpected letter from Uncle Sam. Back to 1-A. When the Navy turned their backs on Bruce's request for reentry as an officer candidate, he said he couldn't hold it against them. The Air Force Officer Training School was only accepting pilot trainees with perfect, 20/20 uncorrected vision. My husband had been wearing glasses to correct distance vision since fourth grade.

"True." His delayed response to the mention of OTS was

unexpected. "They did promise me entry into OTS if I enlisted as an airman. Anyway, this is our best shot for now, babe."

Bruce shifted in his seat and stretched his neck from side to side to relieve the tension. Whatever weight bogged me down, his was heavier. Except for losing the baby. That was a mother's pain. Sometimes the miscarriage seemed like a blessing in disguise—a thought that sent pangs of guilt to my core. *We'll have more children when the time is right.*

As we pulled into the motel parking lot, Bruce suggested I go to the room and settle in while he picked up a pizza. It felt good to take a break. Fresh air filled my lungs and my mind.

"Look at those flowers." Bushes of coral azaleas were in full bloom everywhere.

"Beautiful," said Bruce, absentmindedly.

"You know, I just might look into the Selma Ladies League that Mrs. Bader mentioned. It sounds like a big sorority." I sighed at the thought of sorority sisters. "The Selma Ladies League might be fun and a chance to meet people like me."

"If the Selma Ladies League has members younger than eighty!" Bruce laughed as he snatched the newspaper from the back seat and handed it to me. "*The Selma-Times Journal* is looking for delivery guys." He pointed to the ad he had circled.

"A paper route. Does that mean we have to buy you a bicycle too?" My eyes widened.

"Maybe I can pick up a used one and ask Santa to bring me a brand new one." He had that gleam in his eye. "But only if I'm a good boy."

His teasing excited me and spurred a longing to be in his muscle-bound arms. As if Bruce read my thoughts, he pulled me close and kissed me hard. With a deep breath and closed eyes, I absorbed the moisture of his kiss, the scent of his cologne, and his touch.

"I'll go talk to the newspaper folks tomorrow. Here's hoping the position is still open."

In the light of day, the motel didn't look quite as dingy as it had the previous evening.

~

I plopped on the freshly made bed and spread out the newspaper. The front-page headline glared: "Ho Chi Minh Challenges the Vietnamese People: Fight to Win." Last week a national poll had reported that only 31% of the American people supported the escalation of the war. Another 28% believed the U.S. should pull out of Vietnam. The rest didn't care. American boys—and their wives—were giving up their lives for less than a third of American citizens.

Like hammering a nail into a block of wood, the numbers and the threats of Bruce's deployment were an incessant haunt. Talking aloud, I asked myself, "If so many people are against the U.S. involvement in Vietnam, what are we doing there?"

Unanswerable questions and no choices. During our military commitment, OTS or not, we would be told what to do and when to do it. We were supposed to be fighting for freedom, but the U.S. wasn't being attacked. And somehow even away from the incessant rain, rice paddies, and minefields Bruce and I seemed to have lost our own freedom.

As I flipped through the pages looking for photographs, an article, a notice, something, anything about the fire in the forest, an ad caught my eye: *Substitute Teachers Needed Immediately, Selma Public Schools.* This sort of job would be a short-term commitment, and I decided to talk it over with Bruce.

On the last page, I noticed a small headline: "Fire and Police Calls." The brief report read: "Yesterday, the Selma City Fire Department rapidly extinguished a small forest fire on the north end of town. A few trees and dilapidated dwellings were damaged with no loss of life or limb." That was all. No hint of further investigation into how the fire started nor any mention of those who lived in the dilapidated dwellings or the man on the stretcher, for that matter.

I sat staring dumbfounded at the newspaper then picked up the phone. After getting an outside line, I placed a long-distance call to Sandy, Tri-Zeta sorority sister and second maid of honor at our wedding. Waiting for Sandy to pick up the phone, I thought about how Lucy wanted to be the only maid of honor. *What a battle that was!* The scenario made me grimace.

Sandy was the only person, other than Bruce, who knew about my pregnancy before the wedding. She was the only person I could talk to about my miscarriage. We shared the news with my parents and others, afterward. *And then there was no good news to share.* But today other issues were heavyweights. Sandy would be an objective sounding board.

"It was all so suspicious — the mechanic, the white guys running from the forest, the white robe on the injured guy. The newspaper didn't even say there would be an investigation. Just reported about a fire on the edge of town and scorched dilapidated dwellings. Those dwellings were homes for lots of people who were running for their lives."

"What does Bruce think you should do?" Sandy asked.

"He thinks we should stay out of the politics here. Just keep our heads down," I said, repeating some of my husband's words.

"He just cares about your safety," said Sandy. She still dated one of Bruce's fraternity brothers and loved Bruce too.

"I just can't ignore what we saw and not report it to somebody. Maybe the fires were started on purpose, in some sort of retaliation."

"Claire, you'll do what is right. Please be careful."

After we talked a little more and promised to call soon, I

made my decision and dialed the motel operator. "Please connect me with the police department." My palms were sweaty, and I cleared my throat more than once. Bruce would be back with dinner any minute and he probably wouldn't approve of my decision.

"You alright, ma'am? Are you in trouble?" The operator sounded alarmed.

"Oh no, sorry. I'm fine. Just fine. Just had a question to ask an officer."

Within a few minutes, I was connected to the main operator at the police headquarters. It took several transfers before the detective in charge of arson investigations answered. Uncertain if it was my Northern accent or the topic of my call, but his well-mannered Southern greeting soon dissipated when I asked about the fire and the people who lived in the shanties at the edge of town.

"Ma'am, you need to leave police and fire business to the professionals. We have investigated the situation and found nothing that would hint of arson, except a few corncob pipes. Likely, some careless old nigras." I had heard that before. He grunted in distrust before continuing. "Ya' said you're new to our beautiful Selma. That right?"

Just as I was about to answer, Bruce bounded through the door. I swallowed hard, offered a sheepish grin to Bruce, and replied with a wave at my husband, "Uh, my husband and I just got into town." Bruce stood suspended midway between the door and the bed. "We're, rather my husband, is stationed at Craig Air Force Base."

Bruce put the pizza on the small table and raised his hands in the air as he knit his brows, wondering who was on the other end of the line.

"Well, ain't that nice now." I pictured a mocking head wagging side to side as he spoke. "We *do* appreciate your concern and thank you for your call." Click.

"Who were you talking to?" Bruce pulled the drinks out of the bag.

"I called the police to check on the fire we saw yesterday." I riveted my eyes toward him.

"Why did you do that?" Bruce collapsed into the stuffed armchair and spoke in a very controlled tone.

"Because there was nothing in the paper about the fire investigation, and because we saw those men running toward the pickups. Somebody needed to say something about it." I could feel the blood rushing to my cheeks as my voice began to crack.

"What did the police officer say?'

"He just pooh-poohed the whole conversation. Said the cause was likely some old pipes from some careless nigras. The same story we heard from the mechanic."

Bruce closed his eyes for a moment as if attempting to select his next words carefully. "Look, I know you meant well. But we have got to lay low, settle down, and get along as best as we can. Promise me you won't do anything more to bring attention to us unless we talk about it first?"

Unsure if I could agree to such a promise, I nodded half-heartedly. "I'll try."

CHAPTER 6

Despite the downpour of a spring thunderstorm, our move into Rohns Manor went without a hitch. Four suitcases and half a dozen cardboard boxes helped.

A week later, on the first evening, after Bruce reported to his assigned Base Civil Engineering section, we lounged in front of the television set. After some jostling of the antenna bunny ears for reception, the picture came in crystal clear. The Atlanta Braves were playing good baseball, and I basked in the comfort of hearing bats cracking and balls whistling.

"Hope our Detroit Tigers have another good season," said Bruce. "Just our luck they'll end up in the World Series while we're here in Hicksville." He stood, reached to kiss my head, and headed toward the bedroom. His new paper route with the *Selma News* meant a wake-up call of 3:30 a.m.

"Be there soon." I was wide awake. Bruce was agreeable when I posed the suggestion to apply for the substitute teaching position. However, when a long-term substitute position was offered on the spot, his attitude registered in the lukewarm category. The job was a contract for the remainder of the school year at Brooks Elementary School. Bruce's response was cautious with genuine concern.

"You've been through a lot, honey. The doctor wants you to rest and take it easy for a while," Bruce had said. I reminded him that it would only be until the end of the school year, two months away. And we'd have more income, which we needed.

I didn't say but having a job would take my mind off my miscarriage. Some words are best unsaid. He gave in.

"If this is what you want, I'm on board. But you should check in with a doctor to be sure it's okay."

Except for a few anxious stomach flutters when I thought about teaching fifth-grade students in an all-black elementary school, I offered assurances about being perfectly fine. My interview with Mr. Harold Parkington, Personnel Director for the Selma Unified School District had gone remarkably well, and I felt confident I could do the job.

"Currently, we don't have any openings in the white schools, Mrs. Zuretski," he spoke and lowered his head, as he peered at me over the rim of his glasses. He hesitated and swallowed hard, then continued, "You should also know that you'd be the only white teacher at Brooks. Actually, the *first* white teacher in any Selma black school." He removed his glasses, and his eyes widened as he sat taller in his swivel chair. With his chin elevated, he glared at me as if stunned at his own announcement. His almost-accusatory demeanor startled me more than his words.

"I'm sure it will be just fine, sir." I nodded my head in a subconscious attempt to assure us both. I knew he had a job to do. Fill in the vacancy. Sharing my positive inner-city teaching experience, I omitted the part about the students being mostly white and younger than fifth graders. Another minor detail— all the teachers were white. I shook off lingering doubts about making the right decision. I was good at teaching. *So the location was not the same. Nothing to worry about.*

Sitting alone while Bruce slept, I studied the apartment décor. Although complete with ample furniture, the emptiness of the large living room space sent a chill through my bones. Still, the cherubs floating above my head near the high ceiling edge made me smile. Hungry for a snack, I grabbed a handful of unshelled pecans. The sack of nuts had sat untouched on the coffee table since our arrival. A thoughtful welcome gift from our landlady.

After several attempts of tugging and chipping at the meat tightly tucked into the pecan shell chambers, I gave up. The edges of the shells cut into my skin and left my fingers throbbing. Maybe Bruce could help crack the pesky nuts while we watched television sometime.

I crept into the bedroom where Bruce was curled up on his side with half-drawn sheets and wriggled in next to him. Snuggled up like two spoons, I closed my eyes. The intermittent clicking of crickets outside our windows was strangely comforting. But sleep continued to evade me. I eased off the side of the bed, slid into my slippers, and quietly retrieved my notebook and fountain pen from the nightstand. I tiptoed back into the parlor, plopped into the corner of the sofa, and spewed the events of the past few days onto the blue-ruled pages. *Someday I'd write a book about this place.* Post-civil rights life in a real Southern antebellum mansion would surely make for an interesting saga to share.

The words I had penned over the past couple of weeks seemed as if they came from someone else — more like fiction than real life. The Texas panhandle trailer home at Sheppard Air Force Base had been the size of a big truck, surrounded by barren red soil that extended for miles. The protective pines and oak trees of the Midwest were as scarce as cacti in the Deep South. I vowed never to return to the godforsaken place and continued to spill my guts. *Should I have listened to the priest after all? Ridiculous. Besides I was pregnant. Mother liked Bruce, but I sensed she wished he'd come from a more prominent family. Dad thought Bruce had such a promising future ahead of him but feared we'd struggle. Dad was right.*

I dabbed at my eyes as other sleepless nights in the trailer came to mind. The lyrics of the same *Harper Valley PTA* tune had relentlessly droned in the background, repeating the warnings and wrath of gossip as I threw up in the toilet. As the melody peaked and waned over the shaky connection, my prayer was to be spared of the wrath and judgmental tones of my own *Harper Valley. I got my wish, though not in the way I had expected. Still, the barefoot and pregnant image no longer fit.* Now I would be teaching in an all-black school. My parents wouldn't approve of any of it.

Still wide awake and struggling to shrug off the nagging doubts, I pulled out a box of linen stationery. A letter to Sandy was long overdue. I sprawled elaborate peacock-blue ink words of glorious description about our Southern manor living quarters. Maybe I was just a little jealous that Sandy had joined the Tri-Zeta alumni group in the Pointes along Lake St. Clair, renting a small place with two other sorority sisters, and was probably having a ball. Yet, as the flow of words filled the page, a sense of relief consumed me. The unexpected turns of my new life held the promise of genuine purpose. I saved my announcement of the fifth-grade teaching job until the end, sharing the interview details and swearing utter secrecy about my teaching of colored children. Though Sandy never knew any people that weren't white, either. I trusted my best friend and missed her.

Lost in the thoughts of the past, I watched the glistening blue words fade to a dull turquoise. Mother and Dad needed to know about the miscarriage and my new job. All the details wouldn't be necessary. Although my parents had watched the march by Dr. King on television, they had never traveled below the Mason-Dixon Line. I doubted they could ever understand what the culture in the South was *really* like during this time. Sealing Sandy's envelope, I thought about how hard it was for older people to change their ideas and vowed to call them the next day.

I placed the envelope on the dining room table, almost tripping on the edge of an unpacked box tucked under the table leg and labeled "miscellaneous." Thrilled at the sudden thought of untouched treasures, I rummaged through wadded newsprint until a pair of silver candlesticks finally were uncovered. To think they had come within seconds of being packed in my grandmother's attic made me breathe a sigh of relief. I unrolled the inky newsprint and held each up to the crystal candelabra. Admiring the glow of the light, the commitment to make the best of our new life in Selma overwhelmed me. *It would get easier in only nine short months* if Bruce was invited to attend OTS. A chill flashed through me and clinched my final thought before I dozed off on the sofa.

~

After a scrunched-up sleep on the sofa all night, my neck was a little stiff. Yet, I felt surprisingly refreshed and prepared breakfast after Bruce returned from his paper route.

"You can pull that moldy plastic shower curtain down when you finish," I shouted over a pan of sizzling bacon.

"What if you can't find another one that fits?" He garbled as he brushed his teeth.

"Already did, and Mrs. Bader approved it. She even agreed to pay, but I didn't tell her it was the most expensive one on the rack. She said she appreciated my housekeeping. Besides, we can't have people over for dinner with that moldy eyesore hanging in the bathroom."

He shoved the curtain into the garbage can. "Sounds like you scored points. Way to go." His smooth cheeks brushed against mine, and he planted a kiss on my forehead.

I sprinkled powdered sugar over the French toast, still hot from the griddle, and arranged the bacon on the side. The eggs would be next.

"In fact," I said, "she invited me to join her at the next Ladies League meeting at the end of May." I flapped my eyelashes in victory.

Bruce lifted a mocking pinky from the handle of his cup. *Laugh if you want to, mister!* Being invited to a gathering of these society ladies would be a nice entry into a brighter social future for us both. *Mother would approve.*

CHAPTER 7

The following Sunday morning we ran into the Baders. Mrs. Bader clutched Billy Chas's arm as he guided her down the front steps. A handsome mother and son in Sunday church clothes.

"I hope y'all are comin' to the parade this afternoon. Today's a special day in Selma." If his smile was any bigger it would have touched his earlobes.

"I did read in the paper that the Confederate Memorial Day is celebrated on the fourth Sunday in April," said Bruce, trying to be cordial.

"Yes, sir. We have floats, horses, marching bands, the works! You should join us downtown. It's always fun." He stopped and looked purposely at us. "And y'all will see our glorious Southern pride." His demeanor lightened, and he smiled in what was the sincerest gesture I'd seen from Billy Chas Bader yet.

"Evra-body is there," Mrs. Bader beamed. I suspected that was exactly why she attended.

"We wouldn't miss it." Bruce gave me an appeasing squeeze and smiled at the pair.

They meandered toward Billy Chas's Corvette, and we watched as he helped her into the front seat. Bruce waved as they drove off.

"Nice of him to invite us," said Bruce, still amused.

After church, we drove downtown and parked our car off Broad Street and near the beginning of the parade. Hundreds of people had already arrived, picked a spot, and had blankets spread on the ground. A band donned in crisp blue uniforms began the festivities, heralding Dixie tunes. Billy Chas followed the entourage in his red Vette with two ladies perched atop the back seat. Both were donned in billowy Scarlett O'Hara-style skirts. He waved to the bystanders along the curbside, while the ladies flapped Confederate flags into the air above their heads.

Billy Chas spotted us and shouted, "Hey, Bruce and Claire!" Bruce saluted. I smiled politely.

The sheriff and a few of his crew, with holsters in gear, filled an official police car behind Billy Chas. Several more of the sheriff's men were scattered throughout the parade route, some with hands on guns. Others donned billy clubs that hung from their belts. Several local members from the all-white Boy Scout troops waved from the next car, while other members proudly carried the U.S. flag, the State of Alabama flag, and of course, the Confederate flag. An older model Chevy was next in the lineup. Not a convertible, but that didn't appear to phase the driver as he beamed a celebratory smile and waived to the crowd from the open window. Tugging at Bruce's jacket, I nodded toward the car.

"Except for those guys sweeping behind the horses, he's the only colored person I've seen so far in the parade," I said just as a rousing group of colored people shouted and cheered. Most waved small wooden sticks with unfurled Alabama flags. Some waved Confederate flags.

"He looks professional. Bet he's high on the totem pole in this community," said Bruce.

I nodded and motioned toward another familiar face in the crowd. "There's the personnel director from the school district, Mr. Parkington." A middle-aged lady, likely his wife, clung to his coat sleeve while waving frantically at Billy Chas Bader, who maintained a winsome grin as he cruised in front of the crowd.

"The guy standing next to Mr. Parkington is Mr. Tilly, my boss at the base," said Bruce as he waved a hand in his direction.

Both men directed their wives through the onlookers until

they were close enough for introductions. Mr. Tilly mentioned how he had heard so much about me, while Mr. Parkington flattered me with his pleasure over reading my transcripts and recommendation letters from student teaching supervisors. He also apologized for not being able to place me in a white school. When he mentioned the white schools, Mr. Tilly stared off in the distance.

Always quick on the draw, Bruce made a joke about it. "Claire has had experience in teaching in inner-city schools. Did she tell you about her subbing days in a high school geometry class? A Geometry II class." He winked at me, grinning as he added the course correction.

My math skills were always a source of his ribbing, but I was glad he was being his friendly, candid self with one of my bosses in the school district. Mr. Parkington's eyes lit up. Everyone liked Bruce.

I chimed in. "Now to be fair, that class was filled with rowdy boys, most of 'em only five or six years younger than me." Recalling how tired I felt during those first few weeks of my pregnancy gave me renewed hope. The next time around my energy level would be higher.

"Didn't some kid toss an eraser at another kid, and it flew out the window?" Bruce rallied.

"Well, sort of. But it was more like a game of Keep Away. I had my back turned to the class, copying an assignment on the chalkboard when the flying eraser took an aerodynamic turn right out the window."

It was good to hear Bruce laugh.

"The wooden-handled eraser made a final landing on the hood of the assistant principal's new car. The investigation for the culprit took the rest of that week, as I recall." I shuddered thinking about the pure chaos and havoc the incident caused as Bruce put a final spin on the tale.

"The expression on the assistant principal's face was priceless, though," I said with a grin. The Parkingtons chuckled, enjoying the story.

It was another high school band's turn to woo the crowd and our conversation was no longer mutually audible. Mr. Parkington patted Bruce's shoulder before the couple headed off to greet others in the crowd.

As the parade continued across the Pettus Bridge, the onlookers nearby dispersed. We sauntered off hand in hand.

"Are you worried about this job, Claire?" asked Bruce without provocation.

I hesitated. "A little. Guess I'm just anxious about having my own class." Teaching hadn't been my original career goal, and I recalled a childhood aspiration that I hadn't thought of for quite a while. "My childhood dream was to be a newspaper reporter. Just like Lois Lane." I offered an overly dramatic sigh.

"Sidekick to the famed reporter and superman, Clark Kent." Bruce had heard this story before and was playing along for my benefit.

"That's right. Lois wore suits with high heels and carried a spiral stenographic notebook. And she always had a new number-two pencil with a clean eraser."

"So now you will be a great teacher with dozens of number-two pencils with clean erasers." He put his arm around me. "I know how much you love to write, and you'll have a chance to do that too. You'll be better than Lois Lane."

As I hugged him and looked over his shoulder, I noticed the colored driver of the old Chevy staring in our direction as he waited on the entourage. He wasn't smiling.

CHAPTER 8

Mr. Tilly rolled down the window of his station wagon and waved a hefty hello as he pulled up to Rohns to pick Bruce up for work. Giddy with excitement about my first day at Brooks, I waved back enthusiastically.

"I think our luck is changing." I threw both arms about Bruce's neck and thought about how Southern hospitality was certainly alive and well. "It's so kind of Mr. Tilly to pick you up until the end of the school year." Dropping Bruce's lunch into his arms, I pursed my lips to mimic another kiss.

The sun beamed warm rays through the windshield as I maneuvered the Ford down winding streets lined with willowy trees and flowering Japonicas. The azalea shrubs were so vivid that barely a green leaf was visible. Parking the car at Brooks Elementary School, the sounds of children's laughter echoed beyond the playground. As I walked from the parking lot, heads turned, and voices muffled. Suddenly aware of my whiteness — my differentness — my heart quivered. Several grandmotherly types tended to the children, skin tones ranging from several shades of tan to deep charcoal. I saw very few younger ladies, mothers. Straightening up a notch, I smiled and waved. The morning sun expanded my shadow, and the luscious wet grass was slippery under my pumps. It reminded me of home. I was prepared to be welcomed and felt assured of my decision.

Although I arrived early, many teachers were already walking through the hallways. My smiles were returned with stares and an occasional, mostly curious, nod. My clammy palms instinctively rubbed the side of my sweater. For the first time in my twenty-two years, I was the only white person in the crowd. The hubbub tempered as I neared the office of Principal Gordon Williams. Built like an aging football player, the principal greeted me with exaggerated politeness and escorted me down the corridor to the door of my classroom. I wondered if the personnel director had told him I was white. Of course, Principal Williams didn't say. At least not in words.

After unlocking the door, the principal held it open, allowing me to walk into the room. I swallowed to control a gasp at my surroundings. A dingy calendar dangled askew from a nail on the wall behind the teacher's desk. Bold black X marks covered several of the days in April. An obvious countdown. The number of student desks jammed into the classroom space made me cringe, and I felt my brows meet as no student work or learning posters hung anywhere. It was too early to strip the boards for summer vacation. Before I could ask about supplies, Principal Williams casually glanced about. Apparently pleased that all was in place, he handed me the key to the room, wished me a good day, and made a hasty exit.

The top of the wooden teacher's desk was empty with only a handful of pens and pencils inside a half-opened center drawer. Three or four teacher's edition textbooks sat piled on top of a nearby window ledge. No lesson plans or notes were anywhere in sight. Flipping through the books, I noticed how each series was older than the previous one. The copyright date in the history book was 1957. Twelve years old.

I plopped into the wooden captain's chair and watched the rhythmic progression of the second hand on the clock that hung on the wall in the back of the room. The ticking timepiece reminded me that the students wouldn't converge for almost an hour. While I seriously considered walking out, my attention shifted to a sheet of black construction paper dangling beneath the clock, showcasing a sketch of a single white gardenia. A silver thumbtack held the paper to the plaster. The drawing looked almost like a photograph—each petal of the flower flowed from the stamen to the edges of the paper. The block signature below read: Jackson Willis. Jostled with sudden curiosity, I wondered if Jackson was a student in this class. *Such talent!* I was eager to find out.

"What do I have to lose," I said aloud walking toward the glass cupboard doors to see what other materials were available. A couple of dozen geography books that contained all fifty states lay askew on a shelf. With forty-one names on the attendance roster, students would have to divvy up. Snatching stacks of faded construction paper found piled up under the books, I snipped red and blue strips and tossed them into a box. Perfect tools to pair up teams to share the sparse number of textbooks.

A can of half-used pencils sat on a shelf. As I whittled away each pencil in the sharpener, the aroma of blended graphite and wood levied a sense of familiarity. The finished pinpoint tips added to my list of accomplishments within seconds.

Five minutes until the starting bell and time for a needed trip to the ladies' restroom. A near head-on collision with a black woman a foot taller than me was the closest I'd been to any other person in the building besides the principal. Her violet eyes reflected surprise and took my breath away. She stepped away from the restroom door and considered my petite 5'1" stature from head to toe. I excused myself and smiled. She nodded, stood even taller, and marched down the hallway.

With the same moist palms that the paper toweling couldn't correct and a dry throat that a trip to the drinking fountain didn't quench, I took a couple of deep breaths. Dozens of children had begun lining up outside the exterior doors of my classroom. The sun shone as they huddled together with a collective breath that hovered in the crisp morning air of the early April day. At least temperatures were more moderate here than in the quirky

Midwestern springtime. The contrast made me smile as I returned to the classroom and wrote WELCOME on the chalkboard.

I decorated each letter with a calligraphic swirl, wanting to portray a warm welcome, unlike the greeting that had charmed our entry into town. The shanties we saw along the road as we arrived weren't far from Brooks. Some of the kids likely lived there. I shuddered and prayed that none of them were affected by the unexpected blaze.

Bells clanged and my thoughts dissolved as I opened the doors. Throngs of dark-skinned children with curly heads marched single file into the classroom. I sensed our mutual apprehension, realizing this was the first time the kids had ever seen a white teacher in their school. The thought calmed my angst. With a nervous smile, I repeated my good morning greeting as they bounded through the doorway, then more quietly took their seats.

"My name is Mrs. Zuretski." A bevy of awe-stricken, fifth-grade faces stared up at me. Their chocolate eyes gaped wide with wonder. A stunned silence followed, spreading like a heavy blanket over the classroom. I wrote my name on the chalkboard and encouraged the students to say it with me.

"I just moved here with my husband who is in the Air Force. Let's get to know each other. Shall we?" Moving slowly down each row, I passed out the faded construction paper. "Boys and girls, I would like you to write the name you'd like me to call you on this folded piece of paper." I held up a sample sheet folded in half lengthwise. "Like this—hot dog bun style." A kid in the back row covered his mouth as he shrugged and looked at the girl next to him. She sat twisting one of many braids that hung below her earlobe.

The girl raised her hand and asked, "Can we decorate our name card, ma'am?"

"That would be wonderful! And you can draw a picture of your family, or a friend, or a pet that is special to you. I'll make one too." Three students in the front row dove into the task, gladly accepting the crayons I passed out.

After writing my name on the faded orange sheet that had been left from the pile, I drew a picture of Bruce and me with a big wedding cake between us. Waiting for all to finish, I crushed an urge to glance at plans on my notepad that outlined our first day together. With hooded eyes sneaking peeks at my every move, and the desire to smile trickling across their faces, I exhaled. Staying focused and nonchalant, I drew daffodils around the edges of my name card.

In my best teacher-mode tone, while broadly scanning the room and trying to make eye contact with as many students as possible, I modeled the introduction scenario.

"My name is Mrs. Zuretski." I pointed at my placard. "And this is my husband, Mr. Zuretski. We just got married." I held up the picture of the wedding cake. "I sprinkled the edges with daffodils because they are my favorite flower."

"Where's your kids?" The question came from the back of the room, amidst a sea of blank stares. It was the boy who'd reacted to my directions about the paper folding.

"What's your name?" My knees shook as I forced my intent-to-take-charge tone.

"Jonah, ma'am," he said, with a little less force.

"Jonah is a strong name." I took a breath. "Well, since we just got married, we don't have any children." I took a deep breath. "At least not yet."

I smiled at the boy. "I look forward to learning more about you, Jonah." His mouth fell open as he gazed randomly about. He was a class leader and winning him to my side was important. I'd offer him the attention he enjoyed while maintaining control.

The introductory ice breaker was a success! The children stated their names and seemed to enjoy talking about themselves. I passed out more of the faded paper, explaining how they were going to make their very own book, called a *journal*. I wrote the word on the board and asked if anyone knew what it meant. A hand went up.

"It's a book where you write about things."

"Good, that's right. You're going to write about yourselves. Tell me your name."

"Maribelle, ma'am." She held up her name tag.

"Good job, Maribelle." She beamed.

"Class, while I take roll, I'd like you to decorate your journal cover and write your name at the bottom." Smiles flickered like lightning bugs in the night.

I wrote ABOUT ME on the board.

"And, when you are finished decorating your cover, please write a half-page paragraph about yourself." I held up the loose-leaf notebook paper to show the students what a half page would look like before passing out sheets to each row.

"Tell me how many brothers and sisters you have, where you live, your pets. Also, write at least one thing you are especially good at doing. Are there any questions?"

A hush spread over the room as I handed out the not-so-new sharpened pencils.

I finished taking attendance and walked about, collecting journals. The scuffed shoes and faded clothing worn by each student spoke volumes.

Near the back of the room sat Jackson Willis, the gardenia artist. My heart hurt as I read his name card. His sketch revealed a forest aflame, people running helter-skelter, and a little boy holding the hand of an older woman. Jackson's flare of artistic talent and attention to detail was exceptional and beyond his years. The subject matter made me want to hug him.

"Beautiful artwork, Jackson," I said resisting the urge to ask about the fire. *Later.*

"Thank you, ma'am." He squinted at me, then bowed his

head over his desk, attentive to designing his journal cover. I wondered if he could see well.

I moved to the front of the room and told the class that I looked forward to reading their journals and learning more about them. Shaking the sack filled with the numbered construction paper strips, I said, "We're all going to pick numbers from this bag, so we can organize for a special game."

The kids exchanged puzzled glances.

Once each child had a number, I explained how everyone would have a partner to share our geography books. Smiles all around. Kids were not so different from one setting to another. From my student teaching, I knew kids loved to work together, and the expressions on the faces of these children made it even sweeter.

The morning hours sped by. Just before noon, the violet-eyed teacher poked her head through the door.

She spoke assertively, "Beg pardon, ma'am. You're assigned to playground duty on the playground for the first half of lunch recess." Mesmerized once again by her enormous eyes, now covered with horn-rimmed glasses, I thanked her.

Gathering the children, I slipped on my sweater and led the line outdoors to the playground. Heads swiveled in our direction. Wishing I'd worn a different color sweater, any color but red. I shrugged. I'd likely stand out no matter what I wore.

"Can I touch your hair, ma'am?" A little girl, who looked more like a third grader, crunched her shoulders and squeezed little hands behind her back as she spoke. With blinking eyes, I nodded. The warmth of her request made me tingle. That is until I saw the lineup of several children behind her, awaiting turns to run their fingers through my long coal-black hair.

With at least ten more hands eager to experience the same sensation, I knew the first child was likely assigned to pose the question. My family wouldn't have approved of my thoughts, but my own Irish-Italian ethnic roots and those of my students did share some similarities — we both had naturally curly black hair, even though my Irish eyes were blue. I chuckled and accommodated the children's requests, as many ring games enjoyed by the groups of children chimed in other parts of the playground. I'd never seen kids engaged in such musical gaming: Green Sally Up, Bob-a-Needle, and Draw Me a Bucket of Water seemed to be the most popular.

When the bell rang, the ring games quickly dispersed, and the students marched to their respective teacher-line-up spots. I organized three lines of fifth graders, including another group of students who were not in my classroom. Whispers and giggles followed as the troops paraded back toward the school cafeteria for lunch. This was showtime and I suddenly felt like a star.

On my way to the classroom to eat my lunch, I stopped by the school library to look for a book to read to the students that afternoon. I doubted these kids had many chances to enjoy many read-aloud experiences. No librarian was on duty and few volumes lined the shelves in the small room, but none about black children or black families. I felt myself smirking at no one and wishing I could get a copy of the Newbery Award-Winning book, *The Cow-Tail Switch and Other West African Stories*, written by the black writer, Harold Courlander. I had learned briefly about this book of West African culture — the topic and the author would offer further affirmations for my students. There was no doubt about the lack of funds being allocated for literacy in segregated schools. A couple of copies of *The Hardy Boys* series lay askew on a lower shelf, and I reached for one thinking it was at least age appropriate. As I filled out the index card, several potential student lessons came to mind: creative writing and summaries, vocabulary building exercises, and inference questions to answer with pictures to illustrate. Whether inspiration or a creative surge, the magic of lesson design came easily.

With the classroom door shut, I slipped off my shoes and

propped my feet up against the radiator that wasn't turned on, flipping through the first chapter of *The Hardy Boys*. My cheese sandwich was dry, but I devoured it hungrily. Several folded sheets of paper now lay on top of my desk. One revealed a daily schedule. I hadn't seen it earlier and wondered if Principal Williams had dropped it off while I was monitoring the playground. Apparently, students were assigned to music class during the final period of the day. This allowed extra time in the afternoon to plan what I would do with the class the next day.

When the clamoring bell announced the end of lunch recess, the same violet-eyed teacher opened the classroom door.

"Are you ready for the students, ma'am?" She bobbed her head slightly from side to side, almost taunting.

"Why, thank you. Yes, ready for our afternoon." I straightened my back, consciously asserting my position and trying to remain professional. More affably, I moved toward her. "By the way, my name is Claire Zuretski," I said, extending my hand.

She looked at my hand, which dangled in space for what seemed an eternity. Suddenly, a smile took command of her face, and she grasped my palm.

"I'm Winnie Holmes and have taught fifth grade at Brooks for twenty years." Eyebrows lifted on the last two words of her sentence.

"See you got the fifth-grade schedule I left." She peered around me toward the teacher's desk. "If you need any help, just let me know."

In an instant, her smile dissolved. With eyes narrowed and a no-nonsense scan along the long row of children lined up in the hallway, she scurried back to her classroom. Her gesture was thoughtful, but I knew the pecking order prevailed. The senior-teacher professional attitude and behavior were alive and well from North to South.

My afternoon plan included story time, discussion, writing, and two rows of math problems before the scheduled music class. We slipped into the final remnants that ended a successful day—one I had feared could be a disaster. Students obediently copied the homework problems I had written on the board. Such attentiveness was a teacher's dream, and I basked in my position. Yet, tomorrow was ahead with several more weeks before summer vacation would begin. The reality of having so few materials, no lesson guides, the antiquated textbooks, and only a couple of chalk nubbins piqued my anxiety. Daunting. *Perhaps it would be best not to return. Easy.* My parents could send money. I sighed and vowed not to ask.

As the music period approached, I needed to know more about the basics of the class-changing procedures. Jackson Willis was the first to get his work done. He held a library book close to his face to read while waiting for the others to finish. I planned to ask Winnie Holmes about eye checkups.

I approached Jackson's desk and whispered, "Jackson, do the children take their school bags and coats with them to the music classroom?"

Startled, he looked directly into my eyes. "Yes ma'am."

As I thanked him, a hand from the smallest girl in the class shot into the air. "Ma'am, will you be back tomorrow?" She had a whole head of tiny braids and wore a dress that had seen more than its fair share of launderings. Her pleading gaze and hopeful tone took me by surprise, and a warming sensation tickled my ribs.

"Yes, of course, I'll be back tomorrow." The assuredness of my spoken words surprised me. "So you must do all of your math problems tonight."

Seizing the moment, I continued, "Does anyone know what a contract is?" Not a single hand went up. "Okay. You will need to learn about contracts because they are important and something you will use when you are older." With wide eyes and erect backs against the seats, students were poised to learn the definition of a word that would help them be more like grownups.

Snatching one of the small chalk chunks from the ledge I wrote "contract" on the board and followed with the definition: A contract is a promise to do something you say you will do.

"Please repeat after me." Everyone echoed the definition. "Now repeat the definition to the person next to you." Giggles of glee filled the room as students turned to share. "Now close your eyes and say the definition to yourself, then raise your hand if you can tell everyone what a contract is." Almost every hand went into the air.

The success of the exercise raised my confidence. *This cooperative strategy works every time.* I called upon a small-boned, shy boy seated near the doorway.

"Good job," I said. He stretched a few inches taller in his seat.

"You will need to sign this contract that says you will return your pencil and your homework tomorrow." Again, I wrote the word "contract" at the top of the blackboard with a sentence promising to return the pencils the next day. The contract concluded with the word "Signed" and a blank line. As the children wrote, I stared at the dust motes from the chalk particles that filtered through the sunlight. I hadn't been buoyed by such joy and peace since our arrival in Selma.

When students walked to the coatroom to gather their belongings, I noticed Jackson's limp. One leg seemed slightly shorter than the other.

"Jackson, would you please lead the line?"

"Yes, ma'am." He stood at least three inches taller as he paraded the class to the dimly lit music room where the other fifth-grade class was already seated. The space was a multipurpose room that likely served many functions at the school. Only the melodious tones of the piano, where the teacher was immersed in the melody of his own talent, made it come alive. Aware that he was not alone, he stood upon my entrance and bowed his shiny, balding head politely. I flashed a friendly smile and helped seat my students. He stared agape at the white teacher and the colored children.

On my way back to the classroom, I saw that Mrs. Holmes's classroom door was ajar. Hesitating for a moment, I scraped my hand through my hair, swallowed my pride, and decided to take her up on her offer to help. If I was to get through the remaining days of this school year, I needed an ally. Other than Principal Williams, Winnie Holmes was the only adult who had spoken to me all day.

I tapped on the frosted window glass above the door handle and poked my head through the entry. My senior fifth-grade partner sat hunched over a stack of papers. Feeling meek, I squeezed a sweet-face expression and spoke, "Excuse me, Mrs. Holmes. Do you have a minute?"

Placing her red pencil on the stack of papers, she shot a stunned glare in my direction. As if she had suddenly weighed the evidence and decided in my favor, she rubbed her lips together and spoke, "Yes, please come in."

A rush of adrenaline propelled me forward as the events of the past seven hours flashed by. I didn't want to speak ill against another teacher, but the lazy lout who preceded me as the teacher in this classroom deserved it. My thoughts scrambled to understand how any teacher could leave no lesson plans, textbooks, or notes in their absence. *Even if the person had to quit, due to some emergency, teachers have a professional responsibility to leave lesson plans behind.*

Mrs. Holmes stared at me for several minutes as I struggled in my attempt to let her know my frustration with the lack of decent textbooks. *Crap, there were barely enough pencils. Rather, pencil stubs.*

Removing her horn-rimmed glasses and rubbing her eyelids, she spoke with deliberate emphasis upon each word, "This is how it is here, Mrs. Zuretski. The colored schools don't have many materials."

"That's outrageous!" I was unsure about which was worse, hearing the facts or knowing nothing was done to correct the problem. "How can these children get an education?" I didn't even raise the question about Jackson's squinting and the needed eye check.

"Can't say as I blame your frustration," she spoke with hesitation. "That's why two other subs have floated through that classroom. Teaching at Brooks is hard. Poor, fatherless families. Few supplies. Outdated books." She sighed in resignation of the plight.

Nodding, I remained baffled by why the situation was tolerated.

With a softened tone, Mrs. Holmes continued, "My son, Isiah, is a freshman at Tuskegee University. That keeps me here teaching to pay for his tuition." She looked down for a moment, then raised her head and spoke, "Isiah was among a class of forty-five children. Few materials and teachers that floated in and out, but he made it. He was on the Dean's list first semester." She beamed.

Without warning, my eyes began to fill.

Winnie Holmes studied my face, then flashed a beautiful smile that lit up her entire body. "Say, how would you like to plan lessons together for the next month, 'til school is over?"

"Yes, that would be wonderful." I clapped my hands together. "When can we start?"

CHAPTER 9

A week later, standing back and admiring the students' work I had hung on the institutional gray walls, I noticed a shadow hovering over the span of empty desks before me. Looking up, I saw a huddled form peering through the dusty windowpane. No smile, just an empty stare on a weathered, dark, female face, her head covered with a red bandanna. I smiled and waved. The lady disappeared.

This wasn't the last of the senior, colored women I saw during my first weeks of teaching at Brooks. I'd often look up from my desk to see grannies and their toddler charges staring, only to pull away at my greeting glance. Never did I see a man.

"You love the notoriety, Mrs. Hollywood," Bruce had chided.

The next day, while I listed math problems on the chalkboard, the same lady from the previous day peered through the window. This time she ventured a toothless grin when I waved. I had seen her with Jackson on the playground, and she was likely his grandmother.

When students had settled and were writing in their journals, I sauntered toward Jackson. He was deeply engrossed in shading a forest half-green with trees, deep golden hues, bright orange flames, and a grayish sky above.

My chance soon sprung up. "You really like to draw pictures of nature." I considered my next words carefully. "You drew that beautiful gardenia, my favorite."

A grin crept across his generally serious face.

I continued, "This forest scene is so pretty too. But why are flames shooting into the sky?"

He looked up. "It's a forest fire, ma'am." He quickly returned his concentration to the sketch and continued drawing. "We all was lucky to escape, but I lost my glasses in the rush."

That explains the squinting. "When did this happen, Jackson?"

"Oh, it happens a lot, ma'am." He tugged at a red crayon while keeping his head lowered.

"Do people camp out there and cook over bonfires?" I probed.

"Ain't no campers, ma'am."

I waited. Jackson added more flecks to the flames.

"It's those mens with the candles. I saw 'em one time. Theys all dressed in white sheets, like ghosts, and they was singin' and sayin' lots of words I didn't understand. Gramama scolded me good for peekin' at 'em. She said they was up to no good."

I swallowed hard. The little boy we saw leaving the fire was Jackson Willis. "I'm sorry to hear about this, Jackson." Struggling to keep the pain inside, I tilted my head and smiled.

"I'm just happy you and your family are safe."

I looked directly into his eyes, black as the agates in my father's collection, then changed the subject. "Well, I still can almost smell that gardenia." I grinned and pointed to the flower that hung on the wall.

Practically every tooth in his mouth glistened as he looked back and said, "Thank ya', ma'am."

Turning away from Jackson, I noticed Principal Williams standing at the door. Wondering how long he'd been watching. I walked toward him in greeting.

"You're doing a fine job with the class, Mrs. Zuretski. Glad you're with us."

Before I could thank him, he added a nod in the direction of my teaching partner's classroom and continued, "Mrs. Holmes offers many compliments about your work with the students. Much appreciated."

A new teacher, under any circumstance, would be delighted to hear such a compliment from the principal. It took every bit of restraint I could muster to maintain a professional demeanor. I wanted to dance.

He cleared his throat and continued, "Might you consider comin' back next fall and teachin' full time?"

"I appreciate your kind words. The students are great." I meant it. *True, Bruce and I had to live in Selma, at least until his OTS opportunity (hopefully) opened. But Mrs. Bader didn't know I was teaching at a colored school.* Fearing her reaction, as well as the backlash from the belles in the Selma Ladies League, the details of my position, were a coveted secret.

The grin faded from my face. "Thank you, sir, but I can't accept a full-time position right now. We just don't know how long my husband will be stationed here. We're hoping he'll be assigned to Officer Training School soon." I wondered how much of my conversation with Jackson he had heard.

As his gaze briefly softened, I wondered if my tone was pompous or pitiful. With a sudden flick of his glasses into a vest pocket, he cleared his throat and looked deeply into my eyes. "Well, I do hope you'll at least consider my offer, Mrs. Zuretski." He turned and left.

I had hoped my weak response wasn't offensive and was sure Winnie Holmes had encouraged the invitation from the principal. Since we began our lesson planning, I became the proud owner of a full set of geography books, several packs of loose-leaf paper, and fifty new pencils. My one-time, out-of-pocket purchase at the Ben Franklin five-and-dime store supplemented these meager supplies with extra crayons and a large box of colored chalk.

I needed the job and loved the job but had promised Bruce it would be temporary.

The decision was made. I would teach until June. I closed

the book, shuffled a handful of papers into my bag to finish correcting at home, and left. "We'll get by, somehow," I muttered under my breath and hurried out of the classroom.

Looking forward to spaghetti and meatballs and a bottle of Chianti, all recent commissary purchases, I sped home to Rohns. I scurried with the zest of a newlywed, past the japonica petals floating to the ground, and mounted the stairs, two to a leap. With elated thoughts of the special evening ahead with Bruce, coupled with Principal Williams's comments, I could have flown to the door.

Dumping the last of my parcels into the foyer, I used my hip to shove the massive front door closed. Inches from me stood Mrs. Bader. Her cane, like a third leg, was firmly planted on the hardwood floor, her face firm with dogged determination. Kitty glared from behind her ankles.

"Good afternoon, Mrs. Bader." A straight-lipped glare was her response. I reached back to lock the front door. "Is everything all right?"

"As a matter of fact, everything's not a'right." She spat her response before I could turn the latch.

I leaned toward her. "What's wrong? Can I help with anything?" Her outburst reminded me to talk to Bruce about getting the telephone number of her son, Billy Chas. Wish I'd thought of it sooner.

The afternoon sunlight refracted through the prisms of the beveled glass above the substantial doorway, etching angular formations against the foyer wall. Without moving, Mrs. Bader pounded the onyx cane against the hard floor, raising a thunder that punctuated our brief conversation.

"No white woman in the South would ever set foot in one of those colored schools. Especially a *lady* with a college education." Her eyes bulged as she emphasized the word *lady*. She stretched her upper body forward, while her feet didn't budge an inch.

"Mrs. Bader, I don't understand what you mean. I'm just a substitute teacher at Brooks Elementary School until the end of the year." I raised my chin an inch, irritated at my own apologetic tone. "Actually, I'm enjoying it."

The bulging veins pulsating against the loose skin on her neck caused me to pause. In her youth, she must have been ravishing. She was still elegant and quite spirited.

"I will not have you bringin' nigra children into my home." She spoke with eyes ablaze as she pounded her cane onto the oak floor again. She took a couple of short breaths before executing her edict as a final triumph. Using the cane for balance, she trounced through her parlor door. The fluffy cat scampered after her. In contrast to her outburst, she shut the door quietly. *A perfect lady.*

"Of course not, Mrs. Bader." The words sputtered from my mouth as I slowly turned toward the empty space she left behind. The beat of my heart pounded faster than the synchronized ticking of the grandfather clock at the end of the hall. In slow motion, I retrieved my packages and unlocked the apartment door. I plopped down on the overstuffed sofa and let the tears flow. My nails dug into my palms. *The beauty of the wisteria and azaleas around town sure didn't make up for the attitudes of some people.* How could a perfect day have turned rancid through one single encounter with my landlady? As if it couldn't be worse, I risked the potential danger of destroying a vital link to a more civilized social life in Selma, not to mention the lease on our apartment.

The sun had disappeared, and shadows of pending darkness filtered through the tiny window when Bruce jostled my shoulder. "Wake up, sleeping beauty."

At first, I thought my encounter with Mrs. Bader was imagined. But it was real. I buried my face in Bruce's chest, enveloped by the lingering scent of fabric softener from his shirt. A soothing wave consumed me.

"All of this has been a lot for you, Claire. And jumping into a new job after the move hasn't helped matters."

Feeling the warmth of his breath on my neck, I snuggled into the crook of his embrace, grateful he didn't mention the miscarriage that still plagued us. I covered a yawn.

"Bruce, it's not the job. I love Brooks. The principal even asked me to apply for the fifth grade opening next year."

He moved away and stood up as he towered over me. "Look, you're exhausted. Besides, there is absolutely no way you are going to continue full-time work in that colored school, Claire." His face was reddening.

I struggled to shake my irritation at his assumptions and abrupt behavior. "I wouldn't accept a full-time job now," I said. "It's still nice to know my boss thinks I'm doing well. Plus, it's not so bad to earn a paycheck."

I felt my cheeks burning as I spat out the finance reference that would hit him hard. Bruce felt that the husband should be the breadwinner in the family. It was just what was expected.

"He's just glad to have someone in that room. Don't kid yourself."

I pressed my fingertips against my temples and looked at the floor, struggling with the blow of my husband's words. "That sounds like an insult," I said trying to control my voice.

Softening his tone, Bruce continued, "Claire, look, I don't doubt your teaching ability."

"Really? Well, exactly what do you mean?"

"I told Mr. Tilly you'd only be working at Brooks until the end of the school year."

Rising, I purposefully planted my hands on my hips. This was new information. "What the heck does it matter what Mr. Tilly thinks?" Exaggerated wags of my head from side to side punctuated the question.

"He's my boss and very influential in this town. That's why

it matters. Look, honey, let's not rock any boats. Besides you're pushing yourself too much, anyway. The doc said you need to take it easy for a few months, especially." He reached for my hand.

I folded my arms and slumped back down on the sofa, gazing straight ahead.

Bruce plopped back down on the overstuffed seat. "I really wish you didn't have to work. Period. I should be able to earn us a living." He looked away and mumbled, "It's all about this unexpected mess we're in and having to get along in this town."

"Well, I agree with the difficulty of getting along in this town. I have never seen such blatant bigotry." With an exasperated grumble, I spilled the story about my confrontation with Mrs. Bader in the foyer.

"Why would she ever think you'd bring the kids to Rohns?"

"The historical tours, remember? She told us school groups came through to view the antebellum architecture. The one detail she left out was that only white children come through here. And that is very unfortunate because my students need to learn about the history, art, and the architecture of Selma, too." My voice tone was accelerating, and my heart was racing.

A creaking sound outside in the hallway interrupted our conversation. Bruce got up and slowly opened the door. No one was there. Car headlights flashed outside the front window, and I glanced up in time to see Billy Chas pull away in his signature red Corvette. Two white pickups followed him. Flames from Jackson Willis' drawing burned in my memory, leaving me feeling slightly feverish. My teeth chattered.

Bruce softened, taking me again in his arms. We stood entwined, listening to the trio of vehicles get fainter and fainter. Eventually, only the ribbits of a frog somewhere in the distance remained.

CHAPTER 10

From a deep sleep in the darkened room, plagued by an even darker nightmare, I jolted up in bed. Mrs. Bader shrieked aspersions, throwing pots and pans at us and shouting at us to get out of her home. I tossed the six-inch-deep, feathered quilt aside and squinted at the Big Ben clock. It read 4:00 a.m. At the far end of the room, I saw the fully clothed backside of my husband as he rummaged through a dresser drawer. I was not dreaming anymore.

"What are you doing?" A sharp twinge pierced my lower belly as I retrieved the quilt and punched up my pillow.

"Lookin' for the flashlight. Tire's flat and it feels like something's jabbed in along the rim."

"Hmm. That's an odd spot for a puncture, isn't it?"

"Yeah, it is. Almost looks like someone stuck it in there," Bruce mumbled under his breath as if thinking aloud. He located the flashlight and flicked the switch on and off as he pointed it toward the ceiling. "Gotta run. I'm already late for my route. See you in a few." A quick kiss on my forehead and he was out the door.

I could hear him crank the jack, walk around the car, and slam the trunk shut. Fully awake, I hurried to the back door to wave, but he had driven off. Left in the wake of pre-dawn dimness, only the gentle breezes touched my face through the screen. I turned and locked both doors. Maybe it was my big city upbringing, but the events of the past twelve hours didn't create Southern ease, nor personal comfort.

With a return to sleep alluding me, I pulled my notebook from the drawer and unscrewed the top of my peacock-blue ink pen. Tucked back under the safety of the comforter, and with a fresh page inviting my thoughts, the livid edges of the unexpected events came to life. I embraced the opportunity of the blank page in solace.

Five pages later with blue ink on my callused second finger, I slammed the book shut, wiped my eyes, and tugged at the wooden box that held the pages of my favorite stationery—a going-away present from Sandy. The scent of roses spilled out as I opened the wooden box. The sachet tucked in the corner matched the floral buds that faded beyond the edges of the creamy onionskin.

As I inhaled the familiar aroma, thoughts of Sandy, our sorority good times, fraternity parties, homecoming floats, and beer and pizza at Tito's tumbled restlessly through my head. A full year hadn't even passed since graduation, but it felt like a decade. My mood waxed across the pages of my journal, thinking about how Sandy and I completed our student teaching terms at the same school. She ended up with a third-grade position in an upscale suburb, making respectable money. We grew up living three houses away from each other and now she lived with two other sorority sisters. I secretly envied her freedom and immediately felt guilty. *After all, Bruce had been a real BMOC, a hunk, and now he was mine.* I told Sandy how the most unusual flowering trees and shrubs of color everywhere didn't make up for the attitudes of the white folks I had met so far. *It also didn't make up for being so far away from her and my Tri-Zeta sisters.*

The ink flowed again, as I filled in the details about the attitudes of acrid sweetness that surrounded Bruce and me. She already knew about the fire, the station mechanic, and the fleeing white guys. I had written four more pages in minutes. *You should see the darling kids. Jackson can't get enough books to read. And I have a teaching partner, Winnie Holmes, who has taught me as much in a month as I learned during our whole semester of student teaching.* With final letters of hugs and kisses (*xoxo*) to my distant friend, I screwed the top onto the pen with a sense of satisfaction and vowed to explain all to my mother in our next phone call.

To further shake lingering doldrums, I planned to invite Winnie Holmes to come to dinner at Rohns. Mrs. Bader would never allow such an event. I could just arrange it and see what she'd do. The renewed courage I felt after writing lifted my spirits. The dinner party would also give me a reason to sew a tablecloth with napkins to match the dining table.

Rummaging through the stack of magazines on the floor next to the bed, I discovered a French cooking issue of *Ladies Day* at the bottom of the pile. The beef bourguignon and potatoes au gratin recipe on page thirty-two looked delicious. *Perfect for a dinner party, and Bruce would love it.*

The sun's amber glow had peeped above the horizon. After piling my writing materials and magazine on the unmade bed, I pulled on some pants and an old university sweatshirt. Daylight made the world feel safer, offering less credence to the injured tire and providing the opportunity to go for a walk and get some fresh air.

The wisteria and azaleas lining the entry to the Old Live Oak Cemetery, only two blocks from Rohns, sashayed their morning dance. Cracked cement meandered down the center of the restful park-like cemetery, while a scattering of benches beckoned reflective mourning visitors. Bright rays shone through veils of Spanish moss, draped about the live oaks. A welcome to the living.

Not a soul in sight, including those buried under the plethora of granite and rock. I chuckled at my own humor. Names and dates carved across the tombstones beckoned to me. One man was born in 1845 and died in 1912. He could have been a Civil War soldier. His family could have owned slaves. Life must have been harrowing following the Civil War battles that were fought nearby. Buried in the cemetery was an encyclopedia of stories, asleep with the residents.

Suddenly, the sound of a loud, flushing toilet shook my reverie. I wasn't alone after all. To encounter a stranger in the cemetery at this early hour felt eerie. I slipped behind a nearby tree, stumbling over gnarly roots, and crouched to the ground.

It was a timely move. A door slammed, followed by quick patter, barely audible on the dew-laden grass. The footsteps soon faded, but I held my crouched position for what seemed like an eternity. Finally, I peeked beyond the voluminous trunk and gasped. Clasping a shaky hand over my mouth, I pulled back and crunched lower. Two young colored women had walked out of the restroom. The sign above the door read: WHITE ONLY.

The taller of the two women tugged at the arm of the smaller second woman as she maneuvered a pram across the lawn. The tiny woman stumbled over flat grave markers before they both finally reached the blacktop path. They were the same ladies who had been running through the forest when we first drove into Selma. The taller lady stopped suddenly, looking right, and left. I sucked in my breath, ducked back behind the tree, and stayed low. The taller woman rummaged through the contents of the carriage.

"We hafta hurry. You heard Mamiza," she said.

The smaller woman pulled on a pair of glasses and they both glanced about before they continued briskly down the path. Although my crunched toes were becoming numb, any movement was out of the question. *How were these women connected to Mamiza?*

After the two disappeared, I emerged from my hiding place and made my way back to Rohns Manor. To my chagrin, our car wasn't parked behind the back door. Bruce was still delivering the *Selma News.* Hurrying toward the security of our apartment, I spotted Mamiza hunched over a bucket of water and mopping the back porch. A rush of sadness overpowered me as I watched her struggle.

Mamiza offered a slight smile that allowed for a glimpse of her gold front tooth.

"Mornin', Missus Claire." Without missing a beat, she continued emptying the bucket and squeezing the heavy rag mop with her bare, cracked hands.

"Good morning, Mamiza." I wanted to ask how she knew the ladies in the Old Live Oak Cemetery. That wouldn't be wise. Discounting my curiosity and fumbling with the apartment key, I caught a glimpse of an open door to a cellar entrance beneath the stairs leading to our apartment back door. It appeared to be Mamiza's living quarters, but there were no windows. A thin mat lay on the cement floor at the entrance, and a small cot was perched in a corner. A dresser stood propped against the opposite wall with a single wooden chair nearby that was bound together by rope. As if accommodating another sleeper, a pillow and blanket lay tussled on the floor next to the bed.

Mamiza noticed my stare and quickly reached to shut the door. I felt my face redden as I flashed a smile and fumbled with my keyring to unlock the door. Amid Queen Anne furniture, oriental rugs, and polished wooden floors, Mamiza's makeshift sleeping quarters in a cellar was a poignant contrast to the grandiosity of the manor. I had noticed the door below the main part of the manor but never expected anyone *lived* there.

I spent several minutes under the hot shower that morning. Since Mrs. Bader paid the water bill, she deserved to pay an extra price for how poorly she treated people who worked for her. When Bruce returned from his route, he found me wrapped in my bathrobe, huddled around a mug of coffee.

"Hello, there. What's the matter?"

Bruce studied me intently as I explained the odd events of the early morning. Before he could chide me in a tone that would likely reflect his demeanor, a red Corvette pulled up to the carriage house. Billy Chas hopped out and buttoned his jacket. Clutching the mug, I moved to our bedroom. Bruce followed on my heels.

"You could be mistaken about that cellar room, babe," he said as he turned on the bathroom faucet. "Maybe it was some sort of storage space."

"Doubt it," I snapped. "This house is so elegant and stacked with fancy and expensive figurines and knickknacks. That space was special to Mamiza. She sleeps in a place where I wouldn't keep a dog," I grumbled back as I pulled on my underwear.

"It just seems impossible that—"

A loud knock on the back door interrupted Bruce's sentence. We weren't used to backdoor visitors.

He went to the door and opened it. I heard him say, "Hey there. You're out and about early." I assumed he was talking to Billy Chas Bader. "C'mon in. How's it going?"

"Jis' fine." I heard Billy Chas clap Bruce on his shoulder. "Sorry to pop in on you like this, but I need a favor." Bruce cleared his throat. "You're an architect, right?" Billy Chas continued.

"Yup. Well, a graduate of architecture school. Did a long internship with a big firm in Detroit. Haven't had much time to do any practicing yet," Bruce said.

"We're adding some space onto the Men's Alliance Lodge, and we could sure use your help. Of course, we're prepared to pay you well." He cleared his throat.

Billy Chas hardly finished the "pay" part when Bruce responded, "I'd be glad to help out. What's the Men's Alliance anyway?"

"Oh, I'll tell ya' more about it. Let's plan to talk over lunch sometime soon. Oh, and by the way, I'm havin' a few friends over to my place for a little ole fashion Southern barbeque next weekend. Sure be delighted if you and Claire would come by."

"That sounds great. I'll talk with Claire, but pretty sure we have no plans."

"Swell. Great to have y'all come over. A couple of my neighbors who are school principals, at white schools, o'course, will be comin.' Be good for Claire to meet 'em," he spoke his last sentence with more deliberation.

As he was leaving, I heard him say, "Here's my phone number and address. Lookin' forward to seein' y'all."

"The barbeque sounds like fun," I said, walking into the kitchen and tugging at my sweater to cover a chill. "His comment about meeting his principal friends was a bit odd, though."

"He's just trying to be friendly and helpful." Bruce studied Billy Chas' address card for a few more seconds, then looked at me thoughtfully. "Although he did wink at me when he mentioned the white schools."

Bruce shoved the address card in his pocket and gently held my arms.

"Maybe we should talk about that some more, Claire. After all, we'll be here for at least seven or eight more months, and if you're going to teach, working in a white school wouldn't be so terrible." He wagged his head from side to side, mimicking an "*it's not that bad*" sort of way. "Gotta get along with folks, hon. And his job offer to work on the Lodge sounds interesting. Great for my resume when we get out of this mess."

He turned and walked toward the bathroom. Without another word or even a glance in my direction, I heard him adjust the new plastic shower curtain that surrounded the tub.

"You mean get along with the *white* folks." My delayed shout was more of irritation than for the purpose of audibility.

With mounting confusion, I thought about how Bruce hadn't wanted me to work a full-time job. And now he was suggesting consideration of Billy Chas's comment about a teaching position in an all-white school. *Just because Billy Chas had offered him a job.* Bruce's duplicity and unexpected actions were traits that initially attracted me to him—after all he was a Gemini. He had agreed to go along with the two-month, part-time work at Brooks. We hadn't gotten beyond that and now he leaned in another direction. For the time being, the conversation was over. But the gnawing in my head wouldn't stop.

Packing our lunches on the counter, I saw Mamiza shake out a woolen blanket and a pillow not far from her quarters. Feathers fluttered as she shook the worn bedding. She slowly turned her head from right to left, and I quickly ducked out of sight below the kitchen window. When I stood back up, Mamiza had disappeared.

CHAPTER 11

Branches of the pecan tree swayed in the empty yard against a backdrop of the golden morning sunlight, while a fluffy-tailed squirrel scampered up the trunk. I wrapped some wax paper around the brown-edged apples and thought of the scene with Mamiza and the two young women in the cemetery a day earlier.

Mr. Tilly was waiting for Bruce in his station wagon. A stout fellow whose face never outgrew pudgy baby fat, he told Bruce he was glad to have company on the drive to the base.

"Better hurry," I said with a quick kiss on Bruce's cheek and handing him a lunch sack.

Bruce hesitated for a moment. "You know, Mr. Tilly wants me to join the Men's Alliance. In fact, he's asked me twice." He chuckled nervously.

"Do you want to join?" Selfishly, I hoped he'd say no, and wondered why Bruce hadn't mentioned this earlier. On one hand, this would give us a chance to meet others, make some friends. Yet, Mr. Tilly and his friends would likely judge my teaching position.

"Not sure yet," said Bruce as he looked past my shoulder.

Changing the mood and forcing a smile, I spoke in an exaggerated drawl, "Well, it's *awful nice* of him to help us, honey. Southern hospitality and all."

"Yeah." He reached down and planted a kiss on my forehead before dashing out the door.

Bruce thought highly of his boss' accomplishments. He explained how Mr. Tilly was a tail gunner during World War

II. I had seen photographs of B-29s and joked with Bruce about how the planes looked like toys with skinny tail ends.

"I can't imagine Mr. Tilly ever being thin enough to fit into those planes," Bruce had laughed.

"Maybe you'll be portly when you are old and have a bunch of kids," I had responded, dreamily wondering what that would be like.

"Yup. Bet I will." My husband had grinned, rubbing his belly.

I rinsed the breakfast dishes, grabbed my apples and bag, and headed out the back door. As I pulled the Ford away from Rohns, the leafy vermillion shrubs beneath the curved veranda bannisters eased my consternation. Despite the occurrences of the past few days, the bountiful gifts of nature in this city continued to intoxicate me. The sprawling picturesque backdrops created by Mother Nature were relentless.

My drive to Brooks each morning offered a scenic path through older sections of Selma, even though the historical architecture and landscape of a bygone period faded after the first few miles. The spires, beveled glass windows, stained glass transoms, and fairy tale turrets proudly clung to their former grandeur. Romanticizing, my imagination escaped to the belles of those grand estates—the women who shimmered down winding staircases, like the wooden, carved and highly polished one in the Rohns foyer. Time stood still for folks in Selma reflecting a history I had only read about.

Scarlett O'Hara or Melanie Wilkes? An unleashed passion to put my imprint on society, gaining momentum. A gripping love for my man. Overriding racial conflicts. My mind raced, wondering if my new life as Mrs. Claire Zuretski was going to be plagued with stereotypical opposites. Yet perhaps there was no better place to find out just who I was than in the land of the sharp-edged, velvet-tongued females. A dangerous thrill of the unknown pulsated within me.

Mustering the confidence of a trooper, I strode toward the front entrance of Brooks. The caramel-toned grass of winter had given way to verdant emerald threads along the path. Sprinkles of white clover poked through the blades—their freshness didn't change from North to South. Among the sweetness of the lush surroundings and twang-like speech patterns, I found familiar remnants of my own midwestern roots.

The kids on the playground chanted eagerly as they tugged and pulled one another 'round about in a circle. "*Ring around the rosie, a pocket full of posies... Auntie May, Auntie May... we all fall down.*" Like kids everywhere. No difference. Universal childhood glee.

Auntie May was likely the robust lady with a head of cascading curls that didn't look real. She tugged and adjusted her poncho as at least a half-dozen little girls continued to encircle her and chant. Although her chapped hands kept clapping as she laughed with the children, I was sure this playful lady was eager for the bell to announce the beginning of the school day. Several more women hovered together simultaneously laughing and chatting in shortened phrases I barely understood.

Drifting past the joyful members, the chant stopped, and I felt a mass of eyes tailing my back. Taking a deep breath, I waved my hand and smiled. It was a relief to see a return greeting and a flutter of small fingers. My whiteness never faded, and it continued to separate me. *Would there ever be a time when my skin color wasn't noticed?*

Near the entry, stood the lady who had peered through the window on my first day: Jackson's grandmother. She leaned against the stone with arms wrapped around her oversized coat, wearing the same bandanna over coarse silver ringlets that poked out at her temples. Today, Jackson stood close by her side, tucked into a jacket a size too small. A bright red, plaid scarf, which had been wrapped several times around his neck, dangled over the front of his chest, reaching to his kneecaps. Although no words were exchanged, the tilt of the lady's head and soft eyes spoke volumes about the love she had for the boy.

I had made up my mind to let them know that Bruce and I had seen them the night of the forest fire. *The entire event could not go without some attention.* I unlocked the classroom door. With the precision of an engineer, I approached the chalkboard and wrote the date and my name in perfect cursive letters, attending to proper slants and curves.

"My lands. I have never seen a teacher in this classroom *before* the students arrived."

Startled, my head spun toward Winnie Holmes, arms loaded with books, wearing her usual dark suit and white blouse. No nonsense.

"Need to be ready for the day. I want the students to know that their best is expected."

She didn't return my smile, but her eyes softened, reflecting a hint of respect as she slowly nodded and walked away.

I spent a few more minutes sketching flowers with long stems, filling in the petals with the precious yellow chalk I had bought. When the second school bell clanged, I walked to the back door of the classroom to welcome the lineup. It was a lucky draw to have the exterior door in this corner classroom.

Jackson stood at the door, a proud grin covering his face. "Missus Zuretski, ma'am, this is my gramama." At last, I had met the coveted lady, so lovingly escorted from the forest fire. I desperately wanted to share my joy about her safety and Jackson's.

Before a quick, "Hello, I'm happy to—" could escape from my mouth, the woman thrust a big brown paper sack between us. It was rolled down many times from the top to the bulging bottom.

"Ma'am, hope y'all like pee-cons." Gramama's gaze clung to the bag, averting my direct eye contact. "Thank ya' for teachin' my Jackson. He a smart boy." Jackson lowered his head and strolled into the classroom.

"He sure is. Talented too."

Reaching out to accept her offering, I noticed the cuts on her fingertips, surely from pecan picking and plucking. Jackson's grandmother had worked hard to offer this gift today. A paper sack had never been held with such sanctified ceremony.

"How very kind of you, ma'am." Humbly, I reached out, and peeked into the bag. "I know how much work it is to get the meat out of pecan shells." Holding the sack, I hugged it to my bosom.

"May the good Lawd bless you and your work with these here babies, ma'am." She bowed her head as she spoke and ambled off toward the door.

He already has.

Breathless, I watched her leave, knowing her words of blessing would never be spoken in public schools up North. Swallowing hard and taking a deep breath, I entered the classroom, paper bag tucked under my arm. Jackson sat in the front row, now engrossed in the pages of his most recent book. I didn't get the chance to ask her about the fire. Another time.

The day passed quickly as I assessed each individual student's reading skill. The scores were all below the fifth-grade level. Appalled that no one had addressed this problem earlier, I discussed the results with Winnie Holmes. Even Jackson, who devoured books at every spare moment, was the only student reading at barely the fifth-grade level. I knew Northern schools employed reading specialists to help struggling students. Without support and attention to their reading skills, they would not be successful in school. Even become high school dropouts.

Since I was not a particularly welcomed visitor, I decided it was time to voice this topic to my peers in the Teachers' Room. "None of the students in my class are reading at the fifth-grade level. And who does student vision checks here?" I pulled back the wax paper that held my cheese and bologna sandwich.

"Welcome to our world, and there's no one to check vision," said a stout lady who continued to grade workbook papers without even glancing in my direction. "Many of the parents, if they are both living with the kid, can't write their own names. For certain, the gramamas wouldn't even know how to hold a pencil." I flinched as I thought of Jackson's grandmother.

"How can students understand history books written at a fifth-grade level if they can barely read at a third-grade level?" I decided not to bring up the fact that the books were outdated and ended with the launching of Sputnik, twelve years earlier.

The room fell silent. The music teacher, in his black suit and bow tie, tugged at his shirt collar as if the temperature was too warm. The art teacher continued to nibble on a cookie while idly sketching a nature scene, as if she hadn't heard my question. Two kindergarten teachers continued to smile and nod at each other. That's what kindergarten teachers did. Every other head spun in my direction.

A teacher with corkscrew white hair, sitting at the head of the table finally boomed, "Honey, you's in the Black Belt. There ain't no specialists in this buildin'. Less you count the janitor." She spoke with the exaggerated pace of a first-grade teacher and punctuated her final words with a single nod of her head.

The bellow of laughter that followed competed with the whistle of the tea kettle on the stove top. My cheeks felt hot, yet I was grateful for the humor diversion. The exit was only a few feet away and I fought an urge to flee. Instead, I flashed a smile and raised exaggerated eyebrows. I was a white greenhorn and knew it. The teacher's comfort level to speak to me with such familiarity offered an odd mixture of welcoming. *None of this would be possible without Winnie Holmes.*

The art teacher gently placed pastels on top of her drawing

pad and passed me the box of cookies. She blinked and gazed into my eyes as she smiled. I didn't want a cookie, but it seemed rude not to accept. With appreciation of the camaraderie, I nibbled on the sweets, as the realization of our limited resources continued to dampen my spirits.

As the children paraded back to their classrooms, the Black Belt was another term needing an encyclopedia check. Bruce had also referenced Black Belt to Mrs. Bader. Did the teacher's comment mean that everyone in the white schools had reading specialists to help students who struggled? Or, as Bruce had suggested, was I jumping to conclusions? This time, I didn't think so. Every kid should be able to learn to read and not just be passed along from grade to grade until they dropped out. Teachers in the schools were supposed to teach kids to read. That was their job.

At the end of the day, I found a paycheck in my mailbox and reminded myself that this was supposed to be the main reason I took this job. With a two-week paycheck, I could buy the fabric to make an outfit for the Ladies League event. That was if Mrs. Bader still meant to honor her invitation. At least, Billy Chas seemed to like us. Mrs. Bader would also likely be at the barbeque on Sunday afternoon. I planned to spend time with her, especially after what happened last week. Somehow, I had to reconcile my discontent and resolve my personal dissonance. I was still working on the *how* part.

I left the building and walked toward the Ford. Besides Principal Williams's car, mine was the last one left, and it was only thirty minutes after the students were dismissed. Chalking the hasty staff exit up to a Friday and a payday, I plopped my book bag on the ground in search of keys at the bottom of my purse. Bending over, I noticed the rear tire was flat and a nail protruded from it. Bruce just had the tire repaired the previous day.

Looking right and left, I saw no one. Chills ran through me, as I tugged at my sweater cuffs and hurried back to get Principal Williams. Struggling to shake away the jitters that trickled through every part of my body, I saw the familiar red Corvette parked in front of the building. Both flummoxed and a little scared, I hurried my pace toward the school building. Before I could get to the door, Billy Chas hopped out of the Vette and stopped me.

"Hey, Billy Chas." I struggled to sound casual and hoped my voice wasn't quivering. "What brings you to Brooks?"

"Hey to you, Claire. I tour our school buildings periodically. Need to make sure all our grounds are lookin' pretty." He tugged absently at his earlobe. "Looks like you're headed back into the school. Did you forget somethin'?"

"Oh, no. Well, yes. I was going to get Principal Williams. Seems there's a nail in my tire and it's flat."

"I can help you with that," he said, with a big grin on his face. "Good thing I happened to be here."

With both a sigh of relief and a sense of reluctance, I accepted his offer. As he jacked the wheel, he commented on how it looked as though the nail had been jammed in the tire.

"You mean someone did it on purpose? Why, why would anyone do that?" I couldn't help stuttering.

"Just by where the nail is placed. It's above where the tire meets the ground." He spoke as if it was more than obvious. "I'm sorry." His eyes looked sympathetic. "This is jis' the kind of thing that can happen when you're in Negro territory. A pretty, young white lady by herself, and rambunctious teens in this neighborhood. Not a good mix."

Abruptly changing his tone, he patted my shoulder and said, "All done. Good as new. See y'all at the barbeque at my place on Sunday." A second later he bounded toward the Corvette.

My tire was full of air, but I felt completely deflated.

CHAPTER 12

As Bruce drove by the scorched forest on the way to Billy Chas Bader's barbeque party, the oddity of finding a second nail in the tire hung like a lingering malady.

"Wonder if Billy Chas will bring up the tire encounter? Or should I say the sheer coincidence encounter?" I shuddered.

"The guy is on the school board. It makes sense he visits the local schools," said Bruce.

"Yeah. Visiting the schools is a part of his job. Still, the fatherly lecture about my safety in the Negro community was a bit much. Funny how Billy Chas showed up both times after we found a nail in our tires too. He also suggested that the placement of the nail looked like it was done on purpose."

Vaguely responding to the last part of my comment, Bruce continued, "You probably just drove over a nail in that old parking lot. It's lucky he arrived when he did to help, honey."

What perfect timing! Right!

Bruce pulled over to the side of the road, turned off the engine, and put his arm around me. "Baby, you're trying hard, and none of this is fair to you. We're stuck in a murky hocus-pocus climate and don't really fit in." He rubbed his forehead with the tips of his fingers on his free hand as if the exercise would erase it all.

"There was nothing more you could have done," I said still thinking about the nail in the tire event. "You got the draft letter and tried to enlist in the Navy Officer Candidate School. You were even accepted."

"Yeah, should've taken it. Damn it." He slapped at the steering wheel.

"Bruce, you'd have accepted the commission if the riots hadn't broken out. The Detroit Planning Commission needed you to do what you do best—plan communities and design buildings." I rolled my eyes skyward. We'd been over this five dozen times.

"And it all backfired into a bureaucratic nightmare that put me in the 1-A draft status with Uncle Sam. Greetings and salutations. End of story."

"You'll be in OTS in less than eight months." I was hopeful. "We just have to bide our time, honey." Although my tone was lowered, I felt the force of my own conviction.

"We have no absolute assurance that I will get into OTS," said Bruce. His eyes were moist. This was the second time I had seen him tearful. The first time was after we lost the baby. I threw my arms about his neck. We embraced and kissed, overcome with the combination of love and pain, until four or five teenagers drove by in a rickety old station wagon and hooted out a back window.

Bruce shouted back, "We're married." We exploded in laughter.

He breathed in my ear. "Let's go back home. Forget the barbeque."

"We can't do that, Bruce, they're expecting us. It would look bad if we just don't show up." I pulled gently away and scrounged through my purse for lipstick.

"Okay. But later, Mrs. Zuretski."

"I'll look forward to that, Mr. Zuretski." I smiled, gently rubbing the lipstick smear from his lips.

As he started up the engine and turned the Ford back onto the road, he glanced at me. "I do have an appointment with the lieutenant in human resources to see what other options we might have."

"That's good! Now, let's go have some fun and then more

fun after the fun." I patted his knee and arched my eyebrows. To hell with the military bondage and all that came with it.

Floral blooms hovered above the early evening dampness, as if in search of a resting place for the night. I thought how lucky we were to be the beneficiaries. The flowers buoyed my mood and affirmed my mindset.

"I've never seen flowering trees like these before," I said, eager to find out what they were called.

"Just as pretty as the multi-colored maple trees in a Michigan autumn." Bruce didn't see spring flowers in the same way.

As we pulled up to Billy Chas's estate, other vehicles, mostly trucks, had already claimed spots. The pickup with the biggest wheels had a rifle mounted in the rear window. Bruce glanced back at the pickups as we mounted the front stairs.

"Hope we're not overdressed for the party," he said.

"Yeah, hope not." I tossed my head in the other direction. I had cut, pinned, and stitched for two days to finish my outfit for the barbeque, and he hadn't even shot a glimmer at the finished product.

When we approached the front door, Mr. Tilly and his wife of twenty-some years scurried up the walkway behind us.

"I didn't know you and Billy Chas Bader knew each other," said Bruce as he turned to greet his boss.

"Everyone knows Billy Chas and his mama, son." Mr. Tilly slapped Bruce's back while his wife smiled demurely at his side.

She nodded in my direction and said, "Hello." Mrs. Tilly was a robust woman who appeared to know her feminine place in Southern society. But I still wondered if she remembered me from the parade.

We rapped the door knocker and a maid greeted us. She took my purse and poncho and led us to the backyard. Younger and stouter than Mamiza, this woman appeared to be in better health. It seemed everyone who was anyone had at least one personal colored maid. I was sure these loyal folks earned little to no pay. Likely, a bare-bones room and board were their primary rewards, considering my glimpse of Mamiza's quarters.

The vehicles out front didn't match the drivers we saw inside. The men were dressed in slacks and button-down collared shirts. As half a dozen women in brimmed hats and floral sundresses glanced in our direction, I wanted to fade into the woodwork.

The green broadcloth shift I had sewn suddenly seemed out of place. The slits in the sides of the dress showcased the matching green Bermuda shorts I had just finished hemming. Dozens of pairs of eyes scanned me from my now frizzing hair to my platform sandals. Somehow, the outfit, even with gold nautical buttons, no longer looked classy. Never mind that it was exactly what my friends back home would wear to a backyard barbeque.

Billy Chas leaped forward to welcome us. He bowed deeply in my direction and slapped at Bruce's shoulder while shaking his hand. From the back of the property, smoke from a slow-cooking pig filled the air, whetting everyone's appetite. Several colored boys were tending to the spit, turning and basting the animal. The tallest of the group directed the grilling crew, stirring a marinade and instructing the others. He looked familiar, but I couldn't place the connection.

"The boys do a fine job with a boar." Billy nodded in the direction of my gaze, as if he'd read my thoughts, almost taking credit for the high-quality work done by the young men. "And I take plenty good care of 'em." He blew smoke from a big cigar into the sky and smiled broadly to reveal a row of perfect teeth. The blue-gray of his eyes penetrated mine. There was no doubt about his good looks.

With deftness, his smile faded. As if controlled by an automatic switch, the smile reappeared as two other couples approached. "Come meet my neighbors." He snatched a fresh bottle of beer as he guided us toward the couples, led by two ladies wearing flowing skirts.

After introductions were done, the men and the women drifted into separate conversations, and I soon discovered the women were my sorority sisters across the miles.

"My lands, can you believe it, Belinda?" The blonde lady, Ruby Miller, clasped her cheeks with both hands and bounced her curls from side to side. "We're all Zetas."

Hugs and squeals celebrated the union of the Southern and Northern sisterhood. Ruby embraced me with genuine warmth.

Belinda Bailey, who appeared more interested in sprucing up her wavy auburn locks than diving into reunion clamor, nonetheless added, "Simply delightful!"

I recalled my sorority pledge requirement to memorize the history of Tri-Zeta backwards and forwards. Tri-Zeta was a popular sorority in the South, with many more chapters than we had up North.

Ruby continued to keep the conversation flowing, taunting Belinda, and smiling broadly at me. Bruce and Billy Chas were laughing and waving beer bottles with the husbands of my new Southern sisters. I thought that we might have made some friends at last, until a creepy uneasiness tugged at my back. When I turned, Johnny, Belinda's balding spouse, whose arm was in a sling, was scanning me up and down.

As we chatted about Zeta events, I spotted Mrs. Bader clustered in a corner with a group of ladies of similar vintage. She patted the hand of another lady with salt and pepper hair done up in a French twist. A third woman, with deep crimson lipstick that bled into the creases of her lip line, did most of the talking. Without too much delay, I planned to navigate toward my new landlady. The encounter in the Rohns Manor foyer had to be mollified.

Grasping an opportune moment, I excused myself from my

sisters and moved toward the chatting threesome. Mrs. Bader didn't look surprised to see me.

"It's mighty nice that y'all could come, honey." She delivered her greeting with a well-maneuvered velvet tongue, complete with unrelenting Southern charm.

I doubted she had forgotten the foyer incident, but polite manners in social settings were in her genes. Mrs. Bader introduced me to her lady friends, and I found myself a captive listener while the Southern matrons spoke of the history of the Deep South. The lady with the French twist looked at Mrs. Bader after a few moments.

"Sylvia, you're so fortunate to have such a lovely couple in your home. 'Specially with all of the turmoil going on these days." She peeked at Mrs. Bader over the frame of eyeglasses, perched on the tip of her nose.

I wondered how much was known about my teaching at Brooks. My landlady nodded and smiled demurely, acting as if our encounter in her foyer never happened. Stunned by her chameleon behavior, I offered a polite grin. *Perhaps Mrs. Bader genuinely was a sweet old lady, and I was wrong?*

"Bruce and I could have driven you ladies to this party." I turned toward Mrs. Bader. I was as eager to steer the conversation elsewhere as I was to show my best manners.

"Why, that's very sweet of you, Claire, but we girls always attend Sunday services together and take turns driving. Today, I was chauffeur." Giggles all around.

When the piles of barbequed pork and the ceramic bowls of potato salad were stacked on the checkered cloth-covered picnic tables, I sought Bruce. Suddenly, servers and maids appeared from everywhere. The young men turning the rotisserie pit swept and shoveled. The one in charge examined their work, attending to scattered coals and untouched debris with the focus of a master. He gently encouraged excellence in the cleanup and garnered a respect that was impressive.

Billy Chas navigated us toward the smallest picnic table setting and positioned our seats next to my Southern sorority sisters. I soon discovered that their husbands were both school principals, with an emphasis on their roles in white schools. *Another coincidence?* Ruby's husband, Bobby, who appeared to be the older of the two, suggested he might be looking for a third-grade teacher next school year.

"Would ya' be interested in applying, Claire?"

Before I could respond, Ruby piped in, "Bobby, hon, we want Claire to join the Ladies League. Now how on earth can she come to our luncheons if she's teachin' in your school?" My Zeta friend perched fists on her thin hips in exaggerated faux mockery of her husband. I was overjoyed at her encouraging suggestion about the League.

"Right, Belinda?" Ruby flung a glance toward her friend.

Belinda turned a coy head and nodded slowly. "Right." She locked large tortoise shell sunglasses into the auburn curls atop her head. As if the sun was too bright, she quickly moved the glasses back over her eyes, but not before I noticed a bluish mark on her upper cheekbone.

"Claire is an excellent cook," Bruce broke in. "*Y'all* must come to dinner some time." Everyone laughed at his Southern touch.

As if she couldn't resist, Belinda removed the fashionable sunglasses again and flapped her lashes like shutters on a windy day. She rested her chin on her thumb and covered her cheek with four fingers as she spoke. "Why that would be divine."

Bruce didn't fall for Belinda's flapping eyelashes, but he was right. I loved experimenting with new recipes, and it would be fun to have an excuse for a dinner party. Bobby's offer did sound appealing, and I thanked him with a grin and an assurance that I'd keep it in mind. Flattered by the sincerity of his offer, I truly enjoyed my current teaching position and wasn't keen to give it up.

A few weeks ago, all I wanted was to be Bruce's wife and a mother. Having Ruby and Belinda as friends almost seemed like a return to college days.

Johnny belched and excused himself. I noticed several empty beer bottles on the table in front of him. Aware that I was staring at her husband, Belinda spoke in almost a whimper.

"Mah poor Johnny."

"How did he break his arm?" I asked. From what I observed, it could have been due to a drinking binge.

"A few weeks ago, a terrible fire broke out among the shanties on the outskirts of town."

Belinda stopped and blinked a couple of times before continuing. Eyes widening, I stared at her, awaiting the rest of the story, hoping to finally get the scoop on what happened.

"My Johnny almost lost his life trying to save the lives of colored folks who live in those shanties. He was driving back from one of his principals' trainin' sessions in Birmingham and came upon the screamin' little coloreds runnin' from the flames. Johnny fell trying to save one little boy and broke his arm. The firefighters offered their gratitude as they hurried the boy into the ambulance." Belinda lowered her head and spoke in a voice I could barely hear, "I hear the little boy is in the burn unit at the Birmingham Hospital."

"What a tragedy! How brave of Johnny! Funny, the newspaper didn't tell that story." I was glad to get my chance to bring this up—maybe Johnny was one of the white men at the fire site.

Johnny suddenly came alive from his stupor. "Yeah, it was mostly nigras. Good thing I happened to drive by on my way home. What a coincidence, huh?" His eyes narrowed and drilled directly into me while a wide grin covered most of his face.

I stared at him. His mismatch of words, tone, and expression left me speechless.

CHAPTER 13

Bruce tapped my elbow. "Think we'd better leave, honey."

He had to catch some sleep before his early morning deliveries and going to the base. Disappointed I didn't learn more about the Selma Ladies League, those questions would just have to wait for another time.

As if on cue, Ruby Miller stood up and swooped her arms around me. "Our League meetings are held on the last Thursday of the month. I do hope you can join us." She stood back and said, "I'm the hostess this coming month, and you could come with Sylvia. She never misses a meeting."

Ruby rolled her eyes and followed with a teasing grin. Even with the theatrics, it didn't feel like she meant her comment as a tease.

"Why, thank you. I'd love to come." Thinking my response was too hasty, I almost bit my lower lip. Patting her arm, I looked directly into Ruby's eyes and smiled sincerely before turning to leave with Bruce.

"Did you see the look in Johnny Bailey's eyes when I mentioned the lack of news about the fire?" I hissed in Bruce's ear as we walked through the foyer of Billy Chas's estate. "And my Zeta sisters and their husbands were the same folks we saw at Dottie's Place. Remember, they were talking trash about the colored people in town? Did you recognize them?"

"Why in the hell did you bring up the fire, hon? And, no I didn't recognize the couples." His glare and tone startled me.

"Because I wanted to know why such a disaster didn't get

printed in the paper." I paused to consider my next words. "The whole event was bigger than it looked on the surface. Seems like everyone is making light of the issue or just plain ignoring it. It's not right."

I slowed my pace as we walked along the broad wooden veranda to the side steps.

"Belinda Bailey said her husband, Johnny, saved a little boy. The boy could have been Jackson Willis."

"Well, it wasn't," Bruce spoke, emphasizing each word. "Will you please stop trying to be the chief investigator here? For Pete's sake, forget it, Claire. It's ancient history."

I snuggled inside my poncho as we approached the side steps of the veranda. Despite the troubling events of the past few weeks playing ping-pong in my head, I did have a good time at the party—despite my broadcloth shift and shorts.

With guests also leaving and approaching the veranda, we tabled our conversation. Off to the side of the porch, Mr. Tilly was talking with Billy Chas while Mrs. Tilly chatted with other women. The heads of the two men tilted inward and their bodies looked tense. I wondered what they needed to discuss at a party that was so serious. Mr. Tilly glanced in my direction. No smile. I wrapped my poncho closer. *Was I becoming paranoid?*

As we moved away from the lingering guests, Bruce took my hand. "I'm sorry. I just want us to have friends—people who are like us." He sighed as he glanced across the veranda toward Billy Chas and Mr. Tilly, whose backs were again turned away from us. "Segregation is blatant and very powerful in this town. We aren't used to it. But we've got to get through this. We must live in Selma. It's our best option."

Although I didn't entirely agree with my husband, he was right about two things: we had to live here, and it was better than Vietnam. Reaching up, I slipped my arm through his and breathed a silent prayer.

As we drove home, I nudged closer to his seat and laid my head on his shoulder. "I had a good time. How about you?"

"Nice to make some new friends. You even met some new Zeta sisters, hon. Pretty neat!"

"Yes, totally unexpected," I replied, thinking how unexpected events seemed to be the norm in Selma.

CHAPTER 14

The Monday morning sunshine crept in too quickly. With the usual dash to get out the door, I left early to meet with Winnie Holmes to work on a lesson plan before the students lined up at the entrance.

After arriving at Brooks, I hurried to my classroom and gathered the ancient teacher textbook editions, then slipped into Winnie's classroom. She sat at her desk, writing with her facial expressions as much as with her hands. I stood watching from the door, overwhelmed by her dedication. This room was her sanctuary, and her students were her life. Lucky for her students. My own students had been abandoned by three separate teachers, but I thought how they were lucky as well. This responsibility might only be short-lived, but I was determined to give it my best shot and show up every day.

"Sorry to be late." I pulled the only extra adult chair next to her desk.

Winnie smiled broadly and looked into my eyes. "It's fine. I'm always up before dawn and have no one else to ready for the day but myself.

"Claire, I'm using your tip about putting each student's name on a wooden stick and then drawing names at random during class discussions. It helps the kids to be more prepared, on their toes. They're answering questions and participating much more."

Sincere appreciation radiated from her deep-set eyes. Not one to lavish praise, Winnie's comment meant more to me than all my student teaching evaluations combined.

She had much more experience, but I proudly had a few tricks up my newly trained sleeves as well. I had taken classes in cooperative teaching and learning and had lots of ideas about actively engaging students in team and group activities. Sharing my ideas with such an experienced teacher built my self-confidence. We were becoming a teaching team and I liked it.

Gathering my materials when the first bell rang, I headed for my classroom with mutual promises to pick up our long-term planning for our combined classes at lunch. Opening the door to welcome my students, my partner's voice boomed from the corridor.

"Stand up straight, heads high. You are *proud* boys and girls." The only sound to be heard at her command were the dozens of shuffling feet marching. Without outdoor access in her classroom, Winnie's students gathered in the corridor. She used the morning lineup as an opportunity to set the tone of high expectations for the day ahead.

"Jeremiah, stand tall and keep that head up." One last correction before she opened the door and began the day.

Watching Mrs. Holmes, I realized why most of her students read at the fifth-grade level and above.

"Self-esteem is earned," I heard her once tell her class. "When you are successful, you feel good about yourself." She set the bar very high, expecting excellence from her students—and she got it. I loved that about her. *No victims, only victors.*

After reading and language arts lessons, my students worked individually on their essay drafts. This gave me an opportunity to prepare for lunch hour planning with my teaching partner. As the time approached, I secured my fifth graders in the multipurpose room and dashed off to meet with Winnie to discuss the student grouping plan we developed when I spoke of my struggles with the reading levels of my students.

"Winnie, how can I possibly help all of my students read at

grade level in just a few short weeks?" I had asked. The results of reading inventories and word recognition revealed how most students were at least a grade level behind.

I explained how that assessment didn't include Jackson. His curiosity was insatiable, and his grandmother was his rock. But with Jackson's parents absent, and a slew of his siblings to take care of, her resources were limited. The thought of how any single teacher could make a difference under such circumstances continued to haunt me. Yet, Winnie had encouraged me to push myself. Her words hung in the back of my mind.

"You know, Claire, you have the potential to become an excellent teacher," she had said. "You are open to learning yourself, and you are a good problem solver. And besides, you like kids."

Coming from Winnie, these words were precious, and I had humbly thanked her and moved our conversation toward another topic she had mentioned. "Tell me more about this skill grouping plan."

Winnie described how the plan was a flexible arrangement. With only two fifth-grade classes, we had the freedom to adjust our schedules. She explained how we would need to assess our students and place them in skill groups.

"As each student advances," she had said, "the student can rotate into another group."

"You mean we'd rotate groups of kids between the two of us?" I had asked.

"Yes. We can move skill level groups of five or six and help kids master the specific skills they need to improve their reading. The students can advance to a higher-level group as they are able." She'd made it sound easy.

"This certainly isn't like the old one-track-for-life reading group," I said thinking about my elementary school reading classes. Student teaching experience hadn't been much different.

Winnie understood the sorting and selecting process. "No,

but I know what you mean about the bluebirds and the redbirds. In fact, once you were labeled, you stayed there. No such thing as flyin' the coop." She had grinned at her own pun.

I had laughed too, but her point was clear.

"Kids in the low reading groups never seem to move out of that category. Labeling kids for life doesn't help them to learn. This plan is flexible and geared to help each individual student," she had said.

Perched on the edge of my seat, I had asked, "Do you really think we can do this?"

Winnie looked deeply into my eyes. "I've been reading about flexible scheduling and have wanted to set it up for a long time." Her eyebrows raised and her violet glimmer soft, she had smiled. "I think we could be more successful than with any other fifth grade I've ever had."

"And no child would be stuck in any one group and be labeled for life." Every muscle in my body seemed to melt into the chair with a release that oozed throughout my body.

We had executed our collaborative plan the following week and minimal results were almost immediately noticeable. Without reservation, we were a team. Even better, the kids were motivated. They liked the rotation and the special attention it afforded. Someone believed in them and had the know-how to make it happen. Winnie Holmes and I were not only their teachers; we were their cheerleaders.

Now a week later, we sat in her classroom to evaluate our progress.

"How's it going?" Winnie asked, watching me unwrap my bologna sandwich.

"Good. No, very good. Even great! Oh, let me tell you about Jackson first," I said. "This child is unstoppable, Winnie." I read her snippets from an English essay he had written about the importance of saving money. Jackson wrote about how he had a bank savings account of $14.58. His earnings came from collecting empty pop bottles and turning them in for cash. He'd been saving to buy a new scarf for his grandmother for her birthday.

Winnie rested her chin atop folded knuckles, then spoke, "My dear, the only hope for our children is the future. Sure, Jackson's blessed by the Lord with many gifts. But all our kids gotta believe in themselves. There is little for them to hold onto in *this town*, 'specially. At least right now." Gently nodding her head in a rare moment of silent resignation, her hint of hope didn't escape notice. Winnie brusquely dropped her hands in her lap and stared pensively out the window, seeming as if she suddenly recognized someone far away.

The bell rang before I could ask any more questions about the lives of the students.

~

With each passing day, the end of the school year drew nearer. Although tempted to accept Principal Williams's offer to continue teaching at Brooks, especially with Winnie as my partner, I purposively avoided encounters with him. My fear of possible consequences affecting my relationship with Bruce and the white Selma community never completely dissolved.

Thoughts of summer vacation with my new friends, my new sisters, lifted my spirits. I pulled out the old calendar left in the desk drawer. A Selma Ladies League meeting was scheduled for the Tuesday after Memorial Day and Ruby had invited me to attend.

I slipped the dog-eared calendar back into the bottom drawer and walked toward the only storage closet. I opened the door and peered at my reflection in the cracked mirror that dangled from a nail, smiling at my reflection. In two minutes, the bell would signal the appearance of eager fifth-grade faces that would watch my every move.

As I flipped the ends of my hair with a brush, I thought about how bright my world was becoming. Yet, more challenges were likely ahead. Feeling grateful that Bruce and I had enough money to live in a nice apartment (sort of) was reassuring. We were making friends. And Winnie Holmes was becoming my new best friend.

As I shut the closet door the mirror fell to the ground and the glass shattered into a dozen pieces. That would signal seven years of bad luck according to Mother's superstitions. I bent down to pick up the pieces and cut my finger.

CHAPTER 15

A floral panorama in full bloom took my mind off my nipped finger as I drove through picturesque parts of Selma. A travel brochure in real life. Approaching Rohns, I noticed the red Corvette was tucked alongside our parking space near the carriage house. Billy Chas was visiting his mama. Flinching, I didn't share the same affiliation with my own family. Lucy would likely be the old maid, doting daughter in Mother's old age. That is, if she could pull herself away from her career.

To avoid an encounter with Billy Chas, I continued my drive along the meandering road. The Old Live Oak Cemetery only blocks away beckoned visitors with towering live oak trees and flourishing azaleas. Navigating the Ford beneath the sprawling, billowy limbs and through the lacy canopy entrance, I parked the car in the shade. This peaceful spot was more like a park than a cemetery. The century-old trees stretched over a multitude of tombstones, protecting fascinating tales and life stories that might never be told.

I pulled the letter from Lucy tucked into my purse and reread the first few lines. Instead of being sympathetic about my miscarriage, she berated me for being insensitive to Mother in my phone call explaining the loss of the baby. She said Mother cried all evening. *Not a word about empathy for our loss.* Numb. Crumbling the letter into a ball, I stared at the parade of colored maids pushing prams along the walkway. Animated and everyday normal.

There she was. The small lady wearing an oversized man's

sweater over a white dress brusquely steered an antique pram down the path. Even without the bandanna, it was easy to see that she was one of the two sisters I had seen in my early morning visit to the cemetery, and the same one running through the trees during the forest fire. The lady pushed at her thick glasses and wiped her brow, then pulled off her sweater and tied it around her neck. I noticed her pregnant belly and flinched. She shoved the pram onto the path and maneuvered toward the entrance. Pram in tow, she dashed across the street and headed toward Rohns.

She seemed inattentive to the baby, presumably in the carriage. I inched the Ford back onto the road and followed, slipping into an alley on the other side of the street to park and get a full angle view. The woman scurried into the side entrance of Rohns Manor and went directly to the cellar door of Mamiza's quarters. Mamiza quickly appeared and hugged the little woman, then turned from her to retrieve a bulging paper sack from inside her quarters and plunked the sack into the pram, tucking the cover and patting down the bulk. The pretense of the young woman pushing a baby through the cemetery, and hurriedly collecting goods from Mrs. Bader's maid gnawed at me like a colony of chiggers. She covered the sack with a blanket, hugged Mamiza a second time, and hurried off. Mamiza pursed her parched lips together, flashed a glance toward the Vette still parked in the back, then quickly closed the door.

Absorbed in the throes of the scene I had witnessed, I almost missed Billy Chas pulling out. I slipped from the alley and into the parking spot he had emptied and scrambled up the back steps, locking our apartment door behind me.

Plopping my book stack on the floor, I collapsed into a kitchen chair, folded my arms on the tabletop, and rested my head in the crook of my arm. Moments later, Bruce jostled my shoulder. I opened my eyes to a dimly lit kitchen.

"You okay, Claire?"

With a stiff neck from my awkward dozing position, I looked down to see my blouse covered in my own drool.

"Yeah. Yeah. What time is it?" I rubbed at the gooey mascara smudges around my eyes.

He switched on the light and sat down. "You were mumbling something I couldn't understand. Did you have a nightmare? Something wrong, hon?" He pulled out his still-pressed handkerchief from his pocket and reached across the table to dab at my eyes and cheeks. Fully awake and alerted to the events of the afternoon, I told Bruce about the clandestine exchange between the young woman pushing the pram and Mamiza. I also told him about Billy Chas visiting in the afternoon and parking his Corvette behind the house.

"Oh, yeah. Billy Chas came out to the base to bring back some sketches they had on the new wing at the Men's Alliance Lodge. He said he tried to drop them off here, but you weren't home."

I swallowed. "Oh. Well, why would Mamiza sneak a big paper sack to that girl we first saw in the woods? She was the same person we saw downtown, and the one leaving the cemetery. Two out of three times, she was with her sister. This time she was alone. It was funny that she pretended to be pushing a baby in a pram. And she was pregnant." I dropped my head and took a breath. "Do you think I should ask Mamiza about it?"

"Claire, please!" His tone and his purposeful consideration of his next words stopped me. "We need to stay out of the racial divide in this town. I don't want us, especially you, to get involved." *How many times had I heard a version of this message?*

He stood up and walked to the cupboard, pulling out a box of spaghetti, as if that was the end of the subject.

"We're already involved," I said, slowly picking up my books from the floor and walking out of the room. "I'm gonna take a shower," I tossed my words over my shoulder from the hallway.

The patter of warm water soothed the tension that lurked between my shoulder blades as I replayed how we argued over something out of our control. I dried off and tugged on warm pajamas.

Feeling calmer, I returned to the kitchen to see that Bruce had dinner on the table, complete with candles in the immense silver candlestick holders. Captured by his charm, I giggled.

He buried his face into my damp hair and whispered into my ear, "I know all of this hasn't been easy. I'll make it up to you. Promise."

I couldn't resist my husband's sweet humility, as I succumbed to his embrace and absorbed his scent.

"We're going to make it, Bruce. I love you."

"And I love you. Very much." We kissed and then he pulled my chair out smiling broadly as he spoke, "Madam."

We chatted away, hungrily devouring the spaghetti.

"I'm going to miss my students. They've made so much progress over the past month."

Bruce put his fork down and looked at me. "They've made progress because you're a good teacher."

"Thank you. I think so too," I said swirling the wine in the bottom of my glass. I repeated the story about the little girl on the playground who patted my hair. I recalled how her onyx eyes flashed behind thick lashes, peeking up to see my reaction to her gesture. "She was so cute, Bruce. When I asked her how my hair felt, she smiled a toothless grin as she lisped that it was 'weely thof.'" He smiled broadly, his eyes traveling down my long wet wavy locks.

Prickly needle-like pokes tingled my skin as I watched a proud and gentle grin spread across my husband's face. "Truly, I couldn't have done it without Winnie Holmes as my partner. Let's invite her over for dinner. I would love to have you meet her."

"Whoa! That's a hospitable idea, hon." He took a gulp of his wine and laughed. "But Mrs. Bader would probably throw us out if we brought a colored person into her house. Especially if it was a social visit."

"I've been thinking about inviting her over ever since I found out she lives alone. But you have a point." I nodded, remembering Mrs. Bader's tirade in the foyer. "It doesn't seem right that we need to have her blessing on who we invite to dinner, though."

I swirled the final remnants of my spaghetti on my plate.

"It's a bad idea, Claire. We can't afford to be tossed out of Rohns." He took a bigger swig of wine and scooped another forkful of spaghetti into his mouth.

"Well, I'm beginning to think that our Southern friends are not the only hypocrites in town." I forced a smile but surprised myself at the acrimony that had seeped into my voice.

"Now wait a minute. I resent that, Claire." He laid his fork on top of his spaghetti. "Since when have you become a champion of civil rights, anyway? We're not part of the local culture here. I've never seen you so adamant about a cause. It's not like you."

"I'm not adamant about any cause. You go off to the base every day and see people like you everywhere. My only real friend is Winnie Holmes. Plus, it's not right that some kids should have a better educational opportunity here than others."

Bruce looked at me as he listened, eyes glued on mine. "Look, honey, what you're saying is honorable. And I know Mrs. Holmes has been a great partner, but school will soon be over, and you do have the Selma sorority sisters. They want you to join their group. You'll probably never see Winnie Holmes after school is out unless you run into her downtown or something. Please be reasonable. We've gotta survive here. Go with the flow. Okay?"

Although not in complete agreement, I knew Bruce was thinking of us, and we had OTS on the horizon. *Maybe.*

"Okay," I concurred, standing up to take the dishes to the

sink, most of the spaghetti on my plate uneaten. I'd figure it out. Somehow.

~

Bruce stayed up late to watch a rerun of *Here's Lucy* with me. I made popcorn and we laughed until we almost choked. By the time the news came on, Bruce was asleep in the corner of the sofa. I watched his chest rise and fall as he dozed. Filled with love for him, I wrapped the brightly colored Afghan my grandmother had sent me from some exotic Italian port around my legs. As I deliberated the precariousness of my situation, I couldn't imagine tuning in every afternoon to watch the soap operas that Ruby and Belinda raved about. Though I did catch an episode occasionally—to stay in the loop. Belinda told me they even scheduled their college classes around *Days of Our Lives* so they could all watch it together in the parlor of the Tri-Zeta sorority house. Some girls even cut classes rather than miss a single program. A choice that never entered my mind.

Chewing on a hangnail, I tuned out a commercial. Yes, I had given up some dreams, but for the first time in my life I had a professional job, was respected, even liked. I also had a loving, sexy husband. I wrote into midair with my finger, "Life is not so bad here, really." I punched a period at the end of the spatial sentence with my closed fist.

Reaching over to nudge Bruce, I noticed the headlines on the newspaper strewn across the coffee table. The news was about the latest battle in Vietnam. I'd thought little about this dark topic lately. Heat tingled my groin as I rubbed Bruce's well-formed muscles, hard from years of rowing and football. Not wanting to admit it, but the rigors of basic training program probably helped.

"Honey wake up. Let's go to bed." He reached up and hung a loose arm around my neck while pecking my cheek.

We mounted the great white fluffy cloud of bed coverings spread over an array of springs and a flat wooden base. Dozing in Bruce's arms, it was unlikely I'd notice if there had even been a full-sized watermelon tucked underneath the mattress.

~

Drenched in my own perspiration, I awoke at 3:00 a.m. glad to be rid of my nightmare. In my dreams, Bruce was pursued by a militia of Viet Cong in the middle of the Tet Offensive. After the assault on the South Vietnamese, the forces attacked the U.S. Embassy where Bruce was assigned. A wave of relief washed over me as I realized we were both safely in our bed.

Slipping from Bruce's hold, I rolled over, twisting and turning to find my dozing niche. It didn't work—still wide-awake. After a half hour, the alarm went off on Bruce's side, calling him to the delivery routine. I hopped out of bed too.

"Where are you going?" he muttered, still half-asleep.

"With you. I'm tagging along on the route today. It's Sunday and we can take a nap this afternoon after church."

The paper route sprawled across several miles of rolling Selma lawns. Bruce handled the delivery with the deft efficiency that marked his style. As he approached each home, he rolled down his window and tossed newspapers on doorsteps, lawns, and sidewalks. If one landed on a lawn, he'd hop out and retrieve it in a second and either replace it with a fresh copy or wipe the dew on his pant leg.

As we approached the final street, the horizon ignited with a blaze to announce a new spring day. I lay my head against the headrest to absorb every morsel.

"It's only been two months since we arrived in Selma and it feels like we've lived here forever," I said.

Suddenly, Bruce opened the car door and made a hasty dive for a paper that landed in a birdbath. Barks and growls shrieked through the air. Two bloody-eyed mongrels, more than half the size of Bruce's six-foot frame, barreled from the house in determined pursuit of my husband. Barely dawn or not, I leaned on the horn. Bruce tugged at the door and jumped into the front seat with no time to spare. The canines bared their yellow teeth and lunged toward the car as Bruce shifted gears and burned rubber.

With a victorious grin, he said, "Forgot about those pups. They're not always around, but we have met before. Only not so up close and personal."

"You were lucky," I said, a hand to my forehead. "Good thing you played running back in high school." Out the side-view mirror, the dogs disappeared, while still bellowing their warnings. I scooted closer and touched his knee. "I really wish you didn't have to do this job." Bruce should be working to save historic districts or designing buildings. Not outrunning dogs for newspapers before breakfast in Selma, Alabama.

He shrugged a shoulder. "It's not that bad. Besides, it's not forever."

As we traveled back to Rohns, couples and families congregated on church doorsteps, chatting, laughing, and bouncing beautiful babies. Dressed up, all white, and all worshipping God in their own way—Baptist, Southern Baptist, Presbyterian, and a slew of denominations in between. Not a black face to be seen in this section of town.

We usually attended the only Catholic Church in Selma—all white faces. Today though, we drove out into the country to a small church surrounded by miles of farmland with tiny white nodules poking puffy heads above the dark soil. A sprinkling of shanties abutted the cotton fields, a stark contrast to sprawling old plantations. These weathered, unpainted shacks had sagging roofs and usually a single rocker or a couple of wooden chairs sitting precariously on wobbly front porches. A black grandpa teetered in a rickety wicker rocking chair, holding a maize-colored cat that filled the space between his knees. He puffed a corncob pipe, synchronized with each motion. When I waved my arm out of the open window, his blank, empty stare turned into a toothless grin, and he waved his straw hat in the air as if we were family coming for a visit. Surprised, I hadn't expected a response.

Bruce commented that he was an old guy and probably couldn't see the color of our skin.

"We don't know that for sure," I said. "He might just be friendly."

After church, we stopped at a roadside stand where three little girls were selling lemonade. The sign read five cents a cup. Bruce handed them a dollar bill and took the two cups. Their tightly bound black braids flapped in every direction as they jumped up and down and thanked him again and again.

When we got home, we undressed, enjoyed afternoon delightfulness, and fell asleep in a final embrace. Awakening to the dim light of sunset, I warmed up the leftover spaghetti and dove into lesson preparation for Monday morning.

"I'd best get goin' on this right quick," I had said to Bruce while sitting cross-legged over a stack of papers and books. I chuckled at the thought of how Winnie Holmes would surely reprimand a student if she heard such dialect and grammar. But on the playground, the black Southern English shortcuts could be heard everywhere. Some people believed that black kids couldn't be successful in school because of this alternate language pattern. Not a language expert, but I knew the kids in our two fifth-grade classes were learning. In fact, my students were mostly all advancing in their reading skills. Winnie and I discovered what they were missing and taught them, *together*—and the kids had no trouble understanding my English. *Students needed good teachers who believed in them. Period.* Winnie and many teachers I had met in the Teachers' Room fit that profile.

Bruce looked up from the stack of drawings spread over the massive dining table. "Cheer up! Just think, in a few more weeks you'll be free of all this." He waved his hand in magic wand fashion over the texts and lesson-planning notebook that lay open next to me on the floor.

He was right. With no lesson plans to prepare and papers to check, I'd be free to do what I pleased—read, sew, write letters. I was looking forward to getting to know my Selma Zeta sisters and going to the Ladies League luncheon the day after Memorial Day.

"I'm going to miss Brooks, though," I said, chewing my pencil eraser.

"Time to put that behind you, honey," said Bruce as he returned his attention to the rolled-up tubes of drawings.

The Ed Sullivan show droned on in the background. But my favorite, *Julia*, wouldn't be on until Tuesday night. Actress Diahann Carroll played the character of Julia, a black working mother whose husband had been killed in a reconnaissance flight over Vietnam. She was a role model for women, black and white. *If only everyone would think of that, and we could work together.*

Bruce was happy with the addition plans for Men's Alliance Lodge. For me, something was missing.

CHAPTER 16

With his hands behind his back and his ample waistline peeking out from beneath his unbuttoned jacket, Principal Williams stationed himself at the front entrance of the school each morning, poised to greet every teacher. Except for an occasional scratch at his mustache, his stance was steady.

Teachers marched into the building, laden with books and bags, and nodded their respectful responses: "*Mornin', sir, a'right.*" The mantra-like litanies dribbled like a drop of honey that might spill from a biscuit and onto one's finger.

Cordial greetings and respectful nods hinted at my marginal acceptance into the Brooks community. Even if I walked on water, I'd never be part of the inner circle.

Principal Williams always smiled and said my name. "Mornin', Mrs. Zuretski." On one recent occasion, he added that he'd soon be scheduling interviews to fill the fifth-grade position. I smiled recalling his final words as he raised his bushy eyebrows with an eager grin. "Sure you don't want to apply?"

Again, citing the excuse of Bruce's possible orders, I politely declined. He had nodded his understanding, flashed a smile, and turned to speak with a patiently waiting secretary. As I moved down the hallway toward my classroom, I sensed my decline had far-reaching impact.

Bruce had reminded me, *several times,* that continuing down this path would only cause us to be socially ostracized. It would interfere with Bruce's work with Billy Chas and the Lodge remodel and maybe his role with civilians at the base. Mr. Tilly was a good friend of Billy Chas. Bruce ended his litany explaining how the principal had a job to do and had to hire someone for the fifth-grade position. Yet, Principal Williams's affirmations and interest in my teaching made me feel like I had a gift, one that was treasured. Not to mention my personal fulfillment.

Unlocking the rear door and glancing toward the playground, I saw Jackson perched on the first step. His slender fingers clenched a book, and his curly head huddled close above the pages. The sight warmed me from head to toe. Just a few short weeks ago, he was reading books at a third-grade level and now he was reading *The Hardy Boys.* His grandmother, an ever-present sentinel at his side, stood nearby and clutched a large sack. I waved when she looked up and wondered if she toted more pecans. She smiled slightly, but quickly looked down at her feet.

When the morning bell rang, Jackson was first in line. I greeted the students and gave orders for a straight line—a strategy learned from Winnie. My young charges marched as quietly as possible. I wondered if they thought about how each new school day brought us closer to summer vacation.

As the students filed in, Jackson's grandmother ambled up to my side and lifted the large bag out towards me.

"I made this, ma'am, and sure hope ya' like it."

I inhaled deeply, doubting the family had extra resources to buy gifts. "Why, thank you. Please come inside where I can open it, Mrs. Willis." The elderly lady slowly preceded me, then hesitated, awaiting my entry. Again, I gestured, "Please, after you."

Giggles and bustling. Just like Christmas morning, kids awaiting the parental signal to open presents. I placed the well-used brown paper bag on an empty student desk. A hush descended over the seated students and halted the electric energy of a few moments earlier.

"Hmm, wonder what's inside this bag?" With exaggerated eyebrows, I prolonged the opening, enjoying the eager sea of faces. My expression was returned with equally wide-eyed stares. I untied the white string that bound the package, reached inside, and tugged at the soft contents. Over the span of the desk and onto the linoleum cascaded a puffy, colorful quilt. Each square contained a Biblical phrase surrounded by cherubs and angels.

"Praise be to Jesus!" The only words from Gramama. Every head bowed.

Not used to praying in public school, I bowed my head and noticed the shabby house slippers on the tiny feet of Jackson's grandmother. I wondered how much it cost her to make this gift. When we finished praying, my arms instinctively encircled Gramama's tiny frame. Her heartbeat next to mine. The peach scent of her hair balm filled my nostrils as her frail body almost melted into my arms—but only for a fraction of a second.

It wasn't necessary that she make eye contact. "Thank ya' for what ya' is doin' to help my Jackson." Her words were barely a whisper against my ear. She released herself from my grip and walked toward the doorway. "I be seein' ya' after school, son. Learn good, ya' hear?" She ambled through the doorway without looking back.

Fighting an urge to cry, I clutched the puffy fabric close to my body—a space that once carried our baby. This piece would hold a special spot in our nursery—someday. I placed the handmade quilt over the top of the bookcase and remarked how it created a cozy reading corner for our last days before summer vacation. The children were giddy with the idea, and I allowed my smile to cling to Jackson's. I hoped this moment during the last week of the school year would stay with these youngsters forever. *Respect and kindness, especially between two disparate races, had to mean something.*

Shortly before lunch, Principal Williams came into my room, his brows knit and head lowered. "A word in my office during your lunch period, Mrs. Zuretski."

Convinced this was another attempt to get me to teach at Brooks next year filled my belly with more anger than angst at this point. *It was hard enough to leave, yet it would be harder to remain.* Entering Mr. Williams's office and seeing his face replaced anxiety with fear.

"Please sit down, Mrs. Zuretski. I have some sad news."

My knees weakened. "What's wrong? Is my husband all right?"

"This is not about your husband." He motioned toward a chair near his desk. My face must have radiated my relief, but his glare softened for only a second.

He took his seat behind his desk and explained that Jackson's grandmother, Mariah Jesse Willis, was struck down and killed on her way home from walking Jackson to school that morning by some guy driving a truck. His report, presented in an obituary-like manner, abruptly ended.

With a barely audible tone, he gazed out the window, as if trying to see the runaway driver from his chair. "The coward didn't even stop. Jis' kept drivin'."

Mariah was her first name, Jackson's grandmother. As quickly as I whisked away tears falling on my cheeks with the back of my hand, the more they continued to flow.

Principal Williams passed me a box of tissues as I sobbed.

"It can't be… I just saw her a few hours ago…and what about Jackson? What will happen to him?" I asked, finally managing to sputter a full sentence.

"He has aunts and an older sister, actually two older sisters. There's plenty of family to help out."

"No one will be able to fill the void. No one." As images rushed into my mind, words were disconnected. "He worshipped his grandmother, and she lived for him. Do the police have any idea who could have done this?"

"No, ma'am. Don't even have a license number. Just a white pickup with a rifle perched in the back window. Heard the driver was some white guy." He lowered his eyes.

"Well, that description could fit a third of the vehicles in Dallas County," I said, unable to sit still and recalling at least three white pickup trucks parked at Billy Chas's house the day of the barbeque. Whatever identification was seen would never come out into the open. *Did the driver belong to the Men's Alliance?* The thought crossed my mind.

"What can I do to help?" My sadness competed with a professional desire to do what was needed.

"His aunt can't get here until 4:00 p.m. I have already spoken to Mrs. Holmes, but the two of you need to tell Jackson what happened," Mr. Williams continued, visibly shaken.

I swallowed and dug my nails into the palm of my hand in a lame attempt to halt further tears and process what my boss wanted me to do.

"I don't…I can't." Able to form responses before spitting them out was a skill I was usually adept at doing. But this was different. Stretching taller, I spoke in a full sentence, "Sir, it is just that I have never done anything like this before." Truthfully, I was ten years old the last time someone close to me passed away. My grandfather had a heart attack and died instantly. Telling a little boy that his surrogate mother had just been killed was an insurmountable request.

As if he read my mind, he said, "Look, Mrs. Zuretski, you are young, new to teaching, and new to the South. Some of the attitudes and actions here in Selma go back generations. I can't expect you to understand." His face softened as he leaned slightly toward me.

"You have a lot of growing up to do, but you have a good heart, if you don't mind my sayin' so. Mrs. Holmes understands our people, and she will help you talk with Jackson. The boy needs you right now. Your youthful freshness and bright mind have made a difference at Brooks in barely two months. And that's a fact. These kids are learnin' because of you." He leaned toward me as if determined to make his point clear. "You are a born teacher, young lady. I need you to step up and do what needs to be done here for that boy." He hesitated until I looked directly into his eyes. "And for you as well," he said. His softened tone so wise.

With emotions ricocheting, I blew my nose on the third tissue and dabbed at moist cheeks. Closing my eyes didn't dispel the mounting tension. I wanted to make this nightmare disappear but sounds from the playground filtered into my consciousness. Smack, skip-a-beat, smack, skip-a-beat, the jump rope hit the pavement. The repetitive monotone, *"Teddy Bear, Teddy Bear, turn around…,"* the children laughed as they successfully maneuvered into position without interruption. Their voices were a soothing balm.

Peering into Principal Williams' dark eyes I knew there was no choice but to do what he asked.

Lowering my head, I spoke, "Mrs. Holmes and I will tell Jackson, sir."

The bell rang and Principal Williams rose to his full stature, towering over me by more than a good twelve inches. I had been summoned and would respond to the call.

"Thank you, Mrs. Zuretski. A tough job, but you and Mrs. Holmes will help the boy deal with this tragic news."

As I turned the corner heading toward the Teacher's Room to wash my face, Winnie and I collided. She threw her arms around me. As our cheeks brushed, our tears mingled. Neither words nor skin color mattered. Clinging to me for a few moments, she slowly stepped back and reached for my hands. I sensed how this woman knew the pain of loss—ancestral remnants of century-old struggles.

"That boy needs *you*, his teacher." Winnie stopped before lowering her voice and continuing, "Claire, he needs both of us. Together." We walked toward her classroom; heads bent arms lightly brushing.

CHAPTER 17

Sitting across from Winne, I slipped damp palms along the sides of my skirt and hoped she didn't notice. "I'm Jackson's teacher now, but do you really think it's a good idea for me to break such news about his grandmother?"

Sitting erect and proud in her seat, Winnie's tone changed. "I bet you're also thinkin' I'm black, Jackson's black, and Gramama Willis was black." Gliding into the vernacular, she continued, "We is all Black folk, honey, 'cept for you."

A fiery glare I had not seen before radiated from behind her horn-rimmed glasses. What she said was true, but that had nothing to do with how I felt about telling Jackson his grandmother had been killed by a hit-and-run driver.

"Yes, what you said is true. Look, all I meant was, you know the family better and I don't have any experience with this kinda stuff." It felt like my voice was squeaking, fear and anger battling to take over. I dug my nails into my palms. The last thing I needed now was tears. We had only minutes before the recess bell would summon the students back to the classroom.

Regaining her usual sense of composure, her eyes softened to tender pools as she placed her hand on my forearm.

"Sorry, Claire," she said. "We're a team, and teams work together for the goal, the win. You are making an impact on families—this family, for sure. They never had any white folk be in solidarity with them before. Please understand that."

Her tone was a lowered version of the classroom take-control teacher voice. I sat on the edge of a metal chair with reciprocal intensity, enraptured and tentative. Her words were more than mere flattery.

Winnie raised her thick brows as she continued, "Anyway, if you're gonna be a teacher, ya' gotta sometimes deliver the tough messages. The truth is this beautiful and talented little boy has lost the one person who loved and supported him more than anyone else in the whole world. He needs you, and you can help him."

Tears spilled onto my cheeks before I could dig my nails into my palms again. *My* truth had been that I didn't even want to be in Selma. Now I was faced with a situation that I felt ill-equipped to handle.

Rubbing my cheeks, I looked down at my perfectly painted hot pink toenails. My friend was right. I owed this to Jackson and to Winnie. *I owed it to myself.* I took a breath and steadied my voice. "Okay, Winnie. I'll do it. Can one of his sisters be here when we talk with him?"

She reached out and touched my arm. "Claire, we can't count on the two older sisters. That's why Gramama Willis was also raisin' the baby. The only sibling Jackson has in school is the sister who is three years older and at R.B. Hudson Middle School, clear on the other side of town. The older sister works lots of jobs to help."

She squeezed my arm again. "I know this is hard." Her head gently rocking up and down. "But I'll be right here with you," she said, straight-mouthed and with a blink.

I was startled by the facts I'd just heard about a baby. *Did the baby belong to the older sister?* Winnie had told me about Gramama Willis's daughter, Jackson's mother. She drank herself to death, leaving three young kids. No one knew where Jackson's father was.

My position in this dilemma made me braver. "Who are the parents of the baby? Who's taking care of the baby now?"

Winnie folded her hands in her lap and slowly breathed

in and out. "The baby belongs to Mrs. Willis's granddaughter, Delberta, Jackson's older sister." Winnie watched me closely to see my reaction, then continued, "A neighbor lady has been carin' for the little one every morning while Gramama Willis walked Jackson to school. Principal Williams went over and told the neighbor about the accident."

I sat trying to process the many puzzled layers of what I had just heard. Winnie glanced at the clock and stood. "I know you'll do a good job." She patted my shoulder and continued, "After school, I'll walk your students out of the building, while you get Jackson busy on some project. Let's meet in the Teachers' Room and come back to your classroom together. When it's quieter. Okay?"

With a slow nod in tacit agreement, my thoughts were on fast-forward, wondering how I'd survive the afternoon. I tugged at the bag of miniature Hershey bars I was saving for the last day of school. The events of this day warranted a change of plans. After the students returned and took their seats, I passed out the candy and opened a new *Hardy Boys* book purchased at the base commissary in Texas. *We were saving it for our own little boy, maybe, someday.* Settling into my chair, I began the story, using sound, intonation, and gestures, snatching every tool in my box. The kids munched on chocolate and soaked up each adventure—my engagement allaying my own angst.

The clanging of the first dismissal bell offered relief while a question from Jonah brought me back to the moment.

"How come we didn't do any math this afternoon, Mrs. Zuretski?"

"I am glad you love math so much, Jonah. We'll do extra tomorrow." From the corner of my eye, I saw a tongue jut toward Jonah's direction. Leave it up to Jonah. He had a way of speaking his mind—even if not always appropriate.

Before the students packed up their materials, I reviewed the homework listed on the blackboard and noticed Jackson look toward the frosted window on the classroom door. His grandmother always arrived early. I tensed at the thought.

"Jackson, would you be able to help me take an inventory of all of our books for the end of the year report I must give to Principal Williams by tomorrow?" My request was a timely distraction.

"Yes'm," he said, grinning from ear to ear.

Winnie Holmes was waiting when I opened the door to release my class to her charge. "Why is Mrs. Holmes dismissin' us?" Jonah again.

"I have some business to take care of today, and Jackson is going to help me by counting our textbooks."

I sensed Jonah was about to present an argument about his turn to help. With a quick smile I said, "You can help another time. Okay?" Jonah grinned in satisfaction and gathered his belongings. I set Jackson up for the book-tallying task, handed him sheets of loose-leaf paper, and left to make a visit to the Teacher's Room to gather my thoughts and await Winnie's return, as planned.

Collapsing into an old cushy leather armchair, I made quick mental notes about what I would say to Jackson. *How much his grandmother loved him and wanted him to be successful in school ... her pride ... her joy. And someone in a truck accidentally hit her, the driver didn't see her.* With each endearment, I sagged further into the seat, heavy in painful recognition of the responsibility that lay before me. The uncertainty about the truck driver's motive drove splinters of pain deeper. With unaccustomed numbness, I watched the Roman numerals on the wooden clock until the first-grade teacher, whose favorite pastime was chatting, burst through the door.

Clutching a linen sack in one hand, while she slapped the other just above her ample bosom, she gasped then stared at me. "I heard 'bout Jackson's gramama. Dat is bad. How he takin' it?"

"He doesn't know yet. Winnie and I are going to tell him in a couple of minutes." Thinking how fast news travels, I had hoped Jackson hadn't heard about his grandmother.

"God bless y'all." She lowered her tear-filled eyelids and sauntered towards the restroom door. Gone was her usual effervescence.

When Winnie Holmes and I walked back to the classroom, Jackson was still alone and had counted the books and neatly stacked them in equal piles on a table. He stood at the chalkboard, immersed in drawing, and didn't notice us enter. We stood in awe, watching him create a geometric overlay around the number 36. He artfully sketched a winding path amidst a bed of white gardenia shrubs that led to a large house at the opposite end of the same blackboard. He alternated between arm-reaching strokes and smaller detailed marks of white and blue. *So glad I had sprung for the colored chalk.*

I gently closed the door. A disruption into the sanctity of this child's ardent creation seemed like a sacrilege. Mesmerized by the talent before our eyes, we watched as Jackson continued to draw trees, flowers, and a big pie cooling on a window ledge. He stopped with a sudden jolt, stood back as if something was missing and said, "Almost done."

With a swift maneuver of the remaining chalk stub, he sketched a boy walking along the path. The boy pulled a wagon, filled to the brim with books. "Lots and lots of books," he mumbled as a sheepish grin spread over his face, but behind the veneer was the proud confidence of a talented artist.

"What a beautiful mural, Jackson. Can you tell us about it?" Between my teaching partner and me barely a muscle twitched.

"Yes'm. Dis is the big house I gonna build for my Gramama and me some day when I have a lotta money." The grin ignited into a full-blown smile that encompassed his entire face. "I'm goin' to college and be a teacher and even a school principal. I might be the boss of all the schools in Selma. I'll make sure all the kids, both black and white, have all the books they want."

We rushed toward Jackson and sandwiched him between

us. With smothering hugs, we struggled to keep the salty drops in check.

"Your grandmother would be very proud." My words barely audible.

Jackson pulled back as he riveted his gaze directly into my eyes. "Oh, ma'am, she *is* proud of me. She tells me every day. Where she, anyhow?" His head shifted toward the door and his eyes widened as he spoke.

Surprised at my own composure, I spoke before Winnie had a chance. "Please come and sit down with us for a minute, Jackson. I would like to talk with you."

CHAPTER 18

Jackson never returned to school after his grandmother's hit-and-run death. I gathered his work and final report card, grading him on the success he'd earned throughout the school year—all A's. I also packed up the series of twelve *Hardy Boys* books that I'd hoped to read to my own son one day. Jackson enjoyed this series, and he would devour every single word.

Winnie sat in stilted silence as I placed the books in a box for her to deliver to Jackson's aunt who had a small farm on the outskirts of town.

"Where will Jackson go to school next year?" I asked Winnie.

"R.B. Hudson Middle School, same as the others. His oldest sister, Delberta, works in the kitchen at Dottie's Place and cleans at the public library. But she's looking for more steady work. She'll be at the house at night with Jackson, the baby, and the younger sister who attends Hudson. The aunt will watch the kids all summer. 'Sides, they can help with the crops." Winnie had a knack for making sense out of chaos.

I wondered who the father of Delberta's baby was and why she wasn't in school but didn't ask.

"Hope Jackson will keep reading," I said instead. *Who would be his cheerleader now that his grandmother was gone?*

"You know Jackson. He'll find time to read those books. It was mighty kind of you to buy 'em," said Winnie.

"He has made so much progress this year that I couldn't bear to let him fall behind. If properly guided, Jackson's talent and love of reading could lead him to a better life." The aching panic in my belly over the possibility that his progress over these past months could be lost drained any energy I had left.

I moved a stack of papers aside and carefully posed an indirect question to Winnie. "He wrote in his journal that he has two older sisters, but never mentioned a baby."

"The baby is, well I guess you'd say, Jackson's nephew. It's complicated." She rolled her eyes.

Sensing the complicated part was not a topic Winnie wanted to delve into at this moment, I handed her the box. "I understand." *Life was complicated and not everyone lived the way I grew up.*

Winnie and I promised to keep in touch, and then she left. As I gathered my few belongings, my eyes wandered over to the chalk sketch of the gardenia that Jackson had drawn on the black construction paper. I gently removed it from the corkboard and placed it on top of my papers. It was the first sign of life I'd seen when I entered the classroom weeks earlier. *Perhaps I'd buy a frame for it.* As I picked up my stack, I took one last look behind me, and closed the door on my fifth-grade classroom for the final time.

When I arrived at the front office, Principal Brooks was not there. I laid the keys on his desk and anchored a note of appreciation and good wishes under the ring.

As I left the building, dark clouds hovered above the school as thunder pounded the heavens. Without notice, a flash of lightning whipped through the sky.

"Looks like we're fixin' to get a good storm," said the first-grade teacher scurrying out behind me. "Better hurry on." She was her usual jovial self, ending her admonition with a bellowing laugh. I recalled the time we first met in the Teachers' Room. She had reminded me I was in the Black Belt, and I wasn't sure how to take it. I wasn't sure who had learned more over these past two months—my students or me.

As I dashed toward the Ford, zigzags of lightning continued

to blast from above. Two more shattering bolts and the clouds exploded in a raging torrent. I unlocked the door and slid into the seat. Glad to be out of the tumultuous weather, I pulled some tissues from my bag and dabbed at raindrops. They clung to my damp skin like teardrops that didn't want to let go.

The rain pelted the windshield, pounding a final crescendo on my time at Brooks. Slumping in the vinyl seat, I looked out at the water-logged playground. *And now what?* I jostled my too curly hair. Summer lay ahead and I had a few hundred dollars that were all mine. Bruce and I were making a decent life here in this small Southern town. *Right?* I should feel happy.

I tugged at the rearview mirror to examine my mascara-streaked face and noticed an old shed in the field behind me. Pellets of rain, now slowing, pinged as they pounded its tin roof. It was just an old shed, but today it was also a *watershed.* I laughed at the irony. One of my high school teachers had used the term often to refer to events that changed the course of history.

What would it take to change the course of history in this town? Shrugging, I turned the key in the ignition. Teaching at Brooks was behind me now. *Or was it? I didn't believe in coincidences.*

CHAPTER 19

On Memorial Day, Bruce lounged in front of the television set watching patriotic parades. I sewed my outfit for the Ladies League luncheon — a peachy-pink, two-piece dress. The ensemble would be completed with navy patent leather heels, off-white hose, and a peach straw hat with a navy ribbon. I'd prove I knew how to dress for an elegant society luncheon and fit right in, drinking tea and nibbling on small sandwiches and cookies. Bruce wanted us to be accepted, and he repeated over and over how being a part of Southern society would make our lives easier. I was willing to at least give it a chance.

Struggling to fall asleep that night, I was jolted awake by another startling dream. Wiping the perspiration from my face, I allowed the lazy staccato crackling of crickets outside the window to sooth me back to reality. *It was just a dream,* I told myself. This time it was about the League luncheon. I was all dolled up, laughing, talking, and fitting in. Then I reached to pick up a fallen napkin and spilled a cup of hot tea on my newly sewn outfit. Brown stains appeared as Rorschach inkblots — all glaring at me. I dozed into a semi-sleep again, until Bruce knocked over the alarm clock. A crack of light illuminated the hallway, shining in my eyes through the darkness. This indulgence of a nightlight added to our electric bill, but roaches didn't like light.

After Bruce left, I dampened a warm washcloth and hopped back in bed with the cloth over my eyes. Soothed into sleep at last, I didn't hear his return, nor his departure for work. I awakened to a chorus of robins and blue jays chiming their morning ritual through the bright easterly sunlight. The clock read 9:10 a.m. I slipped from the covers and enjoyed a long, and soothing shower. Preparing for the luncheon was almost as much fun as attending, I thought as I generously spritzed White Shoulders perfume over my body.

I pulled the rollers from my hair and tugged every chunk with a dryer. With the prevailing humidity, the wavy flow wouldn't last, but a few squirts of hair spray might help. A little attention to the eyelash curler, a touch of the mascara wand, and I was ready to go.

Mrs. Bader was waiting in the foyer, and we rode to Ruby's house together. Thankfully, Mrs. Bader didn't mention my teaching status. *Only time would tell if I was forgiven for such a "sin."*

I pulled the Ford up to another grand manor, complete with a signature wraparound veranda. With gushed eloquence, Ruby welcomed us, making me feel like a relative she hadn't seen in a decade. The polite cadence of conversation and chatter brimming with Southern hospitality flowed like hot syrup drenching freshly grilled pancakes. As I entered the French provincial parlor that replicated Mrs. Bader's, well-coiffed heads turned in my direction, discrete and subtle. The small, tight group could easily spot a newcomer. *And I was one of those Yankees.*

A gracious hostess, Ruby continued to make every League member feel special. She introduced me to each lady, proclaiming our eternal bond in Tri-Zeta sisterhood.

"The Mason-Dixon Line cannot separate sisters." She hugged me and laughed at her little jibe.

The Civil War was over. No northern aggression. But her comments broke the tension and polite chuckles followed her lead. Belinda started clapping and so did the others.

Despite the trite digs, Ruby and Belinda shared many similarities with my Midwestern Zeta sisters — smart, accomplished, and full of fun. I missed my college days — serving as president of the Women Students' League and my sorority pledge class, and feature editor of the campus newspaper. I even got chosen for the homecoming court.

The ladies filtered toward massive tables on the patio outside as a maid carried a large silver tray stacked with watercress and chicken salad sandwiches. Mrs. Bader gravitated toward a couple of elderly women, conservatively groomed and with deep rose outlined lips. They chatted incessantly. I sat at a table adjacent to Mrs. Bader, joined by a few ladies close to my own age, and a couple more who desperately clung to versions of their former youthful selves.

Donned in black and white uniforms, pressed and stiffly starched, colored help seemed to float throughout the space. Ignored. Non-entities. I accepted a sandwich from one maid and some cookies from another. A third poured lemonade into etched crystal tumblers then meandered toward two belles who sat with Mrs. Bader. Two more servers, one carrying an elaborate silver tea service and the other a crystal pitcher, glided towards me offering both hot and cold beverages. I took the iced tea offered and thanked the lady who carried the crystal pitcher.

"Yes'm." She nodded humbly, without making eye contact. The two ladies sitting with Mrs. Bader abruptly stopped talking, mid-sentence, and exchanged sharp glances. The maid hurried off to attend to another table.

More serving maids paraded through the swinging kitchen door and continued to circulate. They clutched silver trays covered with mounds of triangular sandwiches. Iced lemon cookies and pecan shortbread were plentiful. With noses pointed skyward, the Selmians accepted offerings without hesitation or gratitude. When offered more goodies, I took two and again thanked the server. This time no one, including the maid, made a sound.

"Why, you've hardly touched your watercress sandwich, honey," said Mrs. Bader as she made a 180-degree turn to speak to me. Although embarrassed as my landlady broke the impasse and singled me out, I smiled demurely.

"I have just been too enchanted with the conversation," I said, smiling at my new table friends.

If my words were a bit too sarcastic, Mrs. Bader didn't seem to notice. She waved slender fingers randomly with an air of irritation that demanded instant service. Pulling out a lemon wafer, the remainder of food on my plate sat untouched.

The flashed velvet smile from my landlady reappeared. "I do love these watercress sandwiches, Ruby. You are so handy."

"Thank you, Sylvia." She rolled her eyes for emphasis. "You'll never know what I went through to get my new maid to make these sandwiches right." Ruby raised her voice to make a point to servers nearby preoccupied with fussing about the tables, plates, and trays.

Ruby's comment made me choke. Mrs. Bader patted my back with a tap that was more annoying than helpful. Before anyone even had to crook a finger, a maid limped awkwardly toward me with a pitcher of water and a fresh glass. As I reached forward, I encountered eyes as black as the center of the daisies that sat in a nearby vase.

"Thank you, Miss." I smiled and connected with those black-eyed Susan eyes.

"Yes'm. Glad to help." She looked directly at me and smiled broadly.

"Yes, very nice, Lily Mae." Ruby spoke in a tone of sincere warmth. She then stood and cleared her throat, almost purposefully recouping her demeanor. "Now please fetch more of those lemon goodies. We do love those cookies, and the tray is getting low."

Her back gracefully turned to Lily Mae and her command was complete.

"Yes'm." As she shuffled away with as much speed as she could muster, I thought how she was younger than her disability suggested.

Confused by Ruby's contrary action, I asked, "Who is that girl?" Ruby had taken her seat and concentrated on the arrangement of her skirt around the legs of the chair. "She's young and very quick," I said.

Although no humor was intended, the women at the table covered their giggles with linen napkins.

"Sweet thing," Ruby said, flashing her charming Southern smile in my direction. "Lily Mae has been with my family for years, and I don't reckon that she ever saw the seventh grade." More giggles. Ruby had completely recouped her stalwart demeanor.

"Once you get to a certain age, or if you have a baby out of wedlock—and most o' these young nigras do—what's the point in goin' to school?" Mrs. Bader piped in, glancing an *I-told-you-so* expression in my direction.

"Well, she could take classes, get a high school diploma, and find a good job." I wasn't going to let this pass.

"Claire, you been teachin' at that colored school too long." Mrs. Bader dabbed at the sides of her mouth unnecessarily and exchanged glances with other ladies in the room. "Colored folk just don't have the smarts to take much to schoolin'. Just not in their nature."

I cringed and struggled to temper my response. "My students at Brooks made good progress in less than three months." It was the truth, and the point was made.

"Three months was probably all the learnin' they had," Mrs. Bader countered. "Those other teachers before you didn't teach anything. Honey, there is a big difference between colored brains and white brains."

The other League ladies nodded in unison, affirming Mrs. Bader's words by pursing pouted lips, dismissing further consideration of the topic.

The two older maids continued to fuss at tables and rearrange the cookies. They were not invisible, and I didn't think they were hard of hearing. The back-handed compliment by Mrs. Bader didn't change my sudden urge to escape and join the birds beyond the terrace as they flitted from hibiscuses to japonicas.

"Do tell us, Claire," begged Belinda.

"Uh, beg your pardon. What did you say, Belinda? I was looking at those little birds. What kind of birds are they, anyway?"

"Oh, I was jis' askin' about that shabby old colored lady who was hit last week by a driver. Newspaper article said she was jay walkin'. I heard her grandkids went to Brooks Elementary. I was wonderin' if you knew anymore of the story." Belinda had a slight edge to her voice. "By the way, Claire, those birds are mockingbirds."

My napkin sprawled as it hit the fluffy rug, and I thought of my nightmare the previous night. Fortunately, the long tablecloth concealed my gaffe as well as my dripping palms. I squeezed the linen fabric that touched my knees to gain control. *I hadn't seen any newspaper article and I had looked.*

"Yes, her grandson attended the school. I wasn't there long enough to know him or the family very well," I lied.

I should have told them about Jackson Willis, and how smart he was and how he would likely be a school principal, maybe even superintendent of schools. Instead, I took another bite of a cream-filled sandwich.

Another petite blonde with a dazzling smile offered unsupportively, "That Negro woman was likely juiced up on some hooch and wasn't watchin' her footing." All the ladies laughed at the mimicking comment as they nodded and unnecessarily dabbed at the edges of their lips with their napkins.

"We don't know all the facts, unfortunately." My cheeks were warm.

The laughing stopped and glances were exchanged around the table. I sensed I had spoken out of turn, but it was too late to stop. "Well, if the article didn't hint at anything more than some careless hit-and-run driver, I think we need more facts. Wouldn't you agree?" Although no one could see it, my knees were shaky. I nonchalantly reached for my iced tea.

"Claire is right. We don't know all the facts. It is very sad, indeed." Ruby patted my arm, wanting to dissuade the rising tension. "Would y'all like a little more sugar?"

Ruby offered the silver sugar bowl around the table. I caught her riveted eye toward Belinda. Almost unnoticeable, Belinda flashed an admonishing eyebrow in return.

Thinking of how I needed to make friends and these ladies were two of my best chances, I grinned and politely took two sugar cubes from the bowl.

"Well, my best college friend, Sandy, has an uncle who is a police officer and hates working traffic detail in a big city. He told us girls lots of stories about chasing careless drivers."

I pursed my lips and shook my head knowing what I said was another second half-truth. The ladies responded with nods. *It worked.*

Soon, the luncheon dishes were cleared, and Ruby called the business meeting to order with a spoon tap against her glass. The agenda was brief with mostly talk about the annual fashion show in the fall and always popular recipe exchange. The meeting was adjourned in short order. Belinda reminded everyone about the League pinochle party at her house in June.

As we were leaving, Ruby pulled me aside. "Sorry, some of the ladies were so harsh about the woman who was killed. That was a tragedy." She held both of my hands.

Stunned by Ruby's candor, I glanced toward the floor. "A tragedy, indeed," I said.

Shifting her stance, she hugged me and continued, "I do hope ya' will come to pinochle. Belinda makes the best mint juleps. Sylvia doesn't play pinochle, but I'll pick you up."

"That would be lovely. Thanks, Ruby. Talk soon." Even

though I felt tormented for not defending Gramama Willis, there was something about Ruby that separated her from the others. She cared. I would be glad to be invited back, especially since Mrs. Bader wouldn't be there.

Ruby stuck her rouged cheek carefully to the side of mine and smacked a loud kiss into space, followed by a trés chic "*mooah.*"

As we drove toward Rohns, Mrs. Bader droned on about who wore what outfit, who had put on weight and the slow help. I was on autopilot. Driving through a wooded area, we passed by the Men's Alliance Lodge. What I saw there dredged up more questions. And suspicions.

CHAPTER 20

Since Mr. Tilly's station wagon sat in front of the Lodge in the middle of the afternoon, I wondered if Bruce might need a ride home from the base. I pushed the accelerator, eager to get back to Rohns. He might be trying to call me.

But there was no call for the rest of the afternoon. I prepared dinner assuming he'd be home around 5:30 as usual. When the grandfather clock chimed a half past six o'clock, I began to worry. Ten minutes later he appeared at the back door, waving at Mr. Tilly as the wagon pulled away.

"Where have you been, honey? I was worried about you," I said.

When he reached to kiss my cheek, I noticed his eyes were red. He also smelled like beer. "Mr. Tilly and I stopped by the Lodge on our way home from the base so he could show me the closed off section they're planning to remodel. He bought me a beer. And that's why I'm late."

He smiled and walked into the bedroom to change clothes. "Dinner ready? I'm starved," he shouted loud enough for me to hear.

I wondered why he wouldn't tell me he was there all afternoon. Adjusting the plates on the table, I pondered my approach regarding the fact that he'd been at the Lodge much longer than he had admitted. I flipped my hair aside. It was likely no big deal.

"So how was the luncheon with the League ladies?" He slipped his arms around my waist. I could still smell the beer.

"It was interesting," I said, smiling then turning away to pull out the forks and knives.

Bruce straightened. "That doesn't sound so good." His expression sobered.

"Oh, the food was good. Ruby is truly the gem." I grinned at my own pun. Bruce looked through the artificiality, waiting.

"Mrs. Bader and I drove by the Lodge on our way back to Rohns and saw Mr. Tilly's car parked out front earlier this afternoon. Assuming you might need a ride home, I dashed here to get your call. But no call."

"I planned to explain, babe. We did look over the site and that was after the guys treated me to lunch. Then, they gave me the pitch about the Men's Alliance. They want me to join."

I sat down. My knees felt wobbly. "What did you say?"

"Told 'em I'd think it over. I wanted to talk with you about it. Plus, with the paper route and work at the base, I don't have much extra time." He looked down at his feet before continuing, "But they hired me to do the renovation plans and are paying well. We need to give the whole Men's Alliance idea some thought before I commit, either way."

Certainly, this twist of circumstances could bring added conflict into our already tampered lives. Bruce's questioning tone allayed my anxiety somewhat. Our dinner was already beyond cold. I decided to let the topic slip away. At least for now.

As we cleaned up the dinner dishes together, Bruce put his arms around me. "Honey, everything okay? We don't need to make any hasty decisions. We'll talk about the Men's Alliance later. I don't know if I'd fit in anyway." He kissed the top of my head and continued in a whisper, "We need to talk about trying to have more babies too."

My discontent had nothing to do with the miscarriage. Still, we clung to each other in front of the tiny kitchen window. The only sound was the wind jostling the budding pecans. Neither of us spoke of the Men's Alliance or when and how we would plan to have those babies.

He buried his cheek into my tousled hair, then gently tilted my head back and bent for my lips. My breath was spent as Bruce swept me into his arms. Seconds later we were atop the mountainous bed. What seemed like minutes became the entire night.

I awoke to a cup of coffee and toast served on a tray atop the feathered duvet.

"You have an obstetrician appointment today, right?" Bruce placed the food on the nightstand.

"Later this afternoon. Just routine. Nice that the office is nearby and within walking distance."

I grinned. The walk would be welcome, even though it would be in the wrenching heat of the afternoon. Mr. Tilly couldn't be Bruce's chauffeur forever.

"Call me if you need anything. I'll take off at lunch and be home. Try to get a little more rest." He nodded and turned to walk away.

I hopped out from under the quilt, coffee cup in hand and followed him to the back door. With a quick reach to fill the free mug he'd picked up from the gas station, he was gone. The warped screen door clamored against the frame. Before I could move to reconnect the hook, his head reappeared.

I mouthed a return affectation, blew him a kiss, and poured a second cup of coffee, then plunked into a kitchen chair. The *Selma News* lay on the kitchen table. We wouldn't even have a newspaper if we had to pay for it. Bruce's one job perk. I thumbed through the society section. Fashions in pinks, yellows, and blues splashed the pages, summertime sales abounded, almost as plentiful as the azaleas and blue salvias around Rohns Manor. Selma had a colorful landscape, but no department stores within miles. The nearest box stores were in Montgomery. Not a single mall, no movie shows, no nightspots. Nothing but a couple of small all-purpose stores and a mini version of a Winn-Dixie supermarket.

My daily horoscope did little to boost my mood—no prophesy to ease my anxiety about the Selma Ladies League, or temper my angst over the Men's Alliance, or suddenly lift our military orders. The only affirming note was encouragement to "… stick with your gut and do what you know has to be done. Happiness will be achieved if you listen to your heart." I laughed. *Hadn't I listened to my heart too much recently?* I shook off the plaguing doubts. They weren't going to help.

I poured more coffee and mindlessly flipped through more local reports, supermarket sales and scores of sports outcomes. Meandering through the pages resurrected my emotions about how little was mentioned of the hit-and-run death of Mariah Jesse Willis. A woman's life had been erased in a flash, without as much as a follow-up investigative report. A cherished life gone in seconds. A young boy left without his grandmother. My insides deflated like a punctured balloon.

The classified ads came last. They usually held no interest for me, but a bold print in a corner caught my attention. It read: "Teacher Needed for Disadvantaged Adult Classes." The course was part of the school district's night school program, scheduled to meet once weekly at the Samuel Boynton High School. Pay was fifty dollars a week. We could use the extra money, and the convenience of the night schedule would mean our car was available. Plus, no one would even know. My daily horoscope might be right. I tucked the paper under my arm and walked into the living room to dial the district personnel office.

"Good mornin', Selma City Schools. This is Lacey speakin'. How may I help ya'?"

I recognized her voice as that of the same lady I'd met when I had filled out the application a couple of months earlier. After exchanging the required pleasantries, I asked about the ad. I cringed as I said "disadvantaged adults" aloud.

"Well, howdy-do, Mrs. Zuretski. I will put you through to

Mr. Parkington. He can answer your questions. One moment, please ma'am."

Within a few seconds, Mr. Parkington boomed his charm. Before I could respond to his greeting, he popped the question, "Have you changed your mind about the full-time fifth-grade position at Brooks?"

"No, sir, I haven't changed my mind. My call is about another teaching position. The one advertised in today's edition of the *Selma News*." Taking a deep breath, I continued before he took advantage of my pause to banter on about Brooks, "That would be the evening teaching position for Disadvantaged Adults. Is it still available?"

A slight cough and then some ambient mumbling. The position was likely filled.

"Yes, ma'am. Still available." He cleared his throat. "That class is funded through a federal grant. Suppose it's come about due to the new Voting Rights Act passed in 1965. I'm expecting the grant to extend the entire fiscal year. 'Til the end of next June." He hesitated, dragging the words *voting rights* in a whispered tone. I wondered who he expected might hear him but understood how conversation about race was delivered with either emotional aggression or hushed whispers.

Mr. Parkington continued, his voice escalating, "Basically, the colored folk who attend will be needin' to learn to write their names and do some readin' and 'rithmetic. But I won't kid ya'. This isn't an easy job, Mrs. Zuretski. These folks have had little schooling and they likely won't take to learning easily." As if it was the fault of the people themselves, he punctuated his last sentence with a forced laugh.

Giving him the benefit of the doubt, I attributed his isolated chuckle to his anxiety over a white woman asking about this position. Since it wouldn't have been the first time

I misunderstood a drawl, I repeated what he said, "Did you say they would need to learn how to write their names?"

"I sho' did, ma'am. That is, if they don't need to learn the alphabet first. There's our federal dollars at work." He sounded triumphant, as if he was proud of his delivery and expected me to back out.

I pursed my lips, thinking that all adults should be able to read and write. Informed citizens benefitted everybody. Sensing my logic wouldn't be popular, I withheld further comment.

"What about materials?" I knew Bruce wouldn't be excited about this job, but he'd be more upset if I needed to spend our money on supplies.

"Let me see here." Paper rattled in the background. "Yes, there are both English and arithmetic workbooks."

"How about paper and pencils?" I posed the question considering my fifth-grade teaching experience at Brooks.

"It doesn't say here, but I am sure we can cover that. Probably won't be many folks who sign up for the class anyway. Federal government thinks differently, apparently." He wasn't going to give up on the point of the federal dollars.

I thanked Mr. Parkington and ended the call, promising to get back to him after I talked with Bruce.

In a conundrum, I grabbed a broom from the narrow closet and stepped into warm rays of morning sunlight. Activity was a distraction that allowed time to think over the challenges this opportunity would likely present. Tweeting birds kept me company while I swept the wooden porch. At first, I thought of the old wives' tale about sweeping once you have passed your due date. *It will encourage labor when it needs to be encouraged.* Why I thought of this, I don't know. Likely the nagging sense of sadness. As I began to move the broom from left to right, my spirits lifted. In fact, I considered asking Mrs. Bader for a new broom. *Better do it before she finds out about my interest in teaching colored adults.* Word seemed to travel fast in this small town.

"Why Missus Claire, ya' don't need to sweep them steps. I be fixin' to do it." Mamiza's voice made me stumble over a stone. She bowed gently as I perched both palms atop the broom. That was the most I had heard her speak since our arrival at Rohns.

"Thank you, Mamiza. That is very kind, but I really don't mind. It is only a few steps, and it feels good to be in the sunshine." I smiled. She had never used my name before.

Mamiza smiled back, revealing her one gold tooth amid a missing space and an array of stained ones. "I be glad to do that sweepin', Missus Claire."

This would be a chance to talk with Mamiza and find out more about her and the ladies with the pram. "How about I finish the steps and you do the walkway, today?"

"A'right." She turned away with a slight smile and went back to her sweeping regimen.

As I piled the dirt, I thought about asking Mamiza if she'd be interested in joining my new adult learning class but hesitated and asked instead about her family. Did she have any children? How long had she worked for Mrs. Bader?

She told me she had five sisters and two brothers and that she had been with Mrs. Bader since Billy Chas was a baby. Her smile at the mention of his name took my breath away. I could hardly resist an urge to hug her. I inhaled deeply and plunged forward with my invitation.

"Mamiza, a reading and arithmetic class is starting up at the Samuel Boynton High School in a couple of weeks. Gonna be held on Thursday nights, starting at the end of June. Would you be interested in joining the class?"

Suddenly, her cleaning picked up speed. "No, ma'am. I was workin' in the cotton fields since I was just a little 'un. My mama and daddy was sharecroppers, and they was poh. Me and my brothers and sisters had to help out. 'Fraid I didn't get much schoolin'."

"Hmm. Would you sign up if I was the teacher?"

"Oh, land sakes! No, ma'am. I could nevah do dat. But I 'preciate it." She now had backed her steps further up the walkway. "Thank ya', ma'am," she said, avoiding my gaze. One would think I'd asked her to join me in robbing the City National Bank.

Mamiza cleaned up the last of the branches and wispy Spanish moss foliage and clutched the broom handle under her armpit. "Ya' have a fine day, Missus Claire." She nodded in my direction and moved toward the back door of Rohns.

I was aware that my suggestion had crossed a line and prayed that Mrs. Bader hadn't overheard the conversation. She might hold it against Mamiza. With a churning stomach, I finished the sweeping and headed toward the rear steps of our apartment to prepare for my doctor appointment. It hurt to think that my questions had likely offended one of the dearest people I had met in all of Selma.

~

My shower was quick. I snagged one of my big toes against one of the ancient gargoyle feet supporting the tub. If those grimacing enamel faces could talk, the tales they could tell! I wrapped my toe with a washcloth doused in cold water, appreciating an opportunity to bathe. I wondered what showering accommodations Mamiza had in this towering mansion.

Tucking damp hair into a bun, I shoved the medical referral from the base into my purse. I didn't want to be late for my first appointment with my new obstetrician. His office was nearby, a short stroll from our Rohns apartment and a chance to enjoy the beauty of competing floral scents and splashes of color. The shadowy flailing of the Spanish moss dangling from the live oaks flapped like angel wings.

The waiting room in the doctor's office entertained an outdoor patio atmosphere. Lemonade, iced tea, and plates of cookies sat on silver trays atop a highly polished buffet. Four women, in various stages of pregnancy, were swallowed in puffy mint green loveseats, dreamily browsing through *Vogue* and *Town and Country*.

Helping myself to the refreshments, I found a single chair away from the stuffiness of the space. I picked up the *Selma News* and reread the ad for a teacher of "disadvantaged adults." The name of the course was not very welcoming. If I was hired, I would change the name to "Adult Literacy and Learning."

After half an hour, a bubbly receptionist with long pink nails came into the waiting room to announce that the doctor would be delayed at least another hour. He was delivering twins. Amidst the expelled breaths of mixed emotions from the moms-to-be—states of utter jubilation to sheer terror—I rescheduled my appointment.

Halfway up the block, I realized I had forgotten to drop off the referral from the base doctor, so I reluctantly turned back. To avoid walking through a group of clucking women at the front entrance, I retreated toward the sidewalk that ran alongside the building, ignoring the familiar COLORED sign. Since I merely had an envelope to leave, I didn't think it mattered which door I used. I tugged at the warped, windowless door at the end of the walkway. As I entered the closet-sized space, I almost tripped on a small, tattered throw rug. Certainly not the safest entrance for pregnant women.

A wooden shutter clapped open and a thin lady, wearing large glasses but no makeup and no smile, barked her greeting, "You came in the wrong door, ma'am. White women come in the front door." She raised a single admonishing eyebrow as if one should certainly know better.

"Just wanted to drop off these forms. I had an appointment, but Dr. Brown was detained."

The telephone rang before she could accept the envelope in my hand. As she took the call, I scanned the room behind her. The décor was a sharp contrast to the waiting room I had just left. The dimly lit space had wood floors with a few straight-backed chairs strewn about. No cushions and no windows. While two black expectant mothers sat staring into empty space, another perched on the edge of her skimpy seat, her spine as erect as she could manage, especially with a protruding large belly. I watched her thoughtfully turn the pages of a dog-eared issue of some magazine.

I left my paperwork with the receptionist who wasn't shy about revealing her disgust with the behavior of a Yankee and headed back toward Rohns. The colored waiting room weighed heavily on my mind. Like a scene from *Uncle Tom's Cabin*, only this was real life, and it was 1969. I shuddered at the overt discrepancy between the lifestyles of whites and blacks that prevailed.

~

That night, I made Bruce's favorite meatloaf dinner using a recipe I had mastered, along with garlic-seasoned mashed potatoes. After he dove into a second helping, I broached the topic that raced through my mind all day.

"I would like to apply to teach this adult education class at Samuel Boynton High School." I folded the paper with the ad part upward and extended it toward him. "It is offered in the night school program, once a week. I'd only be gone a couple of hours."

Bruce looked at the address in the classifieds. "This school is not in the best section of town, Claire."

"Negro schools usually aren't," I said raising my eyebrows and wagging my head from side to side.

He put his fork down with a thud as if this was the end of the discussion. "You can't go there at night by yourself."

"Now you sound like Billy Chas Bader," I said. "Today at the doctor's office, I saw one of the most miserable scenes I have experienced since we arrived here," I jeered my response as the heat flowed into my cheeks.

"If people were educated, maybe life would be a whole lot better for everyone in this town. And you are worried about where the school is located? I can't believe this," I shouted and tossed my fork into the sink.

"Claire, be reasonable. There is no way you're going to teach illiterate Negro adults." He pushed his chair back and walked out of the kitchen.

We didn't speak for the rest of the evening.

CHAPTER 21

With cool *goodnights,* we had curled to opposite sides of the bed. This was the first time since our wedding that we hadn't expressed our love before going to sleep. Tossing and turning, with covers on and off, I wrestled with my desires. I wanted this job, and I wanted my husband to be happy. We needed to talk this through. That's what husbands and wives should do.

I lay quietly curled to one side until Bruce left for his paper route, then shuffled into the bathroom and splashed cold water onto my face. The reflection in the vanity mirror revealed blood-shot eyes and a creased forehead, like someone who'd partied a little too hardy. Only this wasn't pay back for a night of fun. *How could I make him understand?*

I mulled over the argument in my head, recounting each detail as I prepared a peace offering of omelets and apple muffins. Bruce savored each bite, though he barely acknowledged my presence.

I broke the ice. "Honey, I really want to accept this job. I think I can help those people learn to read and write. And it's only for a couple of months. If you are worried about me traveling alone, you could drive me." The job would also bring us a little extra money, but I decided to skip that justification.

Bruce stopped chewing and leaned toward me, both elbows on the table. "Claire, do you realize what you teaching the colored adults might mean for us? For starters, Mrs. Bader will likely kick us out of here. Secondly, I'm working with Billy Chas on the remodel of the Lodge. Those guys are all members of the Men's Alliance — all diametrically opposed to integration of any kind. You do know that, right?"

I lowered my voice. "Of course, I know that. But *they* don't have to know. No one on this side of the tracks needs to know about my teaching."

He dropped his head, looked up and studied me in silence for what seemed like several minutes. "Okay, but only because it means so much to you and only over the summer months. From what I hear, half of this town spends summers down on the coast anyway. We'll need to be very careful, and I will drive you."

I took his hand in mind and thanked him for understanding. "This is important to me." Surprised at my own words, I realized how much I was discovering about myself. We had dated for a couple of years and had spent eight weeks in Europe on a University-sponsored student architectural tour. Didn't we know each other down deep, to our very core? *Apparently, there was more to learn.*

~

I dropped Bruce off at the Base Civil Engineering Building, and by afternoon, the laundry and household chores were done, and a peach pie was cooling on the kitchen table. With energy peaked by anxiety, some quiet calming catharsis was needed. I decided to sit in the sunshine and write to Sandy. I couldn't wait to tell her all about sweet Mrs. Willis, Jackson, and my new job. As I stepped onto the veranda, I collided with Mrs. Bader, walking slowly toward the screen door. *Glad she was coming inside, and I was going out.*

"Good mornin', Claire. How ya' doin'?"

Before I could muster some reasonable response that wouldn't sound too joyous and cause unnecessary suspicion, she continued, "I bet ya' are happy to have some free time and not be workin' with those nigra children anymore." Her beady eyes riveted into mine. It felt like she was challenging a response rather than posing a friendly question.

Bruce's admonishment checked my impulse to share my real feelings. We couldn't afford to be evicted.

"Why hello, Mrs. Bader." I ignored her question but smiled sweetly. "What are you doing outdoors on this warm afternoon?" *Honey couldn't have flowed with more languid viscosity.*

"I'm afraid I dozed off. I must get to my soaps. I hope I haven't missed too much of *Days of Our Lives.*" She smoothed a thin gray hair that wouldn't stay in place.

"I do believe it's still on. I have some letter writing to do, so I skipped most of the show today. However, when I turned off the television, Dr. Horton's wife, Alice, was pining over her son, Tommy, who is stationed overseas in Vietnam." With raised eyebrows, my response reflected the enthusiasm of an avid viewer, though I could hardly pass for one. Luckily this time, the TV had been on, and I'd caught a few tidbits of information.

"I don't want to give away too much of the story and spoil your fun." I grinned a little more and scrunched my shoulders toward my earlobes. *Again, words I didn't mean.*

"Oh, thank you, my dear. That poor Alice. She must be beside herself. Sorry, honey, I must get inside. I do wonder why Mamiza didn't fetch me earlier. That woman is becoming so forgetful these days. Such a melancholy nigra," she mumbled her final words as she ambled, cane in tow, through the doorway I held open.

Mrs. Bader turned around as I closed the screen behind her. "By the way, I won't be attending the next League luncheon meeting. Belinda always gets carried away with the mint juleps, and I've never cared much for pinochle. Too old to learn now." Her laugh was shrill at her own admission of age, as if a revelation.

"We'll talk before then, I'm sure. Enjoy your soap," I spoke to her back as she continued toward her parlor.

I moved the white wicker chair forward to face the rolling greenery surrounding Rohns Manor and placed my back to the entry. Breathing a sigh of relief after our encounter, I considered the grave possible consequences of my decision to teach disadvantaged adults. Still, I knew it was the right thing to do, and that I could make a difference.

Alone at last, I opened my folder and saw the message on a slip of paper I had clipped from an old Sunday newsletter: *Give all your worries and cares to God, for he cares about what happens to you.* I Peter 5: 7. Woefully immersed in our Selma move, I hadn't talked to God much beyond our Sunday church visits. I vowed to pray more as I allowed my reverie to fill six pages that would be sent to Sandy.

I thought about writing to my mother but decided to call her instead. Surprisingly, she started crying when we talked about my miscarriage on the phone, covering the mouthpiece to say something to my father. I had never heard my mother cry before.

"Tell her we'll come down there." I had heard Dad say in the background.

Mother had never had a miscarriage and didn't know anyone who had. "I'm alright, Mother, really. I had a D & C, and I'm fine. By the way, what's Dad doing home on a weekday morning?"

"He's got a tee time with a client. And, what's a D & C? Is that serious? You never tell me anything." Mother gasped as if I'd smacked her.

I calmly explained the dilation and curettage procedure that clears the uterus lining and is often recommended by doctors after a woman suffers a miscarriage. I almost wished I hadn't called but personally vowed to write a cheery letter. Since I had an appointment with Mr. Parkington, the end of our call was smooth.

Perhaps, it would have been easier to write Mother a letter and not be forced to field her questions. I also didn't tell her about the job. As I hurried to my meeting in the late afternoon with Mr. Parkington, the sun blazed above. I cringed as a brownish-red cockroach scurried across the sidewalk a few feet ahead. The critters were everywhere. I mused over how I'd spent twenty-two years of my life without ever seeing a cockroach.

Mr. Parkington met me in the reception area of the Board of Education building. With a cardboard box on his hip, he pumped my right hand up and down for several seconds. With the influx of military in Selma, one would assume that the school district would have an abundance of applicants. But most officers' wives spent their days eating lunch with other officers' wives. Some might even be teaching—in the white schools, of course. He handed me the box filled with workbooks, mostly for grammar study, basic arithmetic, and spelling. Tucked inside a smaller box were pencils, pens, and some chalk. A couple of erasers were strewn about the bottom.

"Do you have a list of people signed up to take the class? I thought welcoming name cards would be a friendly way to start off."

Mr. Parkington laughed aloud. "Remember these folks are disadvantaged, Mrs. Zuretski. They can't read, they don't write, and they don't sign up for anything. My guess is you'll get a few to show up, come and go, ya' know."

The rush of blood toward my cheeks must have been obvious. He didn't need to emphasize each word as if I was dumb or hard of hearing.

"Sorry. I, uh, perhaps you can write the name cards for them when you meet the folks. Don't think you'll have more than six or eight, uh, students—adults. You have enough materials for about a dozen folks, though. I might also recommend you collect them at the end of the class each week. Just a suggestion.

Whatever you do, I know it will be a big help, ma'am." Small beads of sweat dotted his hairline as he finished his speech

"Good luck." He patted my shoulder and asked his secretary to have me sign the employment paperwork. "Lacey, if we have some name tags lyin' around, could you give them to Mrs. Zuretski? She is very optimistic."

Mr. Parkington grinned, trying to mollify the encounter, then poked at the glasses that now fell beneath the bridge of his nose and disappeared down the narrow corridor. I thought how he was likely glad to be done with the task.

Handing me a clipboard with papers and an attached pen, Lacey said, "Thank ya' for fillin' these out, Mrs. Zuretski." She nodded and reflected a genuine and friendly smile that showed the gap between two front teeth. She reached into a drawer and handed me a packet of name tags, arching her right brow in skepticism. Her boss's behavior had nothing to do with her, yet she likely held the same attitudes as everyone else.

As I looked over the various papers, including tax deduction forms, the printed words on the employment agreement resonated with a disturbing message. The official course title was "Disadvantaged Adult Learners." I thought how there were many disadvantaged adults in this town—and they didn't all have black skin.

CHAPTER 22

My mother's tone was anxious when we last spoke, and it gnawed like chiggers under my skin. By sharing my good news, I'd be making a peace offering. I decided to phone her for the second time in a week. Instead of writing her the cheery letter, I'd tell her the cheery news myself. Mother picked up on the first ring, almost as if she was sitting by the phone about to call me. Probably not. This was her bridge day.

"Hello, Mother, it's me, Claire," I almost sang my greeting with the warm thought.

Deflated by her cool response, I swallowed hard. "Are you alright?" I was determined not to be affected by her mood.

"Of course, I'm fine," she said. "Why wouldn't I be? Today is my bridge day. Did you forget?"

"Well, you just seemed upset when I last called. I was worried about you. Thought I'd catch you before you went to play bridge."

Nothing on the other end of the line.

Not to be deterred, I continued, "Mother, I have some exciting news to share."

"Hmm." That perked her up.

"I have a summer job teaching adults. Can you imagine that?"

"Why would you want to teach older people?" Back to her old self.

My dad shouted in the background, "We can help 'em. Tell her that, Inez." He sounded more distant than ever. *Nothing new.*

Mother cleared her throat. "We can help if you and Bruce need money. You know that." Her last words typically sympathetic.

She lowered her voice, as if there were unwanted ears on the line. "I don't know if I ever told you this." *I'd heard the message she was about to deliver at least a dozen times.* "My own parents helped your father and I when we were first married. I always say that it's the responsibility of one generation to help the next."

My mother had a way of summing up her positional statements by referencing her broader brush of personal experience. As if a lecture on the grander scheme of life was necessary to support her testimony. Today, I felt like she struggled to deter any creeping emotion.

My intensity jarred as a dark object moved to the outer perimeter of my right eye. I spun around to meet the beady eyes of a furry brown field mouse. But not for long. The rodent scurried from the fireplace hearth toward his escape route under the doorway and fled into the foyer. I covered the receiver and jumped on one of the velvet-cushioned, dining room chairs, and smacked a palm over my mouth, blocking the scream that begged an escape.

"Claire, Claire! Are you listening? Oh, I didn't tell you about the contract Lucy landed with Ford," she said moving on with her agenda. "Hello. Are you there?"

I swallowed hard and mustered an enthusiastic response, "I'm here, Mother, I'm here and I heard you. Great about Lucy. Uh, and thank you for offering help, but we're fine. Honestly. Bruce has two jobs and I taught for a few months. Now I have this new job. We have medical coverage and a lovely antebellum plantation here to live in. What could be better?" I raised a palm in the air as if Mother was in the room.

She knew about racial tension in the South. She watched the evening news. That was as far as it went. She didn't need to know about my involvement and Mrs. Bader's tirade in the hallway of Rohns Manor. Some things were better left unsaid, especially now.

My mother continued to tell me about Lucy's latest labor relations project, who was engaged to whom, and the European travels of the girls not committed to matrimony. As she went on, I thought of the unexpected maelstrom that had followed my announcement that I'd be joining Bruce in our move to Selma. After he left for basic training, I accepted my parents' offer and moved back home — same pink flowered bedroom — with a plan to join Bruce six weeks later. They didn't understand why I couldn't remain living with them throughout Bruce's tenure in the Air Force. Just as bad, I had to camouflage my morning sickness, taking lots of walks, and puking on every other shrub in the park.

The litany of why I couldn't be more like Lucy never stopped. When I tried to escape the scrutiny during my junior year in college, further humiliation consumed me. "Mother, it's just an apartment with a Zeta sister. I'll have to live on my own someday."

"How could you ever even think of such a thing? Your sister is five and a half years older, and she still lives with her family," she had said.

"Lucy is married to her law practice, Mother. She has no life." I remembered how every sinew in my body raged as I sailed out the door.

My mind returned to the phone call at hand, but it was the same message we'd already hashed and rehashed.

"Claire, we are all truly worried about you. I mean about losing the baby and all. Are you sure you have a good doctor?" Mother persevered.

Poor Claire!

"Yes, and yes. Mother don't fret. I am fine, honestly. Even better than expected." White lies were sometimes better than the truth. I hoped my mother didn't think we lost our baby because of the move to Selma, but she probably did. All medical reports indicated the miscarriage was no one's fault. Just Mother Nature's way of eliminating a fetus that didn't have a healthy connection to the umbilical cord.

"Wait, wait just a minute. Lucy just came in. She wants to say hello."

I doubted my sister wanted to talk to me, but I said, "Okay." My mother was no longer on the other end of the line.

"Hi, ya', Claire," a cool deep voice said flatly. It was Lucy.

"How are you doing? How's the law firm?" My response was cordial.

"Great—perfect, actually. Did Mom tell you about the Ford contract?" said Miss Know-It-All.

"Yes, she did. Congrats." A response that held more sarcasm than I intended.

"Yeah. I'm the first woman in the firm to land such a big one." She sighed. "What are you up to? Bet you're glad to be done teaching fifth graders."

I dove in before she hit me with another question. "Well, Counselor, I loved teaching the kids," I said, purposively poking at her position. Toning down a notch, I continued, "Also, just about every student was reading at grade level and further by the end of May."

"Well, I would certainly expect they would be." Lucy didn't get it.

"A lot of people don't have the educational opportunities that we had, Lucy. In fact, there are a lot of adults who can't read or write at all." I didn't stop. "And I'm going to help them learn."

No response on the other end of the line.

"Are you there, Lucy?" I asked.

I could hear her breathing through the phone lines. "You aren't teaching Negro adults, are you?" Lucy hissed into the phone receiver.

"Who said the adults were Negro?" I asked.

"Oh, come on," said Lucy. "What white adults would need to learn to read and write? Why are you putting us all through this embarrassment? You are a fool, Claire."

"The class hasn't started, and I haven't met the students. Look, I'm a good teacher and looking forward to this experience. Besides, all citizens should be able to vote. If you can't read and write, you can't become a registered voter." I was proud of my sense of composure.

"Mother and Daddy will be very upset. You should be ashamed of yourself," said Lucy.

"I have nothing to be ashamed of, and I am not a fool." Hesitating, I wanted to say more, but didn't. "I need to go now. Goodbye." I hung up.

I was shaking and there was still the issue of the mouse. Scrambling down on my knees in front of the stone hearth, I checked for some type of rodent nest. Nothing. This was not the time to complain to Mrs. Bader. I needed to stay on her good side. I planned to ask Bruce to set traps under the heater in both fireplaces.

~

Grabbing an apple and an old spiral notebook, I made a hasty exit to the library downtown. I needed to learn as much as possible about teaching adult learners. Anxiety about my newly acquired teaching commitment offered a fine diversion from the stray mouse and from Lucy.

Libraries were havens to me, although my only other trip to this one had been to sign up for a library card. Authentic antique horse troughs stood proudly between gaslights in front of the old structure. The troughs were now filled to the brims with the blooming azaleas instead of equine saliva. The white antebellum pillars with gaslight posts lining the walkway reflected the old

South. The freshly trimmed lawns and gingerbread detail on the building beckoned warmth and hospitality. In awe of the wonderland environment, I moved toward the information desk.

"Hey, Claire. Yoo-hoo!" Voices in hushed tones floated from somewhere in the stacks.

Behind the fiction shelves and holding feather dusters, stood Belinda and Ruby. They flitted a greeting with two or three fingers in mid-air and pushed a cart filled with books in my direction. Donned in sundresses covered by matching blue aprons, they looked like they had planned to coordinate their outfits.

"Yoo-hoo!" I returned the greeting in a whisper. "Do you work here?" I knew better, but still asked the question as they approached the desk.

"Lands, no. We're volunteerin'," said Belinda. She stood erect as her voice elevated a notch. Glances of approval from other patrons were offered in her direction. No batting eyelashes this time.

"They can always use more help." Ruby tilted her head toward me. "Why don't you sign up, Claire? It would be fun. We're here a couple of mornings a week, usually. We could all go to lunch after we're finished." She beamed sincerely as she wrapped a chunk of bleached blonde hair behind one ear.

Belinda snatched my wrist and began to tug me in the direction of the manager's office.

"Whoa, hold on. I'll think about it. I'm here today to do some research. You know local sights and all." Not true. I forced an *I-am-excited-to-be-here smile* and shifted a couple of books to the other hip.

Ruby placed the three books she held on to the pile in the cart. "Oh, sweetie, we can help ya' with that."

"Thank you. I have so much to learn about this city." Hoping I wasn't overdoing my enthusiasm, but help was appreciated.

Belinda rushed over to the reference librarian and told her about my interests.

"We have to get back to the stacks," said Belinda. The comment pleased the librarian. With a wave and Ruby at her heels, she scurried off with the cart in tow.

The rotund librarian allowed her glasses to fall to the chain that hung around her neck and led me toward the shelves where Alabama travel and history books were kept. Black Belt history would be strong background information for a Selma adult education teacher to know. What I really wanted was to learn more about the politics of race in this town, but I couldn't directly request that without raising suspicion. She pulled several books off various shelves and stacked them on a nearby table. I thanked her, tugged at a chair, and began my trawl through the voluminous material.

I flipped through pages with photos of rambling Victorian style residences, not unlike the Tara-*esque* Rohns mansion. Many smaller bungalows and cottages stood along paved highways, with rambling lawns and stately old trees. These homes touted the friendliness of spacious sprawling verandas. Quite a direct contrast to the shotgun houses and narrow dwellings scattered throughout the city streets. None of the photos reflected the dilapidated shacks smattering the outskirts of town where the black tenant farmers and sharecroppers lived.

The Black Belt and the Deep South. The books the librarian had given me didn't show those parts. According to historians, the slaves and their descendants had plenty of fertile soil to grow lots of cotton. The global view of Selma was painted with sweeping strokes of glamour and glory, sorting and selecting the grandeur to be displayed.

Before I could learn more about the civil rights march that took place only a few years earlier, Ruby and Belinda reappeared, tugged at chairs opposite me and sat down. As if their every move was synchronized, they both perched their elbows on the table's edge and positioned their artfully drawn faces in their cupped palms.

"Are you learnin' lots about Selma?" This time Belinda executed an exaggerated gaze in my direction, batting her long lashes. I was being mocked.

"I sure am." I flashed my biggest smile and slammed the book shut.

"Good! You were lookin' too serious for a minute." Ruby reclined back in her chair. "How about joinin' us for lunch at Dottie's?"

"Sure. Love to." My only other trip Dottie's Place had been the morning after the fire. "I'm not finished with my research though and need a little more time to look at these materials."

"We can take care of that." Belinda dashed over to the desk of the reference librarian to request that a hold be placed on my Alabama materials for the remainder of the day.

When we got to the café, my two friends ordered club sandwiches, complete with French fries and a salad. Knowing my wallet had barely enough cash for a cup of tomato soup and a grilled cheese. I skipped the iced tea. Ice water was fine.

They both looked at me after placing my lean order with the waitress. "Had a huge breakfast with Bruce," I said and was relieved when they shrugged a response.

The colored waitress clearing the dishes from a table next to ours looked familiar. When she handed a napkin that had fallen back to a frail elderly gentleman, he briskly ordered her to fetch him a fresh one. She nodded dutifully and walked away, paced carriage and posture erect.

"Ruby, isn't that the lady who was serving us at your luncheon?" I nodded my head in the direction of the black woman.

Wide-eyed, Ruby sent an empty glare in my direction and slowly turned her blonde head toward the waitress, just in time to see the woman hand the man a clean napkin.

"How would I know? My maid Cissy helped me hire extra help for the luncheon. All friends of hers, most likely. They all look alike to me, honey." Ruby turned toward Belinda and they both muffled guffaws into their napkins. This pair continued to flummox me.

Smiling politely, I hated myself for not commenting. The waitress set our lunches before us, and I spooned away at the lukewarm liquid. We talked about how we missed college and the fraternity parties.

Taking a final bite of the grilled cheese and glancing at my watch, I made up excuses to leave. "Sorry, gotta run. Need to get back to my Alabama history and geography study. And I still have some grocery shopping to do before picking Bruce up at the base. This has been fun." *Not completely true, either.*

"Wish you didn't have to dash so soon, Claire. We'll plan a longer lunch next time," said Belinda, blinking her eyelashes yet again.

The colored waitress stacked dishes up to her armpits and deposited utensils into a tub. The burden didn't change her stance. She moved like an African queen—articulate as I recalled and decidedly pretty. However, her assets would certainly not be identified through the lens of Ruby Miller and Belinda Bailey.

CHAPTER 23

As I walked toward the Ford, tiny pebbles from crumbled gravel crept between my toes. My legs were shaky, and I was acutely aware of the rhythm of my heartbeat. The speed of my own pace was tempered by two elderly ladies strolling ahead of me. They sauntered without an apparent care in the world. *Lucky them.*

Teaching "disadvantaged adults" had such a negative connotation. My plan was to help experienced citizens develop skills needed for literacy. The Adult Literacy and Learning title was too stiff—the class should be called Selmians for Success. My choice. An adage my mother often used came to mind. *You can't have your cake and eat it too.* I always wondered, *why not?*

I cringed at the inward punch at my belly for agreeing with the disparaging gestures of Ruby and Belinda at lunch. My courteous behavior was sheathed in supremacy. Deep South, proper ladies, even college-educated ones, would surely not be involved in the politics of segregation. They stood by their men and followed their lead. The actions and attitudes of my Southern sisters gnawed at me and drilled deeper than the more overt biases I saw as I walked down Main Street.

A recent article in the *Selma News* showed how the wife of the city's mayor enjoyed cooking large dinners and sewing for her two daughters. The family photo in the newspaper suggested that she might be ten or fifteen years my senior. She was a native Southern belle, striving to pass along her heritage, the article touted. Ruby and Belinda were carved from the same mold—college-educated, with old family money and married into more of the same. Yet, I never heard them talking about cooking or sewing. They fell into the nouveau Deep Southern belle category, reaping the benefits of being a prize homemaker without the effort. No need for them to toil. A black maid would do it.

I watched the two elderly ladies meander toward a parked car. "Why that is just too much information for me, mah dear," said the taller of the two to her friend.

They both laughed in dismissal of any serious talk. Whoever said it was often good not to know what you didn't know had it right. The ladies reflected the white upper-middle-class women I had met through the League. They didn't want any more information. Their lives were perfectly poised for security and well-being. Not knowing held a peculiar bliss, which I couldn't reconcile.

The excitement of my first real teaching job oozed from my pores, and I ached to tell Ruby and Belinda. I was the only teacher, not a student teacher or a substitute teacher slipping into someone else's shoes. On the other hand, my announcement would be futile, and their lack of understanding immovable. I doubted they could share my glee or even begin to comprehend my pleasure in teaching adults who could neither read nor write. *And how long would it be before they found out about my teaching?* Even more worrisome, what effect would my decision have on my husband? This was a small town and little information escaped the ears of Mrs. Bader. I soothed my angst with the thought that the job was only for the summer.

I pulled a tube of lipstick from my purse, filled in my lips, and ran a comb through my hair. After starting the car, I glanced into the rearview mirror absently speaking aloud and vaguely thinking of my accomplished sister. "Who knows? I might even be able to help change some minds around here."

~

Back at the public library, I skirted past the reference librarian, thanking her as I picked up my stack of reference books, and slipped into a corner carrel. Diving into the mountain of paper and folders, I read about how the federal courts had mandated integration, but local radical agitators resisted the law. I realized that even if my white Southern sisters wanted to make a difference, they would face much opposition, including resistance from city hall, the sheriff, and the prevailing white male power structure. *Yes, even their own husbands.* Even though slavery was abolished a hundred years earlier, the culture and the segregated system were supported by a tradition that wouldn't easily dissipate. The Negroes of the 1960s were the children and grandchildren of sharecroppers and continued to occupy that nook in the thinking of the white Southern folks. It seemed as if the remnants of the slave-like, sharecropper dependency of tenant farmers would never fade. Selma archives reported generations of ancestry, boasting of a combined black-white population over 20,000 strong. The intimation of inclusiveness was not real. To me, Selma citizens were prisoners locked in a time warp of the pre-Civil War days.

As I thumbed through a sea of articles, a reference to the White Citizens Council (WCC) caught my eye. The WCC was a group that consisted of white middle and upper-middle-class Southern male citizens who gathered in response to the Brown v. Board of Education ruling to desegregate schools. *Did the husbands of my Zeta sisters belong to this group? What about Billy Chas Bader?* I shuddered at the thought. Although the population profile of the WCC membership composition differed from that of the Klu Klux Klan (KKK), the WCC was not opposed to violence and intimidation. Furthermore, Selma was the first Alabama city to establish a WCC chapter. The article said the group boycotted agencies supportive of black citizens, with bombings in Montgomery reported. Even stronger, any white person opposed to their philosophy of segregation was considered a "communist."

A muffled echo of chimes marked four o'clock, one hour before the library closed. As I flipped through a few of the more recent newspaper clippings, an article dated only a few months earlier gripped my attention: "Rosen Defies Council." I read the headline a second time. Berta Rosen was a white woman who had moved with her husband, Sol, to Selma from the Midwest over a decade earlier to open a dry-cleaning business. Berta organized the group, Females for Freedom, who were against segregation and whose goal was an education for the colored population. The article said the Females for Freedom were *mostly* white and educated Southern women opposed to the tenets of the White Citizens Council. *Mostly.* This could mean a loss of white domination. Intolerable in the current culture. The Females for Freedom also sought to increase the number of registered voters. I didn't know that fewer than 200 of almost 8,000 Negro citizens of voting age in Selma were registered in 1962. With a buoyancy of delight, I thought how teaching the adults could help change the numbers.

What snatched my attention further was an op-ed that compared *antics* of the Females for Freedom to the Nazi youth movement of a generation earlier. The opinion piece said the *Fems* were trying to encourage bi-racial youth groups to come together and participate in summer camps "…an effort to build a classless society of the future where blacks and whites were equal in all ways." *Why could this question even exist?*

Pouring over the print, I continued. The article suggested that the gathering of young teens of the two distinct races was a gesture that mimicked the Hitlerisms of the 1930s and 1940s —youth brought together to compete, play games, and support the regime.

The remainder of the editorial talked about how the day camps with *unknown financial support* did volunteer work for elderly citizens. During the week-long camps, the kids helped with yard work in the community and reading to older folks in the mornings, with the afternoons spent enjoying picnics and playing games together. Earlier articles suggested the Methodist Church was connected to the *Fems*. However, a current letter from the pastor completely denied any involvement with the group. The op-ed garnered scads of opinions, with names affixed to the letters. Most were in opposition to the efforts of the *Fems*. It seemed to me that the *Fems* were on the right track—helping others and building relationships. The next generation was being prepped to make positive changes happen. *Isn't that what it should be?*

Two volunteers nodded in my direction as they pushed a book cart past my carrel. I smiled, despite the tightness that gripped my insides. This spirited female force had moxie, operating incognito, an underground subterfuge right here in Selma. I wanted to find out more about these courageous women who used their education to make the world a better place. I thought about the stark contrast between the *Fems* and the women in the Ladies League. The ladies in the League used their education to go to lunch. *Who were the Fems?* Other than Berta Rosen, no member names were listed.

Scanning the news section, I found stories about organized groups on all sides of the spectrum. Some articles revealed the diversity of the Student Nonviolent Coordinating Committee (SNCC), which seemed to reflect a more genteel spirit toward the problem. This mostly student-dominated group was committed to non-violence with goals to register and mobilize black voters in the Deep South. The SNCC contrasted with the male-dominated Southern Christian Leadership Council (SCLC) and the Congress of Racial Equality (CRE). At least the SNCC had a more pacifist bent and were prayerful.

Two additional groups were more aggressive and on opposite sides of the race relations issue. Both the National Association for the Advancement of Colored People (NAACP) and the WCC fought through words and actions in support of their respective views. The photos spoke volumes. I shuddered to think of the violence that could be executed under the guise of justice and freedom of speech.

Sinking my frame with an audible *humph*, I closed the folder and scanned the shelves and stacks that surrounded me. I was aware of the empty space. However, this library was one of the first public facilities to allow black people to use its services, Civil Rights legislation required it. I had been here most of the day. Not a single black person had entered the building.

As chimes in the background signaled the library would soon be closing, I shuffled copies of the clippings into a file folder before noticing one that had fallen to the floor. The headline to the side of the article boasted the title of "White Citizens Council" and displayed several men grinning at the camera. I hadn't a clue who they were, but there was no mistake about the building in the background. The sign above the entrance read "The Lodge." It was the same building Bruce was working on for Billy Chas.

"Ma'am, the library will be closin' in ten minutes. You are welcome to check out the materials you are reading."

I jumped and instinctively closed the collection of old newspapers. I glanced up into narrowed eyes of the reference librarian and smiled. "Oh, my goodness, the time has escaped me. Thank you."

My heart was racing, and I almost had to catch my breath before speaking. With trembling hands, I fumbled to gather the materials into a neat pile on the carrel. I wanted to know more about Selma's Females for Freedom movement. And was now confronted with a greater challenge that involved my husband.

I nodded toward the librarian and slowly made my way toward the exit.

CHAPTER 24

"Wish Mamiza would've come with us to class. I invited her." I turned toward Bruce as we left Dottie's Place and headed for the car. "Haven't seen her in days." Silence. He was quiet about my new teaching role. Learning more about his wife every day, perhaps he was trying to allow me some space I wasn't aware was needed.

Bruce finally nodded. Then as if compelled, he said casually, "She may change her mind."

I wiped my brow with the back of my hand. The temperature and the humidity were almost equal. I thought about the box of cherry chocolate candies tucked into my purse and hoped they wouldn't melt before class started.

"She was upset when I suggested she join the Selmians for Success class. Like such an idea was out of the question."

Ignoring my comment, he said, "How many adults do you think you'll have?" I wasn't sure if he was really interested or only pretending to be.

"Who knows? Mr. Parkington didn't sound hopeful about the attendance. All he cared about was meeting the federal government guidelines so the school district wouldn't be penalized."

"Sounds like he's doing his job," said Bruce.

"Oh, sure. But I don't think he cares about whether the adults learn or not." I made my point.

"That's not his job. It's yours." He stared ahead at the road before us.

"It's more than that. It was his whole attitude." Sometimes I thought Bruce just didn't get it.

"I don't see that kind of racial posturing at the base. Of course, there are no colored sergeants in the civil engineering department. Most are white and come from other parts of the country. Hmm. I take that back. The first lieutenant in civil engineering is from Biloxi. Man, he is prejudiced as hell. You should hear the stories he tells."

"No, thanks. I'll pass on the Mississippian's stories." I slipped into the car, encouraged that Bruce at least admitted we were surrounded by prejudice.

"That's what I mean. It's the attitude of the folks who are native to this city and native to the South, not military transplants," I argued. "In fact, even though Detroit is in racial shambles right now, we didn't see such outright segregation."

Stopped at a red light, Bruce continued to look straight ahead, as if talking to the traffic signal. "It's not only here in Selma. You didn't grow up in the southern part of Detroit, sweetheart."

Bruce's mother was killed in a car accident before he started kindergarten. His grandmother and aunt basically raised him while his dad worked long hours at the steel mill.

Bruce continued his story, "One of my best friends from elementary school went to Ball Tech, downtown. His dad thought he should be an engineer, so he sent him down there. This kid told me about a time when he and some of his buddies wanted to get a shake at a sweet shop across from the school. A couple of the guys were colored kids and one spoke up. 'Man, you're kiddin'. The manager will give you whatever *you* want, but they won't serve *us*. We're not white.' My friend told him they were nuts and insisted they all go."

"So, did your friend prove them wrong?"

"Nope. They all went into the shop and sat down at the fountain. The lady said they were making trouble and needed to leave. Can you believe it? They didn't do anything, just five guys wanting to buy shakes."

"That's strange. I never heard anything like that."

"It just depended on where you lived in Detroit. You grew up in an all-white neighborhood. You probably never met a colored person, right?"

I stared at my lap, giving serious thought to Bruce's question. "Yah. You're right. I never met anyone back home who didn't have white skin. Everyone on my block and at my school looked like me. I never really interacted with colored kids until my substitute teaching experience."

"Plus, substitute teaching was different, because you were an adult and a teacher," he said.

I was barely four or five years older than most of the kids in the inner-city substitute teaching assignments. If any student had flunked a grade level, that would make me only two or three years older.

We were in front of Samuel Boynton High when Bruce brought the car to a halt. He placed his hand on my knee and I turned to see the warmth in his eyes.

"We can't change the culture here. Please try to understand that." His head was tilted to the side as he repeated his mantra once again.

"Well, we'll have to see about that." For now, we'd each need to respect our different views on the topic. I planted a quick kiss on his cheek and reached for the door handle. Grabbing my purse and book bag, I stepped onto the sidewalk.

"I'll be right here at nine o'clock sharp," Bruce shouted through the open window as I mounted the steps of the school building.

~

Mr. Clayton R. Grilton sat at his desk in the office to the right of the entrance. The gilded desk placard identified him as "Principal," affirming two separate signs I had seen entering the building. His door ajar, I tapped lightly. Immersed in his work, he appeared not to notice me.

"Excuse me. I'm Claire Zuretski, the adult education teacher. Can you tell me where I might find the classroom, please?"

His head rose slowly until he met my eyes directly, causing me to suspect he knew I had been present the entire time. He lifted his thick dark brows and began a full body scan, ending at what felt like the toes of my high heels. I squeezed the cloth handles of my bookbag and looked him straight in the eye. In a more professional manner, he cleared his throat and raised his chin, then looked down at me, locking his eyes purposefully on mine. As he stood, both his positional power and presence loomed at least a foot above my head. He had obviously expected me and planned to show me who was in charge.

"Well, well, Mrs. Zuretski. You are the newest teacher of disadvantaged adults." Emphasis on the word *newest*. Distracted, I thought how he hadn't looked that tall sitting behind his desk. To my chagrin, I sensed his comment hinted at how others never returned to the job.

"You must be Principal Grilton." I smiled and extended my hand.

With a nod of his bald head, he took a light hold of most of the fingers of my right hand and stared directly into my eyes. "Indeed, I am," he said, quickly withdrawing his hand. "I will show you to your room. Either I or my assistant will be here on Thursday evenings."

As we walked through the doorway, a custodian approached, and Principal Grilton asked him to escort me to room 104. "Good luck, Mrs. Zuretski." The principal had already turned his back to me, and my *thank you* floated behind him.

"Reverend Mease is already waiting for ya', ma'am." The custodian's sense of urgency reflected his respect for the minister. "His son drove him over," he said as if that was key information.

As I entered the room, a lanky dark-skinned man peered over his silver-rimmed spectacles. Even though the temperature and humidity were both about ninety degrees, he wore a suit jacket that was a slightly darker shade of brown than his pants. A white shirt and tie completed his attire. I placed my bag of materials on the teacher's desk and quickly approached the Reverend with my hand extended.

"Welcome to the Selmians for Success class. My name is Claire Zuretski."

He placed his pencil in the holder on the desk and stood, slightly bent over while clutching the worn leather Bible under his left arm. It was the way he held the Bible. Like another appendage. I recognized him. This gentleman was the person we saw escaping the forest fire. The Reverend extended his own hand to me, and nodded respectfully, but averted my eyes.

"Howdy-do, ma'am. I'm Samuel L. Mease, pastor of the Mt. Gideon Baptist Church." He spoke in a softened tone and didn't seem aware I had changed the course title.

With the custodian still in the room, the Reverend's tentative welcome was not a surprise. I gently turned back toward the custodian. "Thank you for showing me to my classroom. By the way, I didn't get your name."

"Much obliged, ma'am. I'm Alvin, ma'am. Will be sure to have the door unlocked next week."

"Wonderful! Thank you for your help, Mr. Alvin," I said.

A small grin crept onto his face as he stood a bit taller and left the room. Hopefully, I had the respect of at least one employee in this building.

Reverend Mease had returned to writing on a large yellow legal pad. This man didn't need someone to show him how to write. Mr. Parkington was wrong, and I wondered why the pastor had enrolled in the class.

Paper, steno notebooks, and pencils were in a large box

labeled, "Disadvantaged Adult Evening Class." I turned the box toward the wall to conceal the words marked in crayon and set out the materials on a nearby table. Finally, I wrote my name on the chalkboard. Reverend Mease continued his writing, deftly flipping through the thin pages of his Bible as if in search of a specific passage. Whether his scan was to seek words of spiritual guidance or to augment his writing was unclear.

Although he appeared to be literate, I watched the Reverend slog his pencil across the page of the yellow pad. I saw beads of sweat dotting his temples as he intensely formed the letters on the page with vigilant care. He squeezed the lead tip of a yellow pencil that had been whittled with a sharp knife. Reverend Mease certainly didn't need an ABC reference card. I took the individual alphabet cards and inserted them into the back of each workbook and slipped the full alphabet banner beneath the box wrapping.

I took advantage of the time before class to get to know Reverend Mease better. "Do you live near the high school, Reverend?"

"My wife and I are alone now. The two of us lives in the neighborhood just up the way. But my work for the Lawd takes me all over the town and into the country. We knows folks everywhere." He grinned shyly, not fully concealing his proud connection to his town and his people.

I grinned back at him. "Well, I hope no one you know was harmed by the fire my husband and I saw in the forest on the edge of town a few months back. We were driving into Selma and saw people running for their lives," I raised my voice recalling the true terror of that experience.

Shuffling nervously in his seat, he replied, "Hmm. I do recall that dreadful day. Fact is, I was on the edge of town there to visit a sick brother, a member of Mt. Gideon. The firefighters got there just in time, praise the Lawd. None of the folks nearby were harmed. A blessing."

I breathed a sigh of relief. "Glad to hear that. How did it start, anyway?"

"They never did discover that, ma'am. Maybe a cigarette or a careless match, or somethin'." His voice trailed off with finality. He returned to the notes on his yellow pad, summarily dismissing any further discussion on the topic.

"Well, I'm glad all were safe," I said.

"Yes, ma'am. Praise the Lawd."

With only a few minutes before class, I excused myself to seek out a restroom. He flashed a hooded glance in my direction, then returned his focus to the Bible. *Almost too eager to do so.*

I admired his dedication. Yet, I pondered why he wasn't more curious about the cause of the fire. He must have known something about the white guys. The mechanic at the gas station wasn't surprised either. Somehow the disinterested concern of this elderly pillar of his community didn't align with the facts at hand.

I wondered what to expect from the other adults. If the class enrollment didn't increase, Reverend Mease and I would be working one-on-one, and that wouldn't please Mr. Parkington.

Upon opening the door when I returned to the classroom, a sweet hovering aroma told me the Reverend was not alone. I'd recognize the powerful *Este Lauder* scent anywhere. The lady wearing the perfume was poised in one of the desks with yards of her brightly colored dress draping onto the hardwood floor. She was likely a few years my senior.

As I approached our new member to introduce myself, the lady leaped to her feet and sidled in my direction. Her horn-rimmed glasses, with fashionably large frames, enhanced the fine bone structure of her creamy caramel skin and saucer-like eyes. "Howdy-do, ma'am. Mah name is Lily Mae Brown."

As I reached my hand toward her, there was something vaguely familiar about her, too. "I feel like we've met before, Mrs. Brown."

"Oh, it's Miss Brown, ma'am. I seen you at Miss Ruby's

luncheon just a few weeks back. I thought you were a mighty nice lady, and that's why I'm here, ma'am." She grinned, then lowered her head slightly.

Word traveled fast in a small town, but I was flattered.

This time the Reverend's glance was an unprompted glare toward Miss Brown's direction. She lowered her head slightly. *Did he disapprove of her compliment toward me?* Dogged determination dispelled my inner sensitivity. It would take time to build trust.

"Thank you, Miss Brown. That is very kind, and I am pleased that you have joined our class." Humility made my words barely audible. I recalled my remark about how smart this maid seemed. Ruby had said she doubted if the maid had ever finished grammar school. Yet, she could look at people with her beautiful eyes and really listen to what they said. I recalled how she carefully attended to her tasks at the League luncheon. Lily Mae Brown had charisma.

I gave my two early-bird students workbooks, steno pads, and pencils. I shoved the dozen duck cloth book bags I had sewn to hold their materials to the bottom of the box. It was past seven o'clock and only two students were present. My blouse stuck to my damp back.

Buying time for the benefit of any latecomers and feeling hopeful that I would have more than two people in the class, I moved toward a desk that was equally spaced between both of my new students.

"How did you hear about this class?" I asked.

The Reverend spoke first, "Ma'am, we've had adult citizenship classes here in Selma since the Voting Rights of 1965. The purpose of the opportunity," he emphasized opportunity, "was to inform us coloreds. Myself, I think it's a little late, but better than not at all, I s'pose." His voice trailed off, and he returned his attention to his writing.

Not intending to evoke resentment, I smiled gently and looked at this man who continued to avert my eye contact.

"Well, I'm glad you are both here, and I look forward to helping as your teacher. And it appears as though we will have a very small class which will give us more time to work together." Grinning broadly, I continued, "I'm excited to be here." *I really was.*

I opened my folder and took out the course description. "Let's look at what this course is about and see where it meets your needs. We can always make changes as necessary."

The two sets of eyes now returned my gaze, then humbly bowed forward, likely unsure of the promise from this white teacher.

I swallowed and hoped they wouldn't sense my fear. "The course description says..." Before I could finish the first sentence, the classroom door creaked open. We all turned our heads to see who was coming.

"Looks like two more ladies are joining our class."

The Reverend looked up and nodded slowly, while Miss Brown was the first to speak. Her massive grin and broad sweeping wave told me everyone knew each other.

I placed my materials on the desk and walked toward the door as the thud of the knob banged against the wall. Mamiza and the tiny woman I had seen in the Old Live Oak Cemetery stood in the entry.

"I hope we isn't late to class, Missus Claire." Mamiza clutched her black cotton handbag with both hands. She looked at me, then down at her feet.

"You're right on time, Mamiza. Please come in." I moved toward the door, grappling to restrain a desire to throw my arms around her.

Mamiza scanned the room and stepped forward. The second woman stood behind her, young and pregnant, with wide eyes staring afar, beyond her glasses. *I was going to meet her at last.*

Both wore starched, crisply ironed, cotton dresses. Like two paper cutouts. No apron, but two patchwork pockets covered half of Mamiza's belly. I thought how they could easily hold every valuable item she might own. Their hairstyles were identical, taut little buns pulled tightly at the napes of their necks. The fluorescent lighting reflected glistening highlights off the smooth, balm-covered tops of their heads.

With a voice that cracked a little more than I expected, I cleared my throat and spoke, "I am so happy you both came." Emphasizing *both*, I extended my two hands toward these courageous women and offered an extra squeeze in my grip. However, I couldn't take my eyes from Mamiza. I had never seen her wear any color but black dresses—fabric that melted into her deep ebony skin. Tonight, the bright tones of yellow and orange cloth that covered her tall slender frame announced the arrival of a more youthful someone else.

Mamiza finally spoke, "Thank ya', ma'am. Missus Claire, dis fine young lady be my grandniece, Delberta Willis. She is, I should say was, my sister's granddaughter. God rest Mariah's soul." Mamiza lowered her head and spoke the last few words of her introduction softly.

The smile fell from my lips. "Mamiza, was your sister Mariah Jesse Willis?"

"Yes'm. Sho' was. Some hit-and-run man dun killed her dead a few weeks back. My sister raised this girl, and her younger sister and baby brother too. Lawd, I don't how they is goin' to do without that woman. Especially Jackson, dat special baby boy."

Our cheeks brushed as my arms encircled each. A waft of jasmine petals tickled my nostrils, and I fought the pooling tears.

"I am so sorry for your loss. Mrs. Willis walked Jackson to school every day." Thoughts of the sack of pecans and the handmade quilt filled me with sadness. "She was a very kind lady, and so proud of Jackson. Such a good student."

"Missus Claire, I knows you was his teacher. My sister talked about you all the time." A shy grin revealed the smidgen of her gold front tooth. No further words were necessary.

Mrs. Bader would not approve of such gestures of familiarity with "nigras," so it made sense that Mamiza would not have revealed this before. The hovering fear of disclosure intimated an ever-present menacing force. Yet today a sister was grieved.

I turned my attention toward the respectfully bowed head of Delberta, who stood before me. I had learned about the visual disorder called nystagmus in a special education class. I noticed how Delberta's eyes shifted from side to side behind her glasses. She likely had contracted the affliction from birth. I imagined how difficult school must have been for her with such a burden, especially without individual training and programs to help her succeed. The visual affliction, combined with a lack of educational opportunity, spelled tragedy.

Nothing was mentioned about Delberta's toddler, cared for by Mariah Jesse Willis. I wondered if the child had this disorder and if it had anything to do with no one talking about him. I cringed to think that the little one would likely not get the necessary medical attention either. And Delberta was expecting another baby. I wondered who had fathered her children.

Now I could start to make sense of this twosome. Mamiza had often walked from Rohns early on Thursdays, her day off. She had likely never learned to drive a car, nor would she have the means to own one. Delberta was barely old enough to drive, and with her eye condition, it was unlikely. They had probably both walked, and I made a mental note to talk to Bruce about giving them a ride home.

I waited until our two newest members had taken seats, then clasped my hands together and said, "Well, let's get started." It was half past seven and we now had a respectable handful of students. I wanted each to write their names on name tags but thought better of this request. It would be good to have their birthdates as well—good reason to celebrate each student. I'd have to figure out a better way. For starters, building trust and comfort upon the courage they had already revealed was going to be most important. Perhaps the students might not return if there were too many demands put upon them all at once.

I asked everyone to call me Claire and inquired about how each of them would like to be addressed. The silence that followed my request startled me. As I glanced at each person, I realized my request had created a sense of suspended disbelief.

Lily Mae broke the icy silence, "Lawd, ma'am, just call us by our first names." The bellows of laughter that followed resonated aptly and cleared the pervasive air of anxiety, including mine.

Reverend Mease said nothing.

The Reverend, Mamiza, Lily Mae, Delberta, and, hopefully, Claire.

"Wonderful, Lily Mae. Good plan." I nodded approval. Poised, and with her chest thrust forward, she grinned at her contribution to the decision-making. The gesture further eased the tension and was exactly what I had hoped would occur. Even Delberta smiled demurely. I was sure she would rather have been in a dozen other places than with her Aunt Mamiza in a classroom with older adults.

Before passing out workbooks that only Reverend Mease would likely be able to read, I wanted to build a greater level of comfort and learn more about each student. "Again, welcome to you all. I'm glad you're here and proud to help you in any way I can. So, let's start by getting to know one another." I tore the cellophane paper from the box of chocolate cherries, soft but still whole, and passed them around. Beaming, Lily Mae again was the first to speak.

"Ma'am, we all know each other and see each other at Mt. Gideon Baptist Church every Sunday and at prayer meeting on Wednesdays."

"Wonderful. Maybe you could share a little about your

families." In fifteen minutes, I learned that the only stranger in this room was me. But learning more about my students was important to me to help them be successful. All acquiesced to the Reverend, respectfully waiting for him to speak first. He cleared his throat and began.

"My wife gave birth to six girls before our son arrived." He lowered his head. "Only five of our daughters survived." The fingers that had nimbly held the pencil quivered as he teased a freshly ironed, white handkerchief from an inner pocket of his brown jacket. He removed his spectacles with deliberation and carefully wiped the lenses.

The Reverend continued, "I grew up in the same shotgun house. Only with no pavement on the roads and no cement on the sidewalks. The federal legislation to fight poverty a few years back fixed a lot of them roads." The Reverend nodded assuredly, clearly grateful for any improvements.

"They used to say you could shoot a gun clear through the front door and pellets would bounce into every room. Yeah, but the Good Lawd keeps real beauty in our lives and lined them streets with glorious oak and chinaberry trees."

"Amen!" Exalted responses came in unison.

The only sound for the next few moments was the tapping of fresh droplets of rain against the windowpane. A bolt of thunder rattled in the distant darkness, while the Reverend continued.

As he spoke, I recalled what we had seen nearby. Delberta also lived in a shotgun house on one of those streets. The neighborhood was within walking distance of Brooks. Since Thursday was Mamiza's day off from Rohns, I suspect she spent her time at the Willis house as well. I considered the chinaberries with renewed insight. If one's eyes remained fixed heavenward, the branches that stretched from the age-old trees did resemble cathedral-like arches. The shotgun houses were now a blur beneath the curved arches that soared heavenward.

Glad he was a member of the class, I thought how proud Reverend Mease was of his literacy. He was a good example for the others.

Lily Mae hopped in next. "Ma'am, I live with my sister. She's in a wheelchair and I take care of her. I jis' want to be able to register to vote and to learn all I need to know to do just that. Couldn't pass the test last time, but 'spect to pass with flyin' colors the next time around." She looked hopefully in my direction.

"I'm glad you've come to this class, Lily Mae. We'll be working on handwriting signatures, addresses, and then onto our letters and words to help read the questions."

Her smile beamed with hope and confident expectation.

Mamiza was next. Before I could call on her, she spoke, "Ever since they passed the Votin' Rights Act, I be wantin' to sign my name so I could vote." Her gold upper tooth gripped a lower lip, considering her words carefully. "Besides that, when I retire, I needs to be able to sign them Social Security checks, and that is why I am here." Everyone laughed and I breathed a secret sigh of relief, glad to have not insisted on having all write their names on tags.

A half hour into our first session, I heard a slight tapping on the classroom door. I thought it might be Mr. Alvin. As I approached the door, however, I almost bumped heads with a robust woman who jerked the doorknob first. I stepped back as she steadied her frame with a large wooden cane in her left hand and limped forward, closing the door with her free hand.

"I do apologize for bein' late, ma'am. My name is Opie Doone. Can I still join yo' class?"

"Of course. It certainly is not too late. Welcome, Miss Doone. I'm glad you're here. Please come in." Before I could pull the warped doorframe shut, Lily Mae ran toward our new member. Reaching out, Lily Mae stretched her long arms toward her friend.

"Opie, you did come. I feared ya' might o' changed yo' mind."

Another familiar face. Opie Doone was the maid whom Mrs. Bader chastised for not sufficiently attending to her needs as we drove home from the League luncheon. I remember how our eyes locked at that event. Her treatment by the other guests had not given her the respect she was due. Opie had been a maven of order during the afternoon fest and had deserved to be appreciated.

"I seen ya' at Miss Ruby's lunch party, ma'am. Please call me Opie. Lily Mae and I done talked and we said we'd come together. Mamiza tole us all 'bout you, Missus Claire. Uh, hmm, well, you is jis' different."

Before she could say more, a thud pierced the air and then a loud crash. This time it wasn't only thunder. A jagged-edged, brownish stone lay inches from my feet. Emptiness, bereft of sound and sight, was all that was visible through the jagged windowpane beyond the classroom.

"Everyone duck!" I shouted, and ran to flip off the light switch, putting the room into darkness as well. I crouched beneath the nearest desk and hoped my students would do the same. Three hammering pounds on the door resonated with my clamoring heartbeat and the oak door banged against a wall frame for the second time that night. I held my breath, squeezed my closed eyelids, and waited.

CHAPTER 25

Cautiously opening my eyes, I was relieved to see the cap-covered silhouette of Alvin in the glow of the moonlight from the window.

"Did the electricity go out?" he asked. He went directly to the light switch and flipped the lights back on.

With my hand against my chest, I heaved another sigh.

"Alvin, someone pitched a rock through that window." I pointed a finger in the direction of the sheared opening left in the pane. I gripped onto the ledge of the bulletin board and stood closer to the wall, as much to steady my weak knees as to allow space for Alvin to pass. Lily Mae and Opie sat aghast; hands intertwined across the aisle of desks. I sensed they were praying.

"Damn." Alvin's tone of resignation suggested that this wasn't the first-time vandalism had happened on his watch. He continued to hold onto the mop handle with a tight fist as his nimble frame charged forward.

"Vengeance is in de hands o' de Lawd." Reverend Mease's voice was barely audible as he instinctively offered words of comfort.

"Sorry, folks. It's a lot of work and money to repair this glass," said Alvin as he looked at his shoes, likely realizing there were ladies present.

I tugged at my skirt and stuttered, "I, I think we should call the police. I'm sure the Lord would agree, Reverend?"

Rain dripped through the hole in the glass as Alvin spoke, "Naw, no need to call police, ma'am. They ain't gonna do nuthin'. Anyways, I'll clean up, here." He busied himself with arranging his cleaning tools, wanting to end any further discussion.

The clock on the wall showed we had an hour left for class. Taking a couple of deep breaths, I smiled and said, "Class, let's take a little restroom break while Alvin kindly cleans up this glass. We still have time left until the end of class, and we haven't heard from Opie yet." I blinked my eyes and smiled broadly at my newest student.

Opie stood at least two inches taller than her already stately frame, clearing the air with a smile that covered her creamy skin and allayed my tetchy nerves. Mamiza and Delberta stood quietly by the classroom door waiting for the other ladies. Lily Mae grabbed Opie's hand and said, "C'mon, girl. Let's get some water."

Rubbing my forehead at the thought of the rock incident, I shrugged away chilled arms. Reverend Mease hadn't left the room and was bent over his yellow legal pad. Since the Reverend could write, perhaps he could help me write the names of the students on the cards I had brought. With renewed excitement about the rest of the evening, I waited until Alvin shuffled out of the room then approached the Reverend.

"Reverend, before the others return, might you be able to help me fill out some cards with names of the students in our class?"

Stunned from his reverie, he looked blankly at me. "Beg pardon, ma'am?"

I repeated my question hoping not to sound bad-mannered.

"Yes, indeed. Glad to. Why all those ladies come to Mt. Gideon evra' Sunday. I have their addresses too."

"If you could bring the addresses to class next week, I'd be so grateful." Maybe everyone didn't have a phone. I decided not to ask. "Do you possibly have their birthdates too?"

With a blank expression, he looked into my eyes. I smiled at him and explained how it would be so nice to celebrate any birthdays while we had class. A small grin accentuated the lines on his face. "I'll see what I can do."

Gleeful, I pulled the cards from my bag and watched as the

Reverend slowly carved each letter on the white cards. Alvin nodded in my direction and pushed his cleaning cart through the doorway just ahead of the four women who came giggling into the classroom.

Thanking the Reverend and collecting the cards, I shouted, "Welcome back, ladies!"

They quickly took their seats, and I made every effort to overlook the rock incident while properly welcoming Opie, "We're so glad to have you in this class, Opie."

"It be my pleasure, Missus Claire." Standing tall, she continued, "I hope to have my own hair salon someday, and I'll need all the learnin' possible to be a businesswoman." With such confidence and determination, I believed her.

"Well, this is the perfect place to start, Opie. I'm so glad you're here. We'll see what we can do to make your dream come true." Her eyes were moist, but she radiated joy.

For the next half hour, we went over the materials from Mr. Parkington. He had suggested that my students shouldn't take the workbooks and materials home, but it was my class. I had other plans.

I retrieved the rolled-up cloth bags tucked inside my sack, hooked the handles over my two arms and said, "Surprise! You'll need something to carry your materials back and forth to class."

Mamiza hugged the volumes to her bosom. "You mean we can keep these books?"

"Of course. They're yours." I placed the colorful pieces on the side table so each person could select their own. The Reverend chose the dark brown bag with black handles.

"Thank ya', Missus Claire," said Lily Mae. "I never had my own book or book bag before."

"Please bring them with you next Thursday. We will be using our materials more in the weeks ahead." Certain to connect with every pair of eyes, I cinched a farewell with my biggest smile.

"Thank you all for coming to class tonight." I felt a small sense of relief and hoped the bags would help to soften the rock incident that all now ignored.

We bid our farewells and I reminded Delberta to be sure Jackson kept up with his reading over the summer. I had doubts that Jackson would receive the academic encouragement he got from Gramama Willis. Yet knowing how much he loved to read, he might just do it on his own.

"Yes'm," said Delberta as she scurried toward the door with Mamiza. Delberta had her own problems to deal with.

Alvin returned to close the room, and I took a moment to find out more about the rock throwing event. "Alvin, I'm sorry you had this mess to clean up. Who are the thugs? And why would they do this?"

"Don't know for sure, ma'am. We had some boys that dropped out of school and who mighta broken Principal Grilton's window a few weeks back. The rock had a skull drawn on it. Never caught 'em, but some o' the neighbors said they saw somethin'. You take care, ya' hear?" He stopped talking abruptly and continued to reorder chairs and desks in readiness for mopping. Although eager to get home, his reticence suggested he wasn't going to share more.

"Oh, I'll be fine." Although unsettled, I was anxious to leave and to see Bruce.

As I opened the door, Bruce was standing in the hallway. He grabbed my book bag and said, "What took you so long? Everyone else left almost ten minutes ago."

"Well, almost everyone." He smiled and followed my glance toward Mamiza and Delberta at a distance leaving the ladies' room. As they walked away, I worried about their safety. Tonight, I shuddered to think that any one of us could be a target. Bruce wrinkled his brow.

"I got here early and parked the car so I could come inside," he continued, beaming. "You should have heard those people. The ladies squealed and giggled. What was in those cherry chocolates, anyway?" He laughed, pulled me close and kissed my cheek.

I threw my arms around him and melted into his warmth, clinging to his chest with my eyes closed.

Mamiza and Delberta had disappeared by the time we reached the front doors. The rain had stopped but the sidewalks glistened. The low-hanging branches near the entrance loomed forth in an eerie silence. I linked my arm through Bruce's as we walked toward the car.

"You okay, babe?"

I glanced right, then left, as we walked into the darkness surrounded by the now onerous greenery. "I'm fine." I squeezed his arm and smiled up into his eyes. "Glad you came inside."

As Bruce started the car, I spotted Mamiza and Delberta walking a couple of blocks ahead and said, "Let's ask them if they want a ride."

"I hope no one sees us." Bruce slowed the car down.

"So, what if they do?" If my husband only knew how their safety might be at risk, he would be more compassionate.

"We have to be careful. What if someone from the base or one of Mrs. Bader's friends sees us pick them up? Especially in the dark."

"Oh, c'mon. What harm can it do if we give these ladies a ride home? It's not a big deal."

"Don't kid yourself. This is a small town and news travels fast." He softened a bit and continued, "Guess there's no harm in asking, this time."

When he pulled up alongside the women, I rolled down my window. "Can we give you ladies a ride home?"

Delberta looked at Mamiza. Mamiza hesitated. I looked at them both.

"Missus Claire. Why, that be mighty nice," said Mamiza. Delberta started toward the car. Before she could take a second step, however, Mamiza looped her arm through her niece's thin forearm and tugged at her elbow.

Mamiza then guided Delberta back onto the sidewalk, asserting her charge of the younger woman. Mamiza reflected a determined glare in a dogged protective instinct. One might suspect we were trying to kidnap them.

"Mighty kind, Mr. Bruce. Thank y'all, but we don't mind walkin'," Mamiza said. With elbows intertwined and their heads tilted toward the cracked sidewalk, they moved ahead.

Bruce nodded and rolled up the window. "Well, we tried. Probably best they didn't accept," he said.

"Well not really, Bruce. There's more that might have influenced their decision to decline."

"What do you mean?" He fixed a concerted glance in my direction.

I knew he wouldn't be happy to hear this news, but I thought he should know.

"Someone, probably a group of teenage kids, pitched a rock through the classroom window tonight. I turned the lights out and we all took cover. No one was hurt, but it was scary."

"That's it. You're quittin' this job," said Bruce emphatically as he gunned the engine and headed toward Rohns Manor.

CHAPTER 26

The week flew by and the negative nattering that followed the rock incident on the first night of class ended in a resolved win-win. I had no intention of quitting my new job because of some neighborhood hoodlums, and Bruce had relented. *He would continue to do the driving, and I would continue to do the teaching.*

I watched Bruce, comfy in his shorts and undershirt in front of the TV, engrossed in the evening news. With a tad sense of guilt, I gently reminded him that I had class that night. He didn't budge.

Raising a living room window to seek a wisp of fresh air in the murky July heat, I heard the oscillating rhythm of the wicker rocker as it crunched against the wooden floor of the veranda. Since it was Mamiza's day off, the grand dame of Rohns would usually be alone, but not that night. The flashy red sports car parked at the end of the walkway also announced a visit from Billy Chas.

"Hush, Mama. Careful." A hissed voice.

No doubt about the speaker. It was Billy Chas. "Did you hear him?" I whispered in Bruce's direction.

"Hear who?" The sportscaster blared out game stats and Bruce's eyes were glued to the screen.

Tucking behind the folds of heavy drapes, I strained to hear the conversation, but the Baders' voices were now only murmurs between rickety rocker crunches.

Moving back toward Bruce, I said, "Let's see if we can slip out the kitchen door and take another route to school tonight."

He stood and yawned. "Why is that?"

"I just don't want Billy Chas to see us leaving and wonder where we're going."

"That is pure paranoia. The guy is visiting his mother. He's not here to spy on us."

"Well, I don't think he'd like it if a white Yankee living in his mama's house was teaching black folks, do you?" I raised my eyebrows.

"Look, Claire, this is getting out of hand. You are so suspicious of everyone. In fact, Mrs. Bader asked me if you were all right the other day. She thought you seemed very edgy." He walked toward the back door, opened it without another word, and unhooked the screen.

Mrs. Bader had a lot of nerve to ask my husband such a question. But Bruce had a point, though. Billy Chas was likely just checking in on his mom. As I turned back into the bedroom to scoop up my purse and bookbag atop my sewing machine, I noticed more cars through the front windows. Curious about why so many cars were in front of the manor, I ducked behind a draped window just in time to see Johnny Bailey crunch what was left of a cigarette on the road. He tugged his trousers up a notch. Those actions reflected the same demeanor he posed at Billy Chas's barbeque. He teetered slightly, heading toward the manor. Too much beer, again.

The knots in my stomach tightened as I made my way into the kitchen and slipped through the screen like a thief on a getaway. I locked the door. Checking it a second time. I climbed into the Ford and told Bruce about the pile of vehicles gathering out front. He steered the car in the opposite direction.

"Also, I don't appreciate Mrs. Bader talking about me behind my back," I said. "I will not be bullied by the Baders." My neck and shoulder muscles felt tight, and my stomach churned.

"Honey, you are making too much of this. She is an old woman, and she cares about you. That's all. And Billy Chas is her son. He's allowed to visit his mama, and so are his friends. He's divorced and probably lonely. Let it go. We haven't told anyone about your job."

I shifted in my seat. "Feeling like we have to sneak out the door makes me uncomfortable. I shouldn't be afraid to help people learn to read and write."

Bruce patted my leg but didn't respond. Daylight was fading as we took a secondary route along the backstreets to the high school. A few white merchants were decorating display windows in preparation for the Fourth of July celebration.

"We've lived in Selma for almost four months," I said thinking about the celebrations that would be taking place back home.

"It seems like we've been here half of our lives." His tone echoed my nostalgia, and he repeated the mantra, "Selma is better than Vietnam."

I scooted closer and planted a kiss on his ear. "Right. We'll be okay. OTS could be just around the corner." My optimistic reminder brought a smile to Bruce's face.

"Hope so," he murmured wistfully. Always the practical one.

We were within a couple of miles of Samuel Boynton High when I spotted Mamiza and Delberta standing at the curbside in front of the 7-Eleven store.

"Turn at the next street. Quick!" The traffic light turned green.

"Why? This road takes us right into the school."

"Just turn!"

When Bruce rounded the corner, the architecture changed from little storefronts to another tar-covered road. Rows of garage-like structures abutted each other. Families were sitting on porches, some in rockers and some on front steps, fanning themselves with newspapers. Little kids played ball and jumped rope on the dirt walkways. A group of teens stopped a game of kick the can and ran in baseball fashion around bases—a couple of designated tree stumps and two inner tubes. Suddenly all eyes were cast in our direction and the teenage boys did not look friendly. Perhaps Alvin was right.

"Well, this doesn't look good," I said.

Bruce backed the car up. We both extended friendly waves at the teens playing kick the can. No response.

"Teenagers. They're just being cool." Bruce shrugged as we drove up the street.

"I doubt it. We're in unwelcome territory," I said, glancing over my shoulder out the rear window and changing the subject.

"By the way, what did you think of those tiny shotgun houses? Quite different from the estate style manors near Rohns," he said. Bruce always had a comment about the architecture of our surroundings. "It's like we're in two different cities. By the way, why did you want me to turn onto this street?"

"I didn't want Mamiza and Delberta to see us." I turned and pointed my finger in the direction of the store, secretly glad that the two women were no longer there.

"Last week you were anxious to give them a ride and now you're avoiding them?" Bruce shook his head.

"I don't want to scare them away from class. If they see us, they might be intimidated."

We pulled in front of the empty school which loomed ominously in the fading light of day. Bruce shifted the car into park. "I'll walk you in."

"I'll be fine." Another quick kiss and I was out the door before he could take any further action. "See you in a couple of hours. Bye." I blew a second kiss in his direction, determined not to show the trepidation I felt.

As I hurried toward the entrance and ran up the cement steps, I could feel Bruce's eyes on my back and was glad he stuck around.

Principal Grilton's office was dark, and Alvin was nowhere in sight. I made my way to the classroom where the door was unlocked. I pulled out the papers and materials, as well as the foil-wrapped brownies I had baked. Mamiza and Delberta were on their way, and I prayed all the other students would return.

As I set materials on the desk, the door rattled. Donned in a colorful muumuu, Opie flounced into the room with the same vigor she had had on the first night and settled my angst from the scene at Rohns.

"Please come in, Opie." I hurried toward her, dropping a yellow pencil that had slipped from behind my ear.

Stooping to retrieve the pencil, I noticed she hadn't moved. With head tilted to the side, she blinked her round onyx eyes a few times. Her grip on the brass doorknob loosened, and she stepped back into the dimly lit hallway.

"Ma'am do beg your pardon, but I be back shortly. I need to use the ladies' room." She turned abruptly and left.

Wondering about the formidable glower and caustic greeting, I nodded blankly, and said, "Okay. Of course." I turned to place the name cards of each student on their chosen seat from our last class.

Seconds after Opie disappeared into the corridor, Mamiza and Delberta entered the classroom. Both were donned in crisply starched dresses with handbags in tow. If they had bonnets and gloves, they would look ready for Sunday church services.

"Evenin', Missus Claire," said Mamiza. She continued to use the formal "Missus" and crooked her head toward the younger woman, anticipating proper respect. Delberta responded with a greeting and a shy grin.

Reverend Mease and Lily Mae Brown were next, chatting together as they entered. I breathed a sigh of relief. At least all the students had returned. The Reverend handed me a folded sheet of yellow legal paper with all the home addresses and birth dates of the students.

"Thank you for remembering," I said to him. He returned a respectful nod and took his seat.

Idle chatter and another ten minutes passed. No sign of Opie. I hoped she hadn't changed her mind and slipped out the front door. We had lost valuable time during our first class. I wasn't about to let it happen again, Opie or no Opie.

With a collective welcome to all, I began our class with a talk about how important it is to learn to read and write well. I pointed to the page number of the introduction in our workbook and asked the students to follow silently while I read out loud.

Other than the Reverend, I still was uncertain of the reading skills of the others, but I would respectfully expect the best and be ready to meet each student at their individual level. I also showed them both the printed and cursive versions of their names I had written on 3 x 5 cards.

"Please copy your names at the back of your books as well." I held up the sample of my own name, cursively written and printed in block letters.

"Which way should we copy it, ma'am?" Lily Mae wanted to be correct.

"Cursive or printing." I pointed to each. "You choose."

"I'll write mine like I learned in handwriting class." Delberta's pride in the minimal education she had and her interest in learning buoyed my own enthusiasm. She hadn't finished seventh grade and her vision problems made the fluency of reading and writing difficult. Accurate examples and graph paper would help her align her writing. I made a mental note to bring some to the next class.

I returned to my one-on-one work with the Reverend and was pleased to see he had made revisions. "This is a good start," I said. "Let's also create three or four sentences in the beginning lines. You want to hook your audience in preparation for the powerful message to come."

He smiled in appreciation, erased, and rewrote.

When I glanced toward Delberta, I saw she had flipped a

few pages ahead of the others and studied the directions on page three. Chewing on a pencil eraser, I watched her tilt her head toward the book. She appeared to devour the words. I saw her lips move in concert with an index finger, guiding each tentative effort across the lines of the workbook page. How much she comprehended would be something I needed to know.

Excusing myself from Reverend Mease, I slipped to Delberta's side and handed her a 3 x 5 card to control her visual tracking across the page. I wondered what might have been possible if Delberta had grown up with an educated mother and father. She was only a few years younger than me, but our lives were oceans apart. At her age, I was taking advanced English classes and in my third year of Spanish.

The Reverend wrote his name in manuscript and cursive, studying each page as he scanned the words.

When I leaned over Mamiza's crouched shoulder, she looked up. Her pencil lead was broken, but she never said anything. I quietly handed her mine, with a mental note to go over the use of the pencil sharpener on the wall at the beginning of our next class.

"Try this paper." I handed three-holed paper to Mamiza and passed it around to the others. "The blue lines help make writing straighter."

I went back to Mamiza and copied her name at the top, wrote it in broken lines three times and asked her to trace and then try on her own.

Lily Mae traced over the letters, checking the alphabet card I had provided. Her literacy was limited. I recalled the care she had shown in serving and handling silver and delicate dinnerware at the Ladies League luncheon. She was hungry for learning. With a little help, I knew she could be successful.

I considered unveiling my newest surprise, hand-sewn pencil holders to match each student's book bag of choice. But I couldn't hand out the gifts with one student missing.

"Where be dat girl, Opie?" Lily Mae spoke my thoughts aloud.

I was about to respond when the familiar clatter of the classroom door announced the return of Opie Doone. "So sorry, ma'am." My spirits leapt. She had returned.

Tiny red lines were noticeable around the edges of her eyes. Opie had been crying. "I do think I'm gettin' a summer cold."

"Come in, Opie." It was the second time I had greeted her, and I flashed my biggest smile. "We've just gone over our class introduction. I'll catch you up while the others practice in the workbooks."

Opie took her seat and adjusted with dignity to an erect posture in the chair. As I proceeded to go over the lesson with her individually, she struggled. I took each letter slowly, showing her where O-P-I-E was on her alphabet card. It was clear why she hesitated to come back to class. I decided to have her practice a series of broken-lined block letters of her name while I circulated among the other students. Periodically glancing her way, I noticed how close her face was to the page, teeth biting her lower lip. Opie likely needed glasses. I made a mental note to talk with Winnie about how I could find out more about eye checkups—perhaps for all my students. Thinking about the magnifying glass in the car glove compartment, I dismissed the urge. Embarrassing.

"Nice work, Opie," I said as I sauntered back toward her desk. Her vision aside, she was perseverant. Opie had not only written her name perfectly but was moving through the handwriting manual, copying pages of other letters of the alphabet.

Noticing the clock, I had almost forgotten about the cloth pencil holders. I opened my bag and lay a dozen cloth envelopes, each with a coordinated color button flap on the table.

"I have a surprise for you, my friends." Reverend Mease peeked over the rims of his specks.

Displaying the brightly colored holders from the sack, I explained how they could be used.

"Why they match our bags," said Opie.

"That's right. There are some that are plain too. Your choice," I said showcasing the options.

"That's mighty kind. Thank you," said Opie. I was sure that if her cocoa skin could reflect a blush it would be now.

Each student had selected either a matching pencil holder or a complementary colored choice, and we said our goodbyes. I took my time jotting notes about the class and reminders for next session. Opie took her time gathering her materials, fluffing her skirt, and pulling on a sweater. She then cleared her throat and ambled closer to my desk.

"S'cuse me, ma'am." I looked up into her knitted brows. "There is somethin' I think you should know. My cousin is Winnie Holmes." She looked down at her shoes.

"Why that is wonderful, Opie. Winnie and I worked together at Brooks." Briefly stunned, I hesitated then went on, "Winnie is also a good friend."

Eyes downcast, she continued as if I had not said a word. "Well, you also need to know that she is the smart one in the family and the only one who has gotten an education. Winnie is the reason I'm here."

"I am so proud you joined this class, Opie." I stood and moved closer to this colorful woman. "It is an honor to be your teacher." In one fell swoop, Opie reached out and encircled her large arms around my entire body, capturing and containing the joy I felt. And then just as quickly she dropped her arms and left the room.

Humbled by what had just happened, I watched her once again disappear into the corridor. Aware that Alvin was nowhere in sight, and the only bright light I could see shown above me in the classroom, I gathered my materials and hurriedly left. Bruce was waiting at the entrance. As I hugged him, I noticed an empty white pickup parked across the street from the high school.

Sitting in the front seat as Bruce pulled away, I casually pulled out my compact mirror and fussed with my hair. "Bruce, I think we're being followed." The mirror served the two purposes, only one being to powder my nose. Crawling like a white Palmetto bug, I noticed the truck about two vehicles behind us.

"Hmm. Wonder why anyone would want to follow *us?*" asked Bruce.

"Good question, Sherlock." I made a nervous joke as we waited for the light to turn green. I reached behind my head in a casual stretch and pushed at the knob to lock my door. I wrapped an endearing arm around his shoulder and locked his door too.

My husband's face became stern. He looked through his rearview mirror, furrowed his brow, and spoke, "Is the culprit driving a pink Volkswagen Beetle with one light out?"

"Very funny. Am I supposed to say *pedito?*" I thought of our old high school competition to see who could find a car headlight burned out and say *pedito* first.

"I'm serious. That's exactly what's behind us right now."

I spun around and saw that he was right, and the white truck was no longer in sight.

Whether relieved or amused by the irony of my own perceptions, I giggled. "Probably being my paranoid self again," I said, patting Bruce's thigh with an effort to be sarcastic.

As I breathed deeply and rested my head against the sticky vinyl headrest, I swallowed hard. What I had seen wasn't a *pink ladybug.*

CHAPTER 27

My passion to learn more about Selma's history had only begun, and I was eager to return to my research. Since it was a Tuesday, Ruby and Belinda would not likely be volunteering at the library. As I drove through the streets, colored women, pockets chock full of wooden clothespins and little children at their feet, hung wash out to dry. Just another steamy, sunny Selma summer day. All so normal and harmless.

Pulling up to the front of the library, I remembered reading that the old building was designed with an ancient Eastern European castle in mind and built by slave labor. Apparently, the library was one of the first public facilities in the South to be integrated. Negroes built the structure but were only recently allowed to go inside and use the services and materials. *It wasn't fair and it wasn't right.*

Entering the reference section, the librarian sat in full command. Her thin, wired glasses perched precariously on the tip of her nose as she buried her head in a sea of papers and files. I chose my words and tone cautiously. "Good morning, Miss Lillian. I'm back to learn more about this lovely, historic city of Selma." I flicked my lashes and produced a most demure smile.

"Well, good mornin'. You are Ruby's and Belinda's friend. Lovely girls." I was certain that her hospitality was more about the influence of my Southern sisters than it was about me. She rolled the chair back from the desk, stood, tugged at her too snug skirt, and led me to the stacks.

The folders of clippings were still as dusty as they were on my last visit. At the bottom of the stack sat a manila envelope with a sticker labeled: "Teachers' March." As I untied the string that held the package together several articles fell onto the desktop in the carrel. The headline read: "Negro Teachers March." Right below the headline was a photo depicting the determined glare of Principal Grilton, leader of the line. The article explained that Clayton Grilton, then the president of the Black Teachers' Union, organized constituents in a march to the courthouse. Every black employee in the school district participated. The article labeled the initiative as a hallmark event, praised by colored leaders as a significant gesture of Negro middle-class professionals.

"I am appalled at the aggressive efforts of the Black Teachers' Union and deeply troubled to see all those educated professional people go against their own children," said the mayor in an interview following the demonstration. "These Negroes are robbing their own from an educational opportunity by making a racket and demanding attention. How will our Negro children be prepared for the 20th century with such a lack of commitment by their own teachers?" The message being portrayed by the local paper offered an opposing twist to the inequities the teachers sought to expose.

I wondered if Winnie Holmes had marched in that entourage. Was this what she meant when she talked about the "tales that a Northern white woman could never understand?" I had planned to call Winnie to ask about materials for my adult learners. Now I had a second reason to talk with her.

Flipping through the worn pages, clipping after clipping told of the darkened destruction of the fair city of Selma. Every story was biased. *So much for the free press presenting both sides of an issue.*

Digesting what lay before me, I rested my head against the carrel, facing the window that revealed an aviary. Allowing the dance of flapping wings to entertain me, I basked in the natural beauty of my surroundings. The only species I recognized was the long-beaked hummingbird, so tiny it could fit in the palm of my hand. Making an appearance, the little fellow fluttered off to perch on a nearby oleander shrub.

The blazing Selma sun promised to clench and bake its residents. I saw women carrying brightly colored shopping bags. Others sauntered along the sidewalk, flouncing floral skirts as they guided baby carriages. One mother unfurled an expandable, dime-store hand fan, and waved it over her baby. She didn't even give a nod to an elderly, colored man who was bent over and sweeping every inch of the walkway a few steps ahead of her clearly in her path. In fact, he bowed and moved out of her way. Gazing straight ahead, she appeared not to notice his presence in the least. *If a force of nature hadn't taken my baby, perhaps I could I have been one of those ladies.* One thing for sure, I would have smiled and returned the greeting to the man sweeping the streets. A wave of sadness washed over me, and I returned to the task at hand.

The racial divide filtered through every piece of life in Selma. It was on the streets, in the schools, hidden behind lacy curtains and grand verandas, shotgun houses, shanties, and bungalows. It even included the free press. The *Selma News* wasn't going to help connect any of the pieces, whether it was before the 1965 march or since. However, a national news chain might.

Knowing it would be unwise to approach Miss Lillian about this topic, I snatched my purse and sauntered through the aisles of books seeking the card catalog. After a little digging, I found files of back issues of the national news magazine, *Global,* from three or four years earlier. I picked up several copies of the magazine as well as some national newspaper clippings and went back to my carrel, making every effort to circumvent Miss Lillian's omniscient space.

As I flipped through archives of parched newsprint, already beginning to yellow, a Pandora's box spewed forth a plethora of reports that didn't jive with those of the *Selma News.* Little was written of the happy, submissive Negro seen in the local rag. Nor did I find articles that touted the plantation-style charm of the uninvolved traditional white Southern belles. A few stories hit upon the polar groups of radical white citizens' coalitions and black power people, also clearly outlined in the local paper.

My biggest find of the day, however, was the untouched secret that surrounded tales of clandestine collaboration. Stories of white women and black women working together to bring harmony to the South abounded. These underground initiatives were led by zealots of a very different nature, according to this report.

In the table of contents from a *Global* issue dated August 1968, an article about opportunities for kids caught my eye: "Youth Programs Bring Awareness." The article described the efforts of women from local church groups who initiated projects to educate and bring greater racial harmony to young people of both races. *Was this the Females for Freedom coalition?* It said this group of women designed retreats to build team spirit and heighten awareness of similarities, rather than differences. The article described how a white mother from a local Methodist congregation requested joint Summer Vacation Bible School classes. In this program, both white and black students from different churches would gather to play team sports, board games, and listen to stories. They would even eat pizza together!

Unfortunately, the plan was quickly doused. The governing council of the white Southern Methodist Church denied her request. Not to be thwarted, the program director took further steps. "I am pleased to announce a two-week summer camp will take place along the shores of the Mississippi River just northeast of Selma," she said.

A big question gnawed at my sense of justice: *If Reverend Samuel Mease knew of this initiative, would he participate?*

The *Global* article waxed on about how most black youth in Selma had never left the city limits, let alone the state. Summer camps would be an adventure, an opportunity for team building, and a way to educate young people. Plans were already in the making for future camps for the summer of 1971. I thought of Jackson and made a mental note to have a chat with Mamiza. She couldn't read—at least not yet—and would not know of such an opportunity. Certainly, this information was not to be discussed on Rohns' grounds and would require the utmost caution.

A fall 1968 issue of a Northern paper displayed colored men dressed in suits and ties, while the women wore hats, gloves, and high-heeled shoes. The headline below the photo read: "Selma Teachers Take Action." I rubbed my dampened palms against my skirt before handling the brittle pages. The report offered a much different view about why Negro teachers felt their voting rights had been compromised. Unlike the viewpoint published in the *Times-Journal,* the Northern newspaper explained that the hours of operation for voter registration occurred only during school hours. This prohibited the Negro teachers from being able to register. The purpose of their solidarity demonstration was a plea for a single day for teachers to be able to register to vote without missing school.

The article went on to explain how the teacher demonstration was a result of high school student activism. The kids saw the injustice and set the stage. In response to the denial of Negro citizens' rights, Black Teachers' Union President Grilton called upon colleagues to act. The article further stated that teachers, dressed in Sunday best attire, marched on Friday the 13th to call attention to this injustice imposed by the city fathers.

I scanned the photo, searching for teachers from Brooks. The aging ink made the shot look fuzzy, but a few faces looked familiar. In the center was the profile of a lady holding her purse on her arm, her chin raised toward Mr. Grilton. It was Winnie Holmes, in a stance of grave determination. So much like Winnie.

"The teachers of Selma are professionals who are prepared to support our children and youth and pave the way for their future," Mr. Grilton had told the reporter.

The report touted the professional demeanor of the marching teachers and explained that even though it was Friday afternoon, the Selma teachers would be prepared for their students in school on Monday—whether jailed over the weekend or not. Every teacher carried personal items, such as toothbrushes and toothpaste, as they paraded through the public streets. Grilton said teachers didn't want to miss classes, but they were ready to stand up for their constitutional rights.

At the bottom of the page, pictures of the sheriff and his deputies, swinging billy clubs in the air above the heads of individuals, loomed as large as life. The sheriff's quotes supported the denial of voter registration for colored citizens.

"These Negroes are disturbing the peace and preventing our black children from getting an education," he claimed.

Continuing my research, a letter to the editor shared a critical view of the aftermath of civil rights legislation.

Dear Sirs:

What we see in towns like Selma is nothing but a besieged Negro community, left in a wake and with no thought of how to deal with the chaos the citizens have caused. The marches and the hoopla raised the expectations of the colored people, bringing to the surface a century of inherited frustrations that had been buried beneath the "yes'm, masta" days. But nothing has changed. There are no improvements, nor plans for further action to bring about reforms for the Southern Negro—male or female. All we see is more brutality and unresolved anger. We see the town's sheriff beating marchers and anyone standing in a voter's registration line. If a black male makes eye contact with a white woman, he can be accused of lascivious thoughts with intent to commit rape. Yet reports of white male transgressions and café au lait little faces in the streets reflect a different set of norms.

Was the march of the century no more than a rabble-rousing expression of a few zealots eager to glean national exposure by crying wolf? Our fundamental objection was that an intense, well-publicized expression of a community to offer national news exposure produced only short-term gains. What is the outcome three years after the Movement? Nothing.

The letter was signed by someone from New York.

On the same page, the words of a local Selma citizen offered the Southern white view of the situation.

Dear Sirs:

I am just fed up with the antics of your newspaper to cause trouble in my hometown of Selma. And I am sick and tired of reading your editorial accusations of the incivility and lack of humanity of the white Southern Americans residing in the cornerstone of this Confederacy. In my opinion, and that of many Selma residents whose families plowed the cotton fields and have lived here for generations, your news report is just another Yankee ploy to dredge up hatred and discontent among the Negroes and whites in the South. Our Negroes are happy and cherished by whites. We have lived in harmony for over a hundred years, until you came here to stir up trouble. Your newspaper is a gossip rag of backlash and sewage from "Le Gran Marche." Just because a rabble-rousing Negro preacher didn't like the way we do things in our town and decided to trample upon the holy ground of our Edmund Pettus Bridge, we continue to endure exploitation.

The only toll the grand old dame ever asked for was an appreciation of her welcoming outstretched arms, ready to embrace our arrival as we crossed the river and came home. On my visits home from my blue tide alma mater, I looked for those powerful outstretched limbs, welcoming us in the distance. When we saw the Pettus Bridge, we knew we were home. Every Friday night, my momma and daddy would take us for a fried catfish and hush puppy supper at the Selma Plantation Inn along the white side of the Alabama River basin. I would look up at that mighty structure and feel safe. That was all before the march.

Now, Sir, the Selma Plantation Inn is closed. Yes, there are a few fish stands and picnic tables, but the glory of the past Southern tradition is gone. It was destroyed by the ravages of marching Commies. The United States of America is fighting to keep Communism out of Vietnam when we should be doing that right here in this country. Right here in Selma!

I say, stop the war on your own land. We are not the enemy. Our Negroes are happy here and we love them dearly.

This writer was a self-proclaimed proud Selma citizen, signed Mary Lou Rader.

The name was familiar, perhaps someone I'd met at the Ladies League luncheon. Carefully following the existing creases on the newsprint and returning the clipping to its tattered envelope, the viewpoint of the white upper-class elite was clear. This included Ruby and Belinda. It was preposterous to suggest Selma's colored citizens were content. They were God-fearing Christians and scared as hell to speak up for fear of reprisal.

The birds outside my carrel window had disappeared and clouds had rolled into the billowy shades of grey. I reread the editorials a second, then a third time. Nothing had changed, commented the editor. If national exposure and thousands of advocates hadn't brought about improvements here, what could? Miss Lillian coughed somewhere in the background, beyond the stacks of books. Sounds from another person caused me to check my surroundings. Hope I hadn't absentmindedly spoken aloud.

A tiny mockingbird, perched on a branch barely touching

the windowpane, cocked his head toward me. I felt a pervasive sense of harmony. Gazing at the feathered creature, I decided to take two important steps: learn more about the peace-building church group and discontinue my membership in an organization that supports segregation. Lunch and a conversation with Ruby and Belinda had to be planned, and soon.

CHAPTER 28

Pondering the tasks that lay ahead brought sleeplessness at night, while the dissonance I felt drained my energy during the daytime. However, my first paycheck from the adult education class gave me an excuse for a real luncheon date with my Zeta sisters. *Why should I need to make them understand my position?* The answer: living counter to what I believed wasn't working for me. My priorities had shifted. To be free of the pretense of Ladies League airs, I needed to let Ruby and Belinda know who I *really* was—or was *becoming*.

We agreed to meet the following Monday after their stint at the library. I rehearsed my spiel, including the parts about Fems for Freedom and the youth camp. I wondered what they knew about the group. They would likely be shocked at my interest in becoming involved, but I was prepared to lose their friendship if they couldn't accept that. Surprisingly, I felt little anxiety about the planned luncheon meeting. I would tell Bruce about it later. He'd only try to dissuade me.

"Isn't it fun to sit and eat and chat?" Ruby mused, as she nibbled on another bite of a tuna salad sandwich and added sugar cubes to her lemonade. The ice clanged against the glass as her spoon stirred the cloudy liquid.

"Yup, and I'm starved," I spoke with confidence, knowing I had the cash to back me up.

"Well, don't eat too much, honey," Belinda piped in as she munched on lettuce leaves. She was always watching her figure, along with every man in sight. Bruce complimented my curves often. *Lucky me.*

The waitress came back with more lemonade, while a colored woman wiped empty tables nearby. "Thank ya,' kindly." Ruby flashed a large, pink-lipped smile and glanced about to see if she recognized any other faces in the space.

We exchanged a few more pleasantries about the heat, their trips to the coast, and our husbands. Ruby was an Alabama delegate to our national sorority organization, and she rattled on about a big Zeta alumni conference coming up in Florida in the spring.

"I'd love for y'all to come, Claire—you and Bruce. My Bobby is coming and so are Belinda and Johnny."

"That is, if Johnny won't be away at a conference that weekend," Belinda practically whimpered. "We all would have such a ball." She reapplied lipstick for the second time since our arrival.

I nodded and forced a smile. *I had to save some money from my job just to go out to lunch, and they wanted us to go to Florida.* This reality felt different than it might have a few months earlier. The old jealousy didn't appear—sorority girl connections or not.

I swallowed a sip of water. "It would be loads of fun to go to Florida. We have never been there." *Truth.*

A colored woman wiped tables, farther from us now. She kept her head bowed, while the white guests enjoyed the fare and chatted with friends. Our waitress deftly moved between tables and juggled plates of catfish and French fries, with bottles of catsup tucked into deep apron pockets.

"You'd love the sandy white beaches. It's so romantic." Belinda playfully raised her eyebrows and crunched her shoulders. "There's lots of shrimp, and we can lie in the sun and get bronzy brown. Imagine how great we'll look in our bathing suits when summer comes." She had the plan all mapped out a year ahead of time.

"Sounds amazing. But I'm not sure we can make the trip." I concentrated on my next bite of the sandwich.

"Why not, honey? Bruce gets leave, doesn't he?" Belinda was persistent.

"We just don't know where we'll be next year, but hopefully Bruce will be accepted into the Officer Training School." Unable to resist the comment, I sat taller in my seat and added, "Besides, we'll likely need to use his leave time to go up north for Christmas."

Ruby and Belinda were embedded in family tradition. They'd understand holiday commitments.

Silence followed, except for the clinking of ice cubes breaking down in our glasses. "Oh, and I'm working." I had said it!

"What? Thought you weren't plannin' on teaching this fall?" Ruby looked genuinely surprised. "Bobby would love to have you full time, though. He just found out that two more of his teachers are pregnant and won't be coming back. I don't think he has filled the openings. I'll talk to him tonight." Ruby proposed a solution for every dilemma.

Before I could respond, a thundering clatter of dishes hit the linoleum floor behind us. Diners spun to glance at the array of white plates and cups strewn about. The colored bus girl was picking up the jagged ceramic with her bare hands. A heavy-set man in a shirt and tie dashed out of a swinging door that led to the kitchen. Apparently, the owner.

"What the hell you doin', girl?" Towering menacingly over the woman, he emphasized each word, as he continued, "You'll pay for this."

With a more genteel tone, he looked about the café and pasted a smile on his bulbous lips. "Do beg y'alls' pardon." With a nod toward the white hostess, who stood with mouth agape, he continued, "Gertrude, please refill all drinks for these nice folks. On the house, 'course."

I sat in stunned silence, reminded of the words from the one editorial about the Dr. King's march across the Pettus

Bridge. The writer had criticized the embedded supremacy of the Deep South and its vicious inhumanity, directly opposite of the flamboyant gentility of tradition and proper courtesies.

As the colored worker struggled to gather the sharp, broken fragments, I noticed her finger was bleeding. I immediately stood up and walked over to the woman, knelt next to her, and handed her my napkin.

"Why, thank ya', ma'am." She accepted the cloth and wrapped it around the wound. A flash of her dark eyes spoke her gratitude even more deeply, while self-conscious movements reflected her simultaneous embarrassment. The room dulled in stunned silence. The owner returned with an empty pail and tossed it near the woman, who was still on her knees, picking up the pieces.

"By the way, that napkin will cost you twenty cents." He folded thick arms over his round middle, glared at the waitress, and leveled a brief, but sullen glance in my direction.

"Yes sir, o'course." She allowed the white napkin to fall away in her efforts to get every jagged shard from the broken dishes. As he waddled off, I noticed the woman tuck her head toward her bosom and mumble, as if she were praying.

"I couldn't let the poor woman bleed," I said slipping back into my seat. My response to Ruby and Belinda was more statement than apology.

"No, you could not." Belinda raised her chin.

I wondered if she was mocking me.

"Let's go back to my house and have some fresh pecan pie." Ruby purposefully folded her napkin into a long rectangle and placed it on the table.

"That would be lovely," I agreed, knowing there was unfinished business to be discussed.

Belinda stretched her neck and hailed our waitress with her broad smile and bat of her lashes. We paid our bills to the cashier and left.

~

Driving behind them in the Ford, I rehearsed my presentation. I planned to tell them about teaching the adults, and how important it was for all people—blacks and whites—to be able to read and write. Voter registration for all citizens was an important constitutional right.

The broken dishes incident at Dottie's Place was unfortunate for the woman. Yet, the incident offered further fodder for me to stand up for what was right. The incident set the tone for my speech. Although I had not formally been initiated into the Ladies League, I would gently withdraw my consideration.

Ruby's maid must have had the day off because Ruby invited us into her kitchen and pulled the pie out of the refrigerator herself. She and Belinda seemed more somber than usual. My reaction at the restaurant probably embarrassed them. No matter, I was attack ready.

As we sat at Ruby's kitchen table, I noticed the quaintly decorated carriage house out back and wondered if anyone lived there. Ruby's Persian cat brushed against my legs under the shiny chrome legs of the table. Even though I was allergic to cats, this gentle encounter was warm and welcoming. With such a genteel setting, and renewed courage, I began.

"Ladies, I have something to tell you. You are my friends and have been unbelievably gracious to me over these past few months. That means a lot. Zeta sisterhood has taken on a whole new meaning for me." My palms felt clammy, but there was no turning back now.

I gazed at the perfect, uncut pie drenched in juicy pecan glaze sitting in the center of the table. Our combined threesome made us seem like 1960s poster girls for the unity of the Northern and Southern branches of Zeta sisterhood. That was as far as the diversity went. Not likely to see a Zeta sister with a skin color darker than ours, especially south of the Mason-Dixon Line.

"Is everything all right, honey?" Belinda spoke first. "You and Bruce aren't getting' a divorce or somethin' are ya'?" She waved her hand in the air and flounced her curls from side to side.

I laughed aloud at her drama. A relief and a momentary diversion from my message to them. "No, silly, we're not getting divorced. But I think you should know something about me. I'm not sure how you're going to feel about this. Something you may not like." I was picking up steam, eager to clear the air.

Before either of them could flip another offhand comment, I dove in, "I am teaching illiterate colored people to read and write on Thursday nights at Samuel Boynton High School."

CHAPTER 29

The teakettle blurted a sharp whistle. The interruption provided time for me to take a deep breath and focus on the faces of Ruby and Belinda. My revelation was out in the open. Resolute with slowly curled smiles at the corners of their lips, they stared back. I likely looked like a fool to these Southern belles.

Summoned by the teakettle, Ruby dashed to the burner and poured hot water into our cups. I watched the color darken while the leaves steeped in little mesh holders. Ruby's tea pouring consumed her attention, and I sneezed. No doubt an allergic reaction as the cat continued to swish and wind its tail about my calves. Ruby was preparing her retort. If she asked me to leave her home, I was prepared.

Ruby returned the pot to the top of the stove and reduced the flame to a flicker. She took her seat and politely passed the sugar bowl to Belinda. They exchanged glances.

"We already knew you were teachin' the colored people," said Ruby. The azure pools of her eyes suddenly riveted into mine.

"Bobby saw your name on the Dallas County Board of Education hiring list for June. He was sorta upset 'bout it, but Bobby and I don't always agree about the place of colored folk in Selma. We sorta agree to disagree." Her chuckle reflected the affection the mention of his name stirred within her.

"Johnny and I don't see eye to eye on this topic either," said Belinda, as she plopped a third sugar cube into her cup. I noticed a large bruise on her upper arm. "His daddy is always meetin' with a bunch of men from the city council to discuss who should be elected on the new council board and what tricks they can pull next. Johnny has been spendin' more time with those men lately, and I sho' wish he wouldn't." As she spoke about Johnny, her eyes moved to examine her perfectly manicured nails.

"You best watch that Billy Chas Bader too," Belinda exploded in sudden recollection, pointing a firm finger at me.

"He's the head of that group and will go to no end to get what he wants. The Coalition of Southern Gentlemen, as they call themselves, expects submission from everyone who is not white and not a male." No flippant attitude this time.

Her comments about Billy Chas especially piqued my interest, but I kept a straight face. "I thought proper ladies didn't get involved with politics in Selma." My hands clutched the teacup in mid-air.

"Look, Claire, times are changin'. Ruby and I don't agree with the status quo in this town. The black student movement at Chapel Hill was a powerful force in the spring of '67."

"Yup. The year we graduated college and were married," said Ruby.

Belinda ignored the second part of Ruby's comment. "The walls that have separated blacks and whites for over a century are starting to crumble and it's the women who will make this a better place to live. Maybe not jis' like when we were growin' up in the 50s, but better than it is right now."

"With more respect—that is, for all people," said Ruby.

I had been wrong about my two Zeta sisters.

"More tea?" Ruby nodded toward my half-filled teacup as I sat taking in their unfiltered comments, not constrained or encumbered by the presence of their husbands and the socially dictated norms of Selma hierarchy. A sense of relief washed over me.

I nodded and returned the cup to its saucer. "Aren't you afraid? What about those women who came here from up North and got involved with the civil rights movement? They were slaughtered by mobs." *Were the lives of my friends in danger?*

"For starters," said Belinda, "the political activism has mostly taken place on white Southern university campuses, and it's been pretty civil. Don't you think so, Ruby?"

Ruby nodded as she returned the teapot to the trivet. She continued, "But let's not forget the barbaric acts committed against women, right here in Selma."

Ruby was referring to the ladies who came from the North to fight the battle.

"The tragedy of those poor ladies who were murdered doesn't make us proud," said Ruby, lowering her head. "Those women had high ideals and thought that they could change the white attitudes about colored folks in the Deep South. Bless their sweet souls. Fact is, though, many black Selmians provided them with protection, hiding them in their tiny shotgun houses."

Wide-eyed, I interrupted her, "You mean the freedom fighters actually stayed in those narrow houses on the dirt roads? The ones near the high school?"

"That is precisely what I mean. Some good women live near there. They continue to help the cause to offer a better life to both the black and the white. Especially for the rowdy teens with no daddies nearby. We're working with 'em." Belinda continued to amaze me as I considered the rock-throwing hoodlums.

The reserve and determination on the faces of my two Southern sisters was an exposé beyond my most imaginative moments. They were not what I judged them to be, and what I saw made me proud to be their friend.

"I don't get it. I just read that the mayor's wife cooks and sews clothes for her daughters. I see other women hanging out laundry on Monday morning, and you tell me that these women are living two lives?'

"Belinda and I, and a few others in the League, all about our age, are working behind the scenes. We're trying to change what's goin' on. Little by little." Ruby paused to clear her throat.

"The Coalition of Southern Gentlemen group that she mentioned is a dangerous bunch. Don't mess with 'em. They're powerful businessmen who put a lot of pressure on this community. They own the town and practically everyone in it. They believe in keepin' segregation as it has been for the past two hundred years. They'll even kill to make sure it doesn't change. We're fightin' against the pressures of the old guard in our hometown. But we know we're not going to make Selma a better place for us and our families if both races don't work together. We want our city to grow, be prosperous and thrive, but not under the influence of these men."

"And not at the cost of inhumanity and injustice to other human beings," Belinda's voice echoed Ruby's at a higher pitch. "We want our children to grow up in a more accepting and peaceful environment." She smiled warmly.

"Precisely," Ruby said.

I reached over and touched Belinda's unbruised arm, captured by her perfectly almond-shaped eyes. "I'd never have guessed all of this. It's taken a while for me to build up the courage to tell you that I couldn't continue to participate in Ladies League activities. And can't support the ideas of segregation and the treatment of colored people the women hold." My voice was rising, and my heart was racing. I dropped my head and said, "Just couldn't keep up the charade."

"Claire, we don't like it either, but bein' friendly and bein' Southern," Belinda mockingly batted her eyes, "will help us to bring more ladies on board."

She named three others from the League that had come around. "Slow, but sure. We will never win an open battle with most of the Selma old white guard—the men or the women. And Mrs. Bader is one of those stalwarts." She raised her thick brows, and her expression went dead serious.

"So, what you're telling me is that it's the younger women

versus the older women in the Ladies League." I struggled to draw some conclusion from this conversation.

"Not exactly." Ruby tilted her head to one side.

"Well, how do I know who is for the change and who isn't? As a Yankee, this puts me in an even worse position."

"It's more about education than age. Basically, those of us who have been to college have learned other ways. Maybe we just think about things differently." Not one to be humble, Belinda suddenly realized she sounded elitist and looked down at her lap.

She took a breath and continued, "Look. Many women in the League have grown up in Selma, got married right after high school, and moved into houses built by their daddies and granddaddies. They don't want any action that will change their comfort zone. Ruby and I could have done that, but we were lucky to go away to the University in Virginia. Southern, but in more neutral territory."

"You moved into a house built by your daddy, Belinda." A jibe, but it was true.

Ruby's tone reflected the pride of their mutual heritage. "We are lucky that we both have parents who want us to have lovely homes, and they had the means to make it happen."

Ruby spoke of the old manor that she and Bobby now owned. "This house was a renovation of an old plantation owned by the Confederate War General William R. Perkins. General Perkins wrote tactical manuals on the War Between the States and began construction of the home in 1852. The library has photos of the original 19th century residence with its grand old columns.

"Yeah, it was one mighty regal-looking Greek gothic mansion." Ruby stretched out her words as her eyes widened. She waved long slender fingers, mockingly, like splayed fans. "All that changed around the turn of the 20th century when they tore up the exterior. I heard that the architects and construction workers found all sorts of treasures when they opened those old walls."

"Did gold doubloons and pieces of eight spill from the rafters?" I exaggerated the question. Seemed like I had read an old *Nancy Drew* mystery with a similar plot. The sudden splash of a deeper friendship endeared me to Ruby and Belinda.

"No such luck." Ruby shook her head. "But they did find silverware and sconces, demitasse spoons, trays. A lot of stuff."

"And don't forget the jar of homemade preserves." Belinda raised an index finger in the air.

"No kiddin'," said Ruby.

The two nodded with feigned grimaces, and we all broke into laughter.

Ruby switched our conversation back to a more sobering focus. "About half of the women in the Ladies League are independent thinkers. The rest follow the old Selma status quo crowd."

"Locked in tradition." I made excuses for these women — but being polite always seemed to come naturally for me or due to my upbringing.

"Yeah, they are. But they are also just plain scared." Ruby slowly stirred another lump of sugar into her teacup. "Their husbands and daddies have businesses here and would buckle under if they were suspected of leaning toward the moderate middle of the integrationist versus segregationist sides of the fence."

"So, what is your group trying to accomplish? Are you working to integrate the schools, churches, and restaurants?" My friends were honorable, and I liked what they'd shared. Still, I wasn't clear on what actions they were taking to achieve their goals.

"We just want people to see each other as human beings. That's all." Belinda's eyes pleaded with me, hoping I'd get it.

The vague answer to my questions made me wonder if, where, and how I fit into their plan. Or if there even was a plan.

"When Bobby mentioned how he saw your name on the

new-hire list at the school district board meeting, I just acted casual-like. But when I told Belinda, we wanted to say somethin' to you because you're doing what we would like to see happen here in this town, Claire."

Ruby looked at me with admiration. "You're teaching and building bridges and that means a lot. Our Selma will be a better city for our children and grandchildren if people are educated and can vote." The expressions on their faces reflected conviction and sincerity.

Belinda interjected, "Many of us feel that the best way to make a difference in our beautiful ole Southern town is to start woman-to-woman. What you are doing with your courageous teaching cracks through the barriers of illiteracy, and that's a gentle, but significant way to begin."

I already knew that and wanted to say so but gave her space to continue.

Not one to dally, Ruby picked up where Belinda left off, "So, dear sister, we have been plannin' to corner you, but you called to meet for lunch and beat us to the punch." She laughed.

"Well, I'm still pretty confused," I said. "So, about this attitude change. How many women in the League support this?"

"Very few. We are not that organized. At least not yet, I'm afraid." Ruby released a sigh. "But we'll get there. As you've learned, most Selma women don't want to be political. Even a few of the educated ones who know better would rather ignore the issues than attempt to make a difference. Intervention by whites is considered reactionary and radical."

"Even *Communist*," Belinda whispered with wide-eyed exaggeration.

Although her use of the dreaded C-word in the same conversation about Civil Rights was no longer foreign to me, I almost knocked over my cup. Hearing Belinda say it aloud was ominous.

"Yes, ma'am! Any person who speaks out for civil rights is a drunk, sleepin' with coloreds, and suspected to be an outright Commie." Belinda spoke louder, as if I didn't hear her the first time around.

"The worst part is that this shortsightedness stands in the way of solving problems between blacks and whites. The solidarity of sisterhood can be powerful—women uniting to make a difference. All we want is a peaceful resolution of the conflict that we all live with daily. We grew up with it. Unfortunately, the few of us involved in this project are an isolated minority." Ruby folded her arms on top of the table in finality.

I sat quietly absorbing the truths that had been spoken. Beyond the open kitchen window, two red-breasted robins splashed and chirped in the birdbath and the lacy curtains barely moved, remaining almost glued to the sill in the humidity of the day. Ruby got up to close the window and switch on the air conditioning unit.

"What about all of the white women I read about in the library who volunteer at the Negro hospital and do other charity work for black folks? Can't they help with racial harmony here?" My renewed sense of energy felt good.

Belinda plopped her pointed chin square in the middle of her palm, while her eyes riveted on me. "Honey, charity is different from solidarity. Sure, lots of ladies are willin' to do volunteer work to help coloreds, but the social barriers haven't changed. Charity is a bandage on the wound. It doesn't cure it." She stopped talking and continued to stare into my eyes.

She jerked her head up and clapped both hands. "You know who you remind me of?"

I sat straighter and swallowed hard. "Who?"

"Well, I'm sure ya' know all about the white Northern college kids who came down to Alabama to fight for voting rights for Negroes. Many were beaten, even killed." Her voice softened.

"Yes," I said. "Of course."

"Well, dear Claire, that Northern co-ed may have been the first white person to teach in the all-Negro Freedom School a few years ago, but we have our very own Selma Freedom School teacher." Belinda grinned as if she was up to something.

"Wait until you see what we have planned for you, mah lovely and talented sister and *teacher*." Ruby emphasized the word "teacher," tilting her head and waving fingers in the air.

CHAPTER 30

"Glad you called, Billy. Good to see you again, Johnny." Bruce shook each man's hand.

Billy Chas added an extra buddy slap on Bruce's shoulder. I wondered if he tightened at Billy Chas's touch.

"And nice to see you, Claire." Billy Chas offered a courtesy bow before we all turned and headed toward the Base Grill.

"Hello, Johnny. I just had lunch with Belinda and Ruby a few weeks back." I feigned enthusiastic friendliness.

The two looked at me as if surprised. I immediately regretted mentioning the luncheon and elaborated, "We met at the library and decided it'd be fun for us girls to catch up about our Zeta times." I gushed and offered a subservient shrug. It worked. The men nodded in approval.

I knew Bruce wondered why Billy Chas had called and asked to meet both of us for lunch.

"Hope there isn't some problem with Mrs. Bader," Bruce had said to me when Billy Chas called to invite us to lunch at the Grill. "We don't want to have to move either." The stability of our living quarters was forever on his mind.

"Sure it isn't anything," I had said, not convinced that it was purely a social opportunity either. I hadn't told Bruce about my conversation with Ruby and Belinda. I wasn't sure of my role in the grand scheme they had in mind. Belinda's vehement warning also plagued me.

Trying to sound casual, I had said, "Why do you think they

want to meet us at the base?" I remembered how Billy Chas and Mr. Tilly seemed tight at the barbeque.

"Just being accommodating to my schedule, I suppose," Bruce had replied. "Plus, the Base Grill is known all over town for its great burgers."

Billy Chas motioned to a table off to one corner, instead of one up front near the window. As we sat down, Bruce got right to the point on his mind. "So how is your mother, Billy Chas? She is getting on in years, but she has so much energy and seems sharp as she can be."

Bruce was laying it on thick, but Mrs. Bader got around quite well for someone who was eighty-plus.

"She always looks so pretty too." I was along for the ride to support my man.

"Lord, no, no. Mama's fine. Why I betcha' she'll outlive us all." Billy Chas thundered a belly laugh as he slapped Bruce on the back.

Although he laughed in agreement, Bruce's glance in my direction spoke to his relief. Billy Chas didn't have news about his mama that would lead to our eviction.

We placed our orders, burgers all around. To my chagrin, Bruce seemed to be enjoying the company. "Say, where is the best fishing around here?"

I didn't know he was interested in fishing.

"The Alabama River. Catfish galore," said Johnny without batting an eyelid.

"You bet," said Billy Chas. "Ain't no better place for fried catfish and hush puppies than along the river shoreline. You'll have to come with us some Friday night."

Fortunately, our burgers and French fries appeared, so my cringe went unnoticed. *The least amount of contact with the Baders and the white males in this town, the better.*

Bruce took a generous hunk and mumbled, "Mmm. These

guys make the best burgers." It was a rare treat for us to eat at the Grill. It certainly beat the bologna sandwich I had packed for his lunch.

Billy Chas nodded in agreement as he swiped at his lips with the napkin and placed it on the table. He snatched a toothpick and gnawed at it momentarily before speaking in a lowered tone, "Bruce, things are pretty tense in Selma these days. Lots of change, movement, transition." His voice trailed off.

Bruce swallowed and stopped eating. With the burger suspended in the air, he looked from Billy Chas to Johnny. Both men had leaned back in the wooden captain chairs and had interlaced fingers across their bellies. Johnny's eyes narrowed.

My husband put his burger down and took a swallow of soda pop before he put an optimistic spin to the comment. "Yup. The Vietnam War and all have turned Selma into quite a metropolis." Bruce cleared his throat.

I resisted a chuckle. *Metropolis, indeed.*

Billy Chas continued as if he was the first to notice, "Our town was glad to be selected for the pilot training program. This base has brought prosperity to Selma."

"Well, the climate makes this part of the country ideal for air flight." Bruce folded his arms and nodded, waiting for Billy Chas to deposit his point in the conversation.

"Yeah, yeah. But we also have other problems. Our racial tension makes living here complicated, especially with people moving in from all over the country. Lots of propaganda ya' know." He waved a casual hand in the air.

"Thanks to the good Reverend King." Johnny practically vomited his comment.

Bruce's expression was stern. My teeth clenched and my jaw tightened.

"Bruce, you're from up North. Not that we're holdin' it aginst ya'." He grinned at his own Yankee versus Confederate comment.

"Oh no, of course not," Bruce responded with reciprocal humor.

"Seriously, buddy, some black preachers, and beggin' pardon, the white Yankee rabble-rousers, have blown the race issue just way out o'proportion. No offense, Bruce. The rabble-rousers are not the fine military citizens like you. They are people who don't understand us here in the South, and think their ways are better."

Johnny sat observing, glancing back and forth from Billy Chas to Bruce.

"I see what you're sayin', but how do Claire and I fit into this picture?" Bruce asked. "The military has assigned us to Selma, over a thousand miles from our family and friends."

Three cheers for Bruce for trying to make some sense of this discussion and put it into perspective for the others. I wanted to add that we'd only been married a few months but decided it wouldn't help my husband's point.

While Bruce paused, considering what — if anything else — should be said, Billy Chas put his toothpick on the plate and riveted his steel blue eyes toward me. "Claire needs to be careful about working with illiterate niggers."

Johnny jerked a single nod, folded his arms across his chest, and stared blankly at Bruce. Both suddenly acted as if I wasn't there.

I placed my fork on top of the cold French fries. Before I could retaliate with a response, Bruce touched my knee under the table and shifted in his seat. "Are you sayin' my wife can't teach where she damn well pleases?" His ears had reddened, and I thought he'd punch Billy Chas. Colored women wiping nearby tables didn't seem to notice. I hoped the lunch crowd didn't either.

"Now, take it easy, buddy." Billy Chas leaned in toward the center of the table. "Look, all I'm saying is that y'all have to be careful. White folk and Negroes don't mix social company in Selma. It's just the way it is, pal."

Johnny scooted his body forward and smiled smugly in my direction. "You're a smart lady, Claire, and I bet you're a mighty talented teacher too. I have at least one vacant teaching position that needs to be filled. The wife of a base lieutenant is expecting, and she won't be coming back in the fall. With military moves and shifting, I'll likely have more openings in the next few weeks. You could have your pick of grades to teach."

Problem solved. Johnny looked pleased. Apparently, he held no grudge over my rejection of his earlier offer to hire me to teach at his all-white school. The reiterated offer still didn't make me feel any better. Although our foursome composed a circle, I felt surrounded and weaponless. The gnawing turmoil I felt wouldn't go away, even if I tried to explain.

Before I could decline, Bruce spoke up, "Look fellas, Claire and I appreciate your friendship and efforts to assure our safety and well-being in Selma, truly. I know there are—well, extenuating circumstances here—for all of us." He had regained composure and delivered his response with careful attention to the words he spoke.

"We'll talk about it. Won't we, honey?"

I nodded, thinking about how quitting wasn't an option for me, if that's what my husband was intimating. We had to figure out how to surmount this hurdle.

"The adult literacy position is short term and ends in a few weeks," Bruce said, noting my nod. He wasn't aware that another class would start in the fall. I crossed and recrossed my legs for the umpteenth time.

Bruce glanced at his military watch. "Gotta get back to work, almost thirteen hundred hours." He stood and quickly unclipped his cap from his belt hook. When I moved my chair back and started to stand, the others arose as well.

Bruce tugged his wallet out of his hip pocket, but Billy Chas held his hand up. "I got this one. Maybe you can pick it up next time, my friend." He stepped back and reached around to slap Bruce's back as he made eye contact with Johnny. His height gave him an advantage and he took extra liberty to flash a secret wink toward his buddy. As Billy Chas turned toward me, I smiled politely, hoping there would be no "next time" gathering.

Reaching to replace his wallet, Bruce missed the pocket opening and it fell to the floor. The other two men continued to walk toward the cashier. While I waited, I noticed that the women cleaning cafeteria tables only a few feet away were glaring at the two men headed toward the cash register. A third woman with a creamy mocha-colored complexion moved purposefully toward the kitchen. I was sure they had overheard a large part of the conversation and were eager to make a hasty exit.

Holding hands, Bruce and I walked back to the Base Civil Engineering office building. "Wow! That was quite a conversation," I spoke in a lowered tone, even though I could no longer see our two luncheon companions.

"I wouldn't exactly use the word *conversation* more like *ultimatum*," Bruce grunted.

He stopped and looked at me. "I swear, Claire, I had no idea that Billy Chas was going to attack you like he did." Punctuated by anxiety or hunger from a half-eaten lunch, his stomach growled.

"I know that, honey, and I appreciate how you stood up to him. He sure is persistent." I took hold of Bruce's other hand and looked directly into his eyes. "But I'm not quitting my job."

Bruce started to respond but two officers walked by. He dropped my hands and saluted. Looking deeply into my eyes, he whispered, "I know how important this work is to you." He paused, then kissed my forward. "Let's talk later."

CHAPTER 31

Crossing the grassy knoll near the flagpole, I saw Billy Chas and Johnny, half-hidden in the shadows of a mulberry tree. Although Billy Chas had his back to me, I could tell his arms were folded across his broad chest. He did most of the talking while Johnny stared at him and dragged intermittently on a cigarette. I backtracked and slipped across the street to the side of the post office, out of sight from the men but within close earshot.

"...but do ya' think he gets the point?" Johnny's voice sounded intense.

"Oh, he's a smart enough guy, all right. Don't kid yourself," Billy Chas spat out the words in frustration. "It's that wife of his who needs to get a clue. She is hell-bent on teachin' niggers. Guess she thinks she's on a crusade or somethin'. You know what, Johnny, that broad reminds me of those Northern women who came down here a few years back."

I covered my mouth to make sure no sound would escape.

"Yeah and look what happened to them. Got what they deserved." Johnny chugged out a deep cough. The menacing tone in his voice made my knees quiver.

"So, what do think we should do now? I gotta get that damn Yankee lady to quit squawkin.'" Click. Johnny must have lit up another cigarette.

"Relax, relax. Hey, buddy, that's the second cigarette you've smoked in ten minutes," Billy Chas said. "You gotta cut back. You're gonna kill yourself."

"Guess I just have too much on my mind of late, with Belinda's Good Samaritan outlook on life in Selma and all."

"Hey, you and Belinda practically grew up together. Your daddies were in the same lodge as mine. Besides, she is mighty pretty." I could picture Billy Chas poking Johnny in the ribs at his comment.

Johnny didn't seem to mind his friend's comments about his wife's looks.

"The important thing is that we're all on the same side of the fence when it comes to a lot of things around here," Johnny emphasized. "Belinda won't cause any trouble."

Billy Chas seemed pleased. "Well, anyway don't worry about the Zuretskis. We have friends. I'll give Carl Tilly a call this afternoon. Let's see if he can put a little pressure on our soldier boy."

"Good idea." I heard a slap on a shoulder, followed by footsteps on the sidewalk moving away from me and toward the base's public parking lot.

Shocked at what I heard, I ducked into the post office and moved to a counter near a window. I pretended to fill out mailing forms while peering through the pane at the two men shaking hands. Billy Chas hopped into his Corvette. Johnny climbed into his white pickup. Seeing the rifle perched in the pickup's rear window jolted my nerves. I remembered Johnny's comment about the white Northern lady integrationists. *Could he and Billy Chas have been involved with the violence and bloodshed surrounding the events in Selma?*

When their vehicles were out of sight, I skipped the Commissary stop and ran to the Ford. I was desperate to get back to our apartment and call Bruce. He had to be warned about Billy Chas's threats, including collusion with Mr. Tilly.

～

The highway back to town was almost empty, allowing me time to ponder our situation. Bruce thought highly of his boss. It would be hard for him to hear that Mr. Tilly could be part of any plot to coerce us into maintaining the status quo in this town.

The phone was ringing as I unlocked the apartment door. Purse still dangling from my wrist, I dashed to pick it up, thinking it could be Bruce. The caller was Mr. Parkington from the school district.

I sat in the chair and listened as he told me that, as expected, the Selma Public Schools had just gotten funding to continue the Disadvantaged Adult class into the fall semester. I was tempted to revise his course title but bit my tongue.

"Might ya' be interested in teachin' agin, ma'am?"

I wanted to shout a big "yes" into the phone but took a breath before responding. "Sounds interesting. I'll have to talk with my husband first. May I call you back tomorrow?"

"Yes, that would be fine. I do hope you'll consider it, Mrs. Zuretski."

I knew he was mostly concerned about getting cash from the feds, only a portion of which they spent on the class. It also made the school district look good, affirming that Selma was all for integration and helping Negroes learn so they could improve their lot.

With a mixed sensation of joy and trepidation, I dialed Bruce's phone number at the Base Civil Engineering Office. Now I had two things to tell him.

Bruce picked his phone up on the second ring. "Hi, honey. I have some good news," I said.

"Oh, yeah? Did the Air Force call and say we could go back to Detroit?"

"Ha, ha. Very funny. But, unfortunately, no."

"Okay, shoot. What's up?" He cleared his throat and suddenly sounded busy.

"Mr. Parkington from the school district personnel office called and asked me to teach the adult literacy class in the fall. They just got definite word from the feds that the funding has been extended. Isn't that great?" Dead silence on the other end. "Bruce? Are you there?" I heard a rustling of papers and Mr. Tilly's voice in the background.

"Bruce are you there? Hello?"

"Nice, nice. That sounds wonderful." His exaggerated tone confirmed that there were other ears close by. "I have to run. We'll talk more tonight. Okay, baby?"

I was getting used to Bruce's limited time for communication. He had to go to bed early. He got up early. He had restricted phone calls at the base.

"Oh, sure. I don't have to give him an answer today," I spoke quickly. "Remember I have class tonight."

"Yup. Okay, see you later."

"Oh, one more thing, Bruce..." The receiver on his end clicked.

I didn't get a chance to tell him about what I had overhead, nor to warn him about Mr. Tilly.

CHAPTER 32

When I arrived that night for the third adult literacy class, Reverend Mease sat hunched over a penciled, yellow notepad. He tapped his chin rhythmically as he studied each word he wrote. The same brown jacket he wore each time was now loosely draped across his legs, still at least two shades darker than the trousers that dangled to the floor. The tan bow tie united both tips of his shirt's starched white collar, edges browned with sweat.

As I sang out my greeting, he spun his balding head in my direction. "Good evenin', Missus Claire." He returned to his notepad.

I plunked my bags on the teacher's desk, pulled out alphabet cards and placed them on each student's empty desktop. Even though the Reverend was the most literate, and only needed help with his grammar and spelling, I still slipped a set in a corner of his desk. Contrary to Mr. Parkington's assumption, the adults in this class were at varying developmental stages of literacy.

Reverend Mease peered at me again over thin, silver-rimmed spectacles and returned to his notepad. The stack of alphabet cards I had passed out were still in their cellophane wrappers.

"Don't ever let anyone think less of you because you're a young person," he said, still attending to the notepad.

"I beg your pardon, Reverend?" I grimaced, hoping the alphabet cards were not offensive to him. "Oh, the cards are just for reference. Always good to have handy," I assured him.

"Fine, fine. No matter. I was just thinkin' out loud, Missus Claire."

In my wildest dreams, I never thought I'd be teaching adults, but didn't think my age should matter. *Everybody is twenty-two sometime.*

"I plan to speak to some young people Friday night, ma'am. I will begin with a quote from I Timothy 1:5-7." The Reverend opened the worn leather Bible and read the passage aloud, without mispronouncing a syllable.

> *Now the end of the commandment is charity out of pure*
> *heart, and of a good conscience, and of faith unfeigned:*
> *From which some having served have turned aside*
> *unto vain jangling; Desiring to be teachers of the law;*
> *understanding neither what they say, nor whereof*
> *they affirm.*

He paused, adding his own paraphrasing, then finished, "But they don't know what they is talkin' about. And they want to be known as teachers." I could see veins bulging at his temple as the Reverend shook his head. "How would these words sound as an opening?" He posed his question, glancing up briefly before making a note in the margin of his yellow notepad.

Stunned at his sudden candor, I wondered if he was talking about me. "I'm not clear about this passage for the young people, Reverend." *Did he think my teaching wasn't sincere, from the heart?*

"This Scripture passage is to remind our youth they have minds, and they can think. And that they sho' shouldn't jump on any bandwagon, even if teachers and grown-ups tells them to do those things that we don't do here. They need to seek the goodness of the Lawd and listen to those who strive to be their mentors."

He smiled directly into my eyes for the first time. "I see that in you, Missus Claire." He nodded slowly. "Would you help me write this clear, ma'am?"

I tilted my head and allowed my gaze to soften before speaking. "How kind of you, Reverend. I must read more of Timothy's writings."

As I sat next to the Reverend and began to help with rephrasing his introduction, I pondered his message, repeating it again in my head. *Was my Christian faith foundational to my work with these people?*

The entrance of Mamiza and Delberta interrupted my thoughts. Delberta wore the same sweater she had wrapped around her when I first saw her in the Old Live Oak Cemetery. Greeting the two, Delberta diverted my gaze, but not before I noticed her puffy red eyes behind the heavy glasses. Mamiza stood beside her niece flailing an orangey-red, oriental, dime-store fan—tails of black dragons sprawled across the folds only partially visible. As a maid for a stalwart old Southern family, Mamiza's colorful side was out of character, but I liked seeing her this way.

Mamiza shifted her weight from foot to foot as she watched the pain on Delberta's face. "Honey, why don't you tell Missus Claire what happened to you while you was cleanin' the library a few weeks back."

"Yes'm," Delberta responded obediently to her aunt, while looking down at her sandals.

Sensing her discomfort, I said, "It's okay, Delberta. You can tell me another time."

"You tell, Auntie." Her voice was barely audible.

"A'right. Well, when Delberta was cleanin' the library floor, two men sittin' under the NO TALKING sign were laughin' and speakin' in loud voices. The librarian hushed 'em but they paid her no attention. Delberta thought they was mighty disrespectful and had been drinkin' too much hooch, but she kept moppin' and doin' her job. Suddenly, one of them mens, the oldest one, jumped up and grabbed Delberta's wrist. He said, 'Did you say somthin' to me, *nigra*?'"

Eyes ablaze as she recounted the emotion of the moment, Delberta blurted, "I wanted to scream, but no sound would come from mah mouth."

Mamiza continued, "Delberta shook her head *no* and cowered under his ole whiskey breath. Even worse, the second guy, younger, was gruntin' and eyein' every part of her body."

Delberta's head was buried in shame as Mamiza outlined the details.

"Did you report this man to the library director?" I looked directly at Delberta. "He sounds dangerous." I wondered what had triggered her emotional state now—weeks later.

"Yes'm. I told the librarian." Delberta defended herself this time.

"What did the librarian do?"

"She said those mens was just that way 'cuz they had been out to the still, and I should pay 'em no mind. Said she'd make a report."

"Girl, finish the story. She did nothin'." Mamiza's eyes widened as she stretched her neck forward. "At least not 'til that crazy man did the same thing to a white lady yesterday. The police took him to jail right away."

"I am so sorry, Delberta. That shouldn't have happened to you." It hurt to realize how this poor girl-mama was used by others in so many ways. "At least the scoundrel got what he deserved."

"The ladies at the library are all nice to me, ma'am. Wasn't their fault," she said.

I had a feeling Delberta's ingratiating words were inflicted from generations of learned acceptance of abuse. She wouldn't or couldn't allow her pain to surface. The hurt she bared was patched up, but not fixed. Much like the hole in the classroom window, concealed with cardboard. The cardboard kept out mosquitoes, but not the Southern summer heat and humidity. *A high school diploma would truly give her freedom and a chance for a better life.*

Shouts from Lily Mae Brown and Opie Doone exploded through the doorway. They were both talking at once. High-pitched laughter punctuated every other sentence.

"Good evening, ladies. Please come in." My smile was genuine as I offered an open palm toward their desks. The voices stopped and blank stares came back at me.

Opie had a paper sack under her arm. I wondered if she'd lost the bag, I had given her. The others all proudly toted the book bags, including the Reverend.

Lily Mae coughed and lowered her head. "Evenin' ma'am." She walked between the rows of desks and slid into her seat. Opie stood glued to the floor, glaring in my direction. It felt like a standoff awaiting a quick draw to determine the winner. Distracted by the Reverend's voice and his half-raised arm, I moved away from Opie.

With his eyes on the yellow legal pad, he said, "Missus Claire, I'd appreciate it if you'd come over and look at my sermon for this comin' Sunday. It is about not taking revenge and comes from Leviticus: 19:18.

Thou shalt not avenge, nor bear any grudge against the children of thy people, but thou shalt love thy neighbor as thyself. I am the Lord.

Grateful for a chance to allow Opie space, I pulled up a chair and leaned into the paper pad. The Reverend clearly had a much better command of the Good Book than his teacher. He summed up the passage and said, "I want my people to see that vengeance will be in the hands of the Lawd. It is not up to us." He repeated the passage from Leviticus one more time, slowly turning in Opie's direction, then looked directly into my eyes as he purposefully folded thin, wrinkled fingers. The Reverend was an ally and I appreciated it.

Opie had moved to a seat toward the middle of the room, slightly removed from the others and not her usual choice. With a yellow pencil woven through the braids piled atop her head, she flipped randomly, disinterested, through the pages of the workbook.

As I moved toward her, she scooted to the edge of her seat. With the first five pages completed in perfect cursive practice, she proudly awaited my attention. I marked *100%* on each finished page. "Nice work, Opie." Kneeling closer to her, I spoke in softened tones in order not to embarrass the others. "This book might be too easy for you."

"Hmm." She pulled the pencil from the top of her head and proceeded to complete the next assignment without further comment.

During our break, everyone moved chairs into a semicircle while I cut the pecan pie I had brought. Opie slipped to the outer edge of the seating, folded her arms, and declined a slice.

"I'm on a diet." She scanned her fingernails as she spoke.

Determined to end the class on a positive note, I shifted the topic. "I do have some news for *y'all*." Blank stares. "Sure hope *y'all* think it's good news." Still no smiles except for a small grin on Delberta's face. The group remained suspended in expectation.

"The Board of Education wants to continue this class into fall semester. Would you all come back?"

Lily Mae was the first to respond while the others stared straight ahead. "Only if you could be our teacher."

"I would love to be your teacher. We're not completely sure we'll still be stationed in Selma, but if we are, I'll be here." My earlobe-to-earlobe grin was genuine, but Bruce and I needed to talk more.

Opie stood up and parked fists on either side of her hip bones. "That be an outright lie, Missus Claire." Every head spun to look at Opie.

"Opie, what are you talking about?" Mouth agape, I folded my hands on my lap to keep them from trembling.

"You knows what I mean. You is pretendin' to be our friend and all the while plannin' to teach white kids." Her eyes bore through me.

"What? Where did you get that idea? I'm not going to do any such thing."

"That's what yo' husband and his white gentlemen friends are plannin.' I do dishes at the Base Grill where you and your friends was havin' lunch. Them mens is trouble. And you was a-smilin' at 'em and listenin' the whole time. 'Specially the one with the fancy shoes."

"I bet that one was Billy Chas," Mamiza interjected with a smile as she spoke his name. "That boy does love his shoes." She had a soft spot for Billy Chas. She had likely raised him.

Every blood vessel on my face seemed to explode against my skin. I wanted to cry, but the anger that churned in my belly wouldn't allow it. I dug my nails into my folded palms.

"Whoa! Just a minute." I took a breath and swallowed hard as I thought about the lunch fiasco with Billy Chas and Johnny Bailey. "I didn't see you at the Base Grill, Opie."

Opie grunted a harrumph sound. "Did ya' 'spect I'd be comin' over and askin' if I could join y'all for lunch? That'd be a good joke." Nodding her head, she spanned the room for support. Every smirk reflected tacit agreement.

I sank into my seat, but not for long. Opie's eruption was unexpected and certainly out of character. Even though her anger was understandable, the trust of my other students was also a priority.

"It's true, I did have lunch at the Base Grill with my husband and two other men. However, let me be clear, I'm not planning on doing what *they* think I should do." I raised my chin to the air at such an accusation. "Please believe me. If we're still here in September, I would like to be your teacher again. That is if y'all would come back."

All that could be heard were the muffled sounds of chirping crickets through the cardboard over the broken window. Regrets for attending the luncheon meeting couldn't take away the fact that it had happened.

Opie stood with hands still posted her hips. "And what if your husband won't *let* you come back? Huh? What about that?" Her words spewed like pellets in an arcade.

"I can understand why you're upset, but Bruce wouldn't stop me from teaching this class."

"We'll jis' have to see about that, don't we?"

She jerked the back of her skirt and stomped out, leaving gaping mouths in her wake—until about ten seconds had elapsed. Then I scrambled after Opie.

"Leave her be." Mamiza's elevated tone halted further steps.

"I'd like her to come back." Looking at Mamiza, flushed and drained, I struggled to stay calm.

"She be all right. Dat girl just needs some time." Mamiza looked at her workbook, raised her brows, and gave full attention to the page in front of her.

CHAPTER 33

Tightly woven crowns of coarse hair, soft as lamb's wool were bowed, hovering over workbook pages. Not another word was spoken. The only sounds were the incessant chirping in the depths of the dark night that loomed outside. Usually chirping crickets were friendly echoes of nature. Tonight, the clucking admonitions were an intolerable nuisance amidst the hush of the classroom.

Apparently, no one needed my help. Although the diligence gave the appearance of intensity, I knew names were being repetitively written, except for the Reverend. His head poured over the worn leather-covered Bible. With a sense of composed purpose, I attacked the paper dishes and tossed them into the metal trash basket.

The ticking of my watch, a gift from Bruce, was even audible. I glided the band off my wrist and feigned an effort of winding and synchronizing my timepiece with the wall clock. Another glance around the room.

Finally, Reverend Mease spoke, "Missus Claire, I'd be pleased for ya' to look at another sermon I've been plannin'. It's 'bout havin' respect for women. The Lawd wants us to respect our women 'cuz they give life and care for his precious chillens. Lawd have mercy, I sure don't want grammar mistakes." He took his specs from the bridge of his nose and wiped them with a neatly ironed handkerchief he yanked from a hip pocket. As he rubbed his fingers between the thin glass lenses, he peered at me under slightly arched, thick brows. A smile reached across his lips for a second. I breathed a sigh of relief and smiled.

Dragging a chair into the space of this holy man, I awaited his next gesture. We both sat, staring at the curly-edged papers before us.

"Reverend, may I?" My nod went toward the pencil-filled pad.

He gathered the pages with his slender fingers and handed them to me.

As I read his opening message, a verse from Romans 6:16, my eyes widened. I read it a second time.

Know ye not, that to whom ye yield yourselves servants to obey, his servants ye are to whom ye obey, whether of sin unto death, or of obedience unto righteousness.

He wrote about being open to the will of God and obedience for the sake of righteousness. Although his viewpoint didn't make sense to me, it was insightful.

He sat on the edge of his seat, staring at me.

"This is very good, Reverend," I said, wondering where the message was going. Despite a few grammatical errors, his thoughts had great depth.

He squelched a hint of pride that filtered through his reserve. "It's the Lawd's word, Missus Claire. I am his servant and only a messenger." His final sentence devoutly stated.

As I read further, he continued to support a viewpoint of turning the other cheek and not seeking revenge. His final passage from Romans 12:19 summed it up more clearly.

Dearly beloved, avenge not yourselves, but rather give place unto wrath: for it is written, Vengeance is mine; I will repay, saith the Lord.

The pastor was clearly telling his congregation not to retaliate. Not to fight back. As I considered his watery eyes, he spoke as if no one was in the room.

"After the march, I would drive out to the edge of town to visit the road camp where poleese kept the overflow of demonstrators taken into custody. I went to pray with them, ask the Lawd to watch over them and make sure they be a'right."

I wondered if his sermon was referring to the physical abuse of his people. Puzzled, I spoke quietly, "Did the sheriff's men beat them in the jail, Reverend?"

"Naw, no ma'am. It wasn't nuthin' like that," he said, to make sure I understood.

Lily Mae must have been listening and interjected, "If Opie was here, she'd tell ya' about Camp Selma, a'right." Her eyes were still riveted on her workbook page, as if considering whether she wanted to say more.

After a few more seconds, she looked up and spoke, "Fact is de whole place was set up like a big dormitory. Like they have at the orphanage. 'Cept it be built for the men who was in jail and for those who worked on road constructions. There was no privacy in that place. No place for a lady to use a restroom. It was all out in de open. Them jailers was mighty low when it come to respectin' ladies. I can tell ya' that." She tightened her lips, then lowered her head.

"You'd think they'd at least put up a couple of curtains," I said.

"Then those jailers couldn't watch." She spat her words and curled an upper lip in disgust as she continued to focus on her workbook.

The Reverend lowered his gaze. No words, no vengeance. The heat that filled my body was a combination of embarrassment and anger. The crickets babbled their tweaks and filled the vacuum of our space once again. I prayed for patience as I recalled Ruby's explanation about how colored preachers did not take a stand on the racial divide. Their work was about following the Good Book and not fighting any secular battles in between. Reverend Mease was clearly not a champion of the Fems for Freedom group.

At the end of class, I busied myself with piling books, jotting a few notes about my students, and making a to-do list for the next class. Mamiza had written her name in cursive on the thinly lined white paper, and I saw that her writing had improved with each attempt. Delberta's reading level was close to that of the Reverend, and she could copy letters neatly and legibly. She still couldn't create a complete sentence on paper. She had written in single-word responses and her spelling was poor, but she beamed with pride over the quality of her penmanship. Lily Mae had feigned study in the workbook pages and had only written her name a couple of times. She had trouble forming the letters, too. She kept shaking all five fingers into the air in quick bouts of recuperation from pressing hard on the lead pencil. And then there was Opie, who had shown promise, but who wasn't in class enough for me to make special lesson plans to help her. Another struggle before me was the need to confront my husband about her accusations.

Alvin's entry reminded me that it was late, and I was sure he wanted to go home for the day. I grabbed my bags and thanked him for cleaning the classroom. As I left the building and dashed toward Bruce and the parked car, rain pelted against my face, and a bolt of lightning shot across the black sky.

"How'd it go, Missus Claire?" Bruce reached to open the door and I flounced into the passenger seat. I shook my head and ruffled my curls, then dabbed at my wet face.

"Peachy keen." I pasted on my exaggerated grin and glared into his eyes.

"Oh, oh! Something smells fishy, and it's not the rainwater."

Before I could say another word, Bruce had pulled the Ford over toward the curb near Mamiza and Delberta, who were walking in the rain. They scooted along the slippery pavement, trying to avoid mud and cracks, while holding the colorful book bags over their heads.

Bruce rolled his window down and stuck his head out. "Mamiza, the rain's getting heavier and there's lightning in the sky. Wish you'd let us give you ladies a ride." Another flash through the sky sent a limb from a nearby tree plummeting to the ground in front of them.

Wide-eyed, the two women dashed into the glistening street and over to the car. I blinked and took a breath as I reached back to unlock the door. Nagging thoughts about Opie's comments would need to go on hold for now. Both women lunged into the back seat.

When I introduced Delberta to Bruce, she nodded, eyes downcast. "Howdy-do, sir."

"Where do you ladies live?" He looked back over his right shoulder at my students who sat stiff as mannikins in the rear seat.

"Mr. Bruce, we jis' live up the way a bit. There be a 7-Eleven store on the corner up yonder. You can just drop us off there."

"Mamiza, it's pouring, and the sky is practically on fire with lightning bolts. I don't mind driving to your house. It's no trouble."

We crawled along the slippery road for several miles in silence with Mamiza directing Bruce to the drop-off. "Okay, Mr. Bruce, right over yonder. Drop us off right there. We only lives 'bout a block up that street."

"Are you sure?"

"Oh, yes sir, yes sir. We'll be home in a flash. God bless y'all."

Before Bruce had barely put the car in park, Mamiza tugged at the door handle. "Glad we saw you, Mamiza. We can pick you up here at this corner every Thursday night. It's on our way," he offered.

Mamiza peeked a glance in his direction, bringing her statue-like stance to life. "Why thank ya', sir. That be mighty fine."

The two women scurried onto the dark street and disappeared up the dirt road. And not a minute too soon. A bolt of lightning soared across the dark sky.

Bruce reached over and gave my hand a squeeze.

I gave a light squeeze back, affirming his kind gesture more than our success with the ladies. Suddenly remembering Opie's comments, I pulled my hand back to my lap. "Bruce, we need to talk." I still hadn't told him about Mr. Tilly. Bruce had postponed our discussion of my teaching another adult education class as well.

"Claire, if this is about the lunch today, I truly didn't know Billy Chas was going to deal the garbage he pitched at us."

We were still sitting in the 7-Eleven parking lot, up the street from the shotgun houses. Mamiza and Delberta had disappeared into the darkness. Bruce turned off the engine.

"I believe that part, and I understand your concern about our safety and wanting to fit in here in Selma. Truly." I paused, considering my next words carefully. "I think we should have told those two guys the truth. Fessed up. One of my students, Opie Doone, saw and heard everything. She thinks you're going to make me teach in the white schools. She confronted me in class tonight and then stomped out." I rubbed away the tears that had tumbled onto my cheeks.

"First off, I don't get what's the big deal about Johnny Bailey offering you a job. You are making more out of this than necessary. The guy wants you to teach at his school, for Pete's sake." He emphasized the *offering you a job* part.

If we had been closer to Rohns Manor, I might have opened the car door and walked home. My husband hadn't heard a word I said.

"Why are you making this all about the job and working in the white schools?" I turned my head and gazed through the passenger window at the blinking neon signs. "Lately nothing about how I feel or what I think matters to you."

Bruce turned toward me and spoke very slowly, "How can you say that, Claire? I care very much about the issues that matter to you. To us."

He proceeded to explain Billy Chas's call and invitation for lunch. "I thought the guy was going to have another party, or something social. You'd like that. The Selma society and parties mean a lot to you. At least they used to." I detected a hint of disillusionment and a tinge of sadness.

Bruce shook his head as if he was confused. "When Billy Chas called about lunch, he didn't say Johnny Bailey would be joining us. But I knew they were friends and didn't really think much of it when Johnny showed up." Bruce's eyes were turned toward me.

I clasped the sides of my face, closed my eyes, and spoke deliberately, "I cannot continue to live two lives in this town. It surprises me that you don't seem to have a clue about how important my work is to me." I was not the same person who'd come here five months earlier.

"I didn't think it was *that* important to you," Bruce said as he switched on the ignition and backed sharply out of the parking space.

"Oh, and by the way, Billy Chas and Johnny are in cahoots with your boss," I shouted, angered by his dismissive tone and behavior.

"What are you talking about? How can you say that about Mr. Tilly, Claire? He is the nicest guy ever. That's unfair and just plain ridiculous." He gunned the engine.

"Oh, yeah? Well, I overheard Billy Chas and Johnny near the Base Exchange this afternoon talking about alerting Mr. Tilly about you. Billy Chas said he'd convince Mr. Tilly to put some pressure on you."

"Why didn't you tell me?" he asked.

I stared straight ahead. The red glare of the stoplight glistened on the hood of the Ford.

"I tried to tell you on the phone, but you cut me short. Billy Chas said I was hell-bent on teachin' niggers. His words, not mine. As if I were on a *crusade* or something. They both agreed that I reminded them of those Northern women who came down here a few years back. They are scheming to pressure your boss to make you force me to conform."

Bruce tilted his head. "Well, that's pretty far-fetched. But Mr. Tilly was in his office with the door shut for quite a while this afternoon. Not typical. He also asked if you might be teaching this coming fall. I told him we were hoping for an invitation to OTS in a few months. Sorry. Trying to figure this out." Bruce ran his fingers through his hair.

"There is nothing to figure out, Bruce, and you don't have to believe me about Mr. Tilly. But I heard what I heard."

I folded my arms across my chest and turned my head toward the passenger window. "Also, as I started to tell you on the phone, Mr. Parkington from the school district office called. He wants me to continue teaching the adult literacy class in the fall."

"What did you tell him?"

"I told him I'd have to discuss it with you. Anyway, I am *not* teaching at the white school. Period."

"That's just great, Claire. Can't you at least *think* about Johnny's offer to teach at his school? That would cinch your response to Mr. Parkington." Bruce grinned. He'd solved the problem as he saw it.

"Sure. A good answer as far as *you're* concerned. What about what I want?"

Ignoring my comments, Bruce continued, "You love kids. Plus, we'll be stationed in Selma for nine months. You may just be there one semester and we'll be gone. We can try to have another baby, and we'll have some extra cash to boot." Bruce's words resonated.

"Did it occur to you that I might prefer teaching these grown-ups who have never had a chance to learn basic reading and writing?" Although this was the second time Bruce had mentioned having another baby since my miscarriage, doing so now felt like a bribe.

"Your thoughts are noble, Claire, but your idealism is hurting us." His tone was lower.

"Are you saying we should allow threats to run our lives?" I hammered back.

"I'm just saying we need to get along in this town, especially with people who look like us. For God's sake, I don't know what's gotten into you. When did you decide to save the world, anyway?"

I had seen that glare of rage only one other time—the day he got the draft notice. I paused before responding, careful to keep my own voice calm. "Since I realized somebody has to do something. Doing nothing and ignoring what needs to be done is wrong."

We drove the last few miles without further verbal sparring. I tried to let the anger dissipate, but my head pounded as loud as the thunder. I couldn't quell my desire to help the "disadvantaged adults."

Bruce patted my knee as we rounded the corner and drove into our muddy rear parking spot behind Rohns. "Just think about it, honey."

"Please do not patronize me," I said, clearly enunciating each word.

~

We readied for bed without talking. When Bruce reached for me, I responded with a slapdash kiss, followed by a curt "good night," and rolled far over on my side of the bed.

The entire day replayed over and over in my head as I gazed at the plaster cherubs on the ceiling, thirteen feet above our heads. With the storm settled, lazy shadows from the full moon showcased the twirls of plaster. I had once commented to Bruce about how they looked like angels hovering and guarding us as we loved and slept. Tonight, they floated in a rhythm of evasion.

Bruce's deep breathing oozed into a muffled snore. When Bruce brought up having another baby again, the flickers I felt the first time he mentioned it didn't happen. And it hurt that he didn't understand my commitment to my work.

I tossed and turned, turned, and tossed, and finally gave up my efforts. I scrambled out of the bed, grabbed the quilt made by Mariah Jesse Willis, and curled up in a stuffed chair. Several books lay on the coffee table, but I had no desire to pick any one of them up.

It seemed like only moments later that I felt Bruce's lips on mine. Four gongs from the grandfather clock in the Rohns foyer chimed somewhere in the background.

"Come on, sweetheart, let's get you into bed."

I allowed myself to melt into Bruce's embrace as we shuffled toward the bed. In the dimly lit room, I noticed a stack of mail on the dresser. The handwriting on the top envelope was familiar. I planned to lay my head on the pillow for just a few more minutes. I dozed to a whisper in my ear.

"I'll be back soon." He left to deliver papers.

CHAPTER 34

Perching beneath the pink blossoms of the magnificent magnolia trees buoyed my spirits. This spot was ideal to meet with Winnie Holmes. It was distant from the fringes of the well-traveled path that wound through the center of the Old Live Oak Cemetery.

Bruce and I didn't talk any more about our lunch with Billy Chas and Johnny or about teaching at an all-white school. No more insistence on accepting Johnny's offer—at least for now. And nothing about teaching the adults in the fall session. We both held a silent pact to agree to disagree on certain points.

Eager to talk with Winnie, my stance hadn't changed. So many questions sat unanswered, including her tale behind the story in the newspapers and her photograph with Clayton Grilton. I wondered if Winnie knew about the camps offered through the Methodist Church. Maybe we could get Jackson into one of the sessions.

Waiting for Winnie to arrive, the gentle warmth of the early Saturday morning sun was welcomed. Its vibrant rays spread across my cheeks. I closed my eyes and slumped back on the wooden bench, jolting at the sudden ping of a twig that snapped nearby. Turning my head, I saw single-striped tails of two chipmunks, furled like fluffy banners, chasing each other around a nearby tombstone. The jagged grave marker looked like an ancient ruin. I chuckled. The person's remains must be resting in special peace, graced that their headstone was a fine toy for some of Mother Nature's tiniest creatures. Cupping my hands above my eyes and squinting, I read the engraving, barely visible through the overgrown ivy. The Old English letters spelled out the name: General William Parsin Rohns, February 3, 1847 – May 10, 1920.

Rohns. With wide eyes, and feeling like an intruder, I spun my head in all directions. No signs of Sylvia Rohns Bader. I knew that she regularly visited her daddy's gravesite, so I hoped that Winnie would soon arrive. I committed the dates of the general's life to memory and planned to look up more information about him on my next trip to the public library.

As I repeated the inscription aloud, Winnie walked up behind me. "My oh my, Claire, you are readin' tombstones. It is known that ancient Selma citizens haunt this graveyard. It is filled with white ghosts."

"That's very funny," I said. She stood grinning back at me.

A few months ago, her comment would have made me uncomfortable. Now it was just another fact, surrounded by the circumstances of time and space and something that made us laugh together. Stepping toward my Brooks teaching partner, I embraced her abundant shoulders.

"I've missed you, Winnie," I said, always mesmerized by her stunning violet eyes that now glistened in the sun. "How have you been?"

It felt right to call Winnie by her first name now, but that wasn't always true. She was at least twenty years my senior. Beyond that, in the Deep South, black people were always called by their first names, never Mr., Mrs., or Miss. Initially addressing her as Mrs. Holmes was my own gesture of respect for my colleague and friend.

"Doin' fine," Winnie replied. "I hear you're busy teachin' grown-ups to read 'n write, and all."

"And I'll just bet your cousin told you all about it," I said.

"Oh, yes, indeed. Opie has struggled with literacy all her life. She's one smart cookie but suffers deeply with the printed word on paper." With a grimace, Winnie shook her head.

If Mrs. Bader or Billy Chas approached the scene and found me with Winnie, the exchange would be uncomfortable, so I got to the practical point of our meeting.

"Winnie, I need some information." I took a deep breath and continued, "I saw your picture with Clayton Grilton in the national magazine, *Global.* You were in a crowd demonstrating for voter registration rights."

I searched her face for some emotion. There was none.

"That is, I'd like to know more about that demonstration," I spoke softly, hesitantly. "The adults in my class want to read and write. But even if they can read and write a little, they still are not registered to vote. How can I teach more than what is in the workbooks? What do they need to know to be able to become a voter in this town?"

Winnie breathed deeply, as if inhaling my questions while staring at the general's tombstone. She nodded her head slowly. "Yes, I have copies of that newspaper clipping and the photo. The national news showed us as we were, and still are. Well-educated professionals peaceably fightin' for voters' rights. The *Times-Journal* ran a tiny piece with the sheriff callin' Negro teachers rabble-rousers and sayin' we didn't care about the kids. The photos were a whole different set of shots too. They made us look menacing and scary." She twisted her lips in disgust.

"Let's sit down," I suggested, walking back to the bench. "I want to hear more about the protest."

Winnie explained the two disparate photos and viewpoints, as well as her knowledge of the citizens' uprising. I sat glued to her words.

"The civil rights marches and teachers' protests for voter rights—including the bloodshed along the path—jolted the roots of our sleepy little town. We got people's attention and we're not going to give up." Her lips were pursed as she looked directly into my eyes. "Still have a long way to go, though."

"What is required to get a voter registration card?" I asked.

"The law says you have to pass a test to get a card. Of course, they charge a fee too!"

"The test makes sense. A person should be informed and be able to read and sign the ballot." It sounded reasonable to me. "It shouldn't cost money to vote, though."

"Nope. And speaking of the test, I'm a college graduate and a teacher, and every time I took that test, I'd fail a couple of questions. The rejection letter said that I failed questions of relevancy needed for informed citizenry. Well, I was not about to let that stop me." She yelped a laugh that cut through my own angst. "I just kept takin' the tests again and again. They always came up with the same outcome—failed. The fact is that the folks in the courthouse handlin' the voter registration kept changing the test questions. They held all the power. I would miss a different single question each time. Honestly, I never told anybody about those tests. My college major was history, and I was just plain embarrassed about getting failin' results over and over. It took me seven attempts before I passed."

As a humble afterthought, she added, "I graduated magna cum laude. Can you imagine that I continuously failed a simple voter registration test? Pretty bad, don't ya' think? Especially when lots of poor white folks are lined up to vote, some of whom haven't even graduated from high school." She stared off over the tombstones.

"It's pretty bad that you got such a raw deal, Winnie. What did you do next?"

She narrowed her eyelids. I knew there was little that could thwart Winnie's determination and perseverance.

"I did the research and started my own citizenship class to help folks learn what they needed to know to be able to register." She didn't hide her bitterness toward the white leaders in the city courthouse. "With permission of the black pastors, I visited all of the churches on a couple of Sunday mornings to tell the congregations about my class."

"Bet a lot of folks were glad to have a class to help them."

"You'd think so, huh? Well, the only person who came was my cousin, Opie. And would you believe she knew all the answers to the practice questions. Even though she is dyslexic and has trouble writin' the words on paper." Although true pride registered on Winnie's face, it didn't make up for the pain of this injustice she had endured.

I was beginning to appreciate Opie's specialness even more. A smart woman, dyslexic, who floated in the shadow of her cousin, Winnie. While Opie's frustration was justified, becoming her outlet didn't make me comfortable. I committed to work on it with her—if she'd let me.

Winnie wasn't finished lauding the praises of her cousin. "Well, that girl has good business sense too. Someday she plans to own a beauty shop, or as Opie's calls it, *a beauty salon.* She plans to have a big sign in the window with red letters that light up and read: OPIE'S SALON FOR LEISURE LADIES. She said another sign would list all the services provided. She has it all planned. Even the color of the curtains and chairs. Lemon yellow."

"Sounds pretty classy," I said with a grin, envisioning the neon sign.

"Yes, siree. She came about that name after she overheard a conversation between two dolled-up ladies walking into the doctor's office she cleaned each evening. One of 'em was complaining that she had to change her appointment at the hair salon because the doctor had to deliver a baby and couldn't see her as scheduled. Can you imagine any woman upset over such a thing?" Winnie's face was stamped with incredulity.

I nodded in agreement.

"The second lady, her friend, moaned how she had the same experience. Then Opie heard her say that three doctors in one building should be able to figure out a better schedule. I guess neither woman looked pregnant. Opie couldn't figure out why they were even coming to a baby doctor's office. From that day, Opie decided her shop should have white class, but serve beautiful colored women. Leisure women of color."

"Wow. I would never have guessed that about Opie. I hope she'll come back to my class so I can get to know her better. Maybe help her realize her dreams."

"Claire, Opie and I talk a lot. And we talk about you, and how women of both races are more alike than different. Fact is, I told Opie that you are more like us than she 'spects. When she met you, she said that I was right." We both chuckled as birds chirped on a nearby wisteria limb.

"Opie believes her beauty salon could help bring white and colored women together. White women could see how colored ladies like the same things they do. Maybe it would help to change things in Selma."

Although I saw little physical resemblance, the two cousins shared the same dream of the sisterhood to make their lives better in the town they loved.

"Winnie, where can I get copies of those voter registration practice questions and the applications?" Teaching my students how to fill out voter application forms was a life skill. "Opie could tell me the answers aloud. I could write the words down and she could copy them."

"Why, surely. You can get them at the courthouse."

"It's understandable why Opie is frustrated, and I can help," I said, planning to get materials from the courthouse before the next class session. "By the way," I said, "did Opie tell you about what happened at the base?"

"No, but I haven't talked to her recently."

"Well, last week Bruce invited me to lunch at the Base Grill with Billy Chas Bader and his friend, Johnny Bailey. I never expected such trouble. Johnny Bailey tried to coerce me into teaching at his school. Of course, I didn't accept. Opie either overheard our discussion or someone told her about the meeting. Either way, she doesn't believe me. Can't say I blame her." I looked away.

Winnie replaced her sunglasses and patted her brow with a handkerchief. "Claire, Opie's trust is tentative. For decades, our people thought that the white man was always right, and they had to be submissive to his wishes. Even today many of our own traditional black preachers still avoid political connections when it comes to guiding their people. In good faith they stick with the Word.

"Of course, there's different degrees of submission. The good Reverend Samuel Mease, pastor at the Mt. Gideon Baptist Church, is probably the most influential and most accommodating in black Selma. My dear, I know he attends your class too. People just want to be treated with respect and equality."

I wasn't really surprised that Winne knew the Reverend was in my adult literacy class. Reverend Mease's biblical references rang true to her comments.

"One day, after the teachers marched, Mr. Grilton asked the Reverend if we could use his church hall for a meeting. The Reverend passed off the decision to one of his senior deacons."

"And what did the deacon say?"

"He said no. Flat out. He said they didn't have enough insurance for an outside group and that was it." Winnie threw her hands up in the air. "We did go back to Reverend Mease to ask for his intervention in our cause. He tole' us that he was a man who spoke the Word of God, not politics and civil rights."

"Maybe he was afraid for his safety and that of his family," I said, considering the Reverend's kind and gentle nature.

"Are you kiddin'? This is the same man who asked a group of men teachers to help him rescue one of his parishioners from jail. He is capable of brave acts when it comes to his congregation. But he isn't gonna stand up to the whites in this town. The Black Ministerial Alliance is deeply rooted in Selma, and it ain't goin' away anytime soon." Winnie shook her head as she looked at the ground.

Sitting in a silence that I knew better not to break, I recalled a story the Reverend shared. He explained he grew up playing ball with white boys, but the races were separated when they went to the Saturday movies. Reverend Mease was sent to the buzzard roost with the colored children, while his white friends sat in theater seats up in the front. He ended his story with a moral cited from Scripture where the Almighty would ensure that justice would ultimately prevail. The other students had resounded "amen" in unison.

I had been intrigued by the buzzard roosts and pressed the Reverend to tell the whole story. "What are the buzzard roosts, Reverend?" I pictured kids perched on the roof of the theater, taking turns crouching on the outdoor balcony and peering through the darkened windows, competing with wild birds.

He explained, "Oh, they was the seats way up at the very top of the movie theater. Ya' had to get there mighty early or ya' might not even get a seat in those buzzard rows. Well, one Saturday my friend, Willy Joe Lythes, a white boy, and me was tossing stones in the Alabama River. It be early in the morning, down near Dusty City Park. We was laughing and flipping those flat rocks as fast as we could turn over a toss. We was even on the same ball team, and I had a good south paw for pitchin'." He grinned at his own skill and was proud of it.

"Well, on this particular Saturday, we both see each other at the movies. It was a full afternoon of *Flash Gordon* and lots o' cartoons. But since there be a metal bar separatin' the white kids from colored kids, I couldn't sit with Willy Joe. He couldn't talk to me, neither. We had just played at the park, but in certain places, we was separate ya' see. I know it hurt Willy Joe as much as it hurt me."

I recalled the expression on Mamiza's face, lips tight, and head nodding as if it was just yesterday that she, too, had sat in the buzzard rows.

How could kids play together one minute and be required to act like strangers the next? As if he could read my thoughts, he had said, "Judge not, that ye be not judged." I thought how the Reverend spoke with the spiritual conviction of the man he was.

With a scornful grimace and realization of the paradox, I nodded. Winnie didn't need to state the obvious. Apparently, one of the biggest obstacles to blacks becoming educated, and gaining the respect of white citizens in Selma, were black preachers. Even Reverend Mease.

"On a brighter note, I know Opie wants to learn as much as she can," Winnie said. "Just like me, she wants to help black women to be free. My guess is she wants to trust you. But the conversation between your husband and those men didn't help." Winnie raised her brows and tipped her head slightly.

"Ya' didn't know she was working in the kitchen at the Base Grill. Besides ya' couldn't have done anything if ya' did know, Claire. You are in a very tight spot, young lady." Her nod left unspoken the power that hate wielded.

I looked at her reflectively. She was right. Billy Chas and Johnny had me cornered that day.

Winnie continued to tell me more about her cousin. "Opie's creamy-colored complexion has opened doors for her that those of us with darker skin can't budge. It is true that the civil rights battles of the early sixties have done little to change daily living for us in Selma. But that has not stopped Opie. She has always enjoyed life and I know she is mighty glad to have the dishwashing job on the military base. Although still separated

from white folks, the base offers a greater sense of acceptance."
Winnie paused to study my face.

"Opie told me the military folks treated our people better.
Maybe because they're only here a while, or because Yanks are
less prejudiced. I dunno. White folks bid her good morning
and sometimes even leave her a tip. The small salary she earns
barely covers her expenses. But she's able to take care o' herself
and her mama. She saves all of her tip money in a big tin can
sealed with a tight lid."

Winnie laughed as she shared stories about Opie. "She
tucks that can away under the loose molding along the closet
floor. She says that way she could get at it from the inside or
the outside. In case of a fire, she could escape with her money."

My friend was on a roll now and didn't stop. "Opie has always
worried about fire takin' her home away. Ever since the days
on the farm when her daddy lay on that tin roof to watch the
vigilantes' fires as he tried to protect all of us girls." A sadness
covered her face.

"Did you live with Opie, Winnie?"

"No, but I spent time with Opie and my cousins when I
was a little girl, after Daddy passed. My aunt and uncle, Opie's
parents, took care of me a lot. 'Specially when my daddy was
called to war. He joined the Army before I was born to escape
tenant farming," Winnie proudly explained as she lifted her
chin and stood tall.

From history classes, I knew that with the onset of World
War II, black men had an opportunity to get out of the cycle
of poverty dealt them by hard farm life.

As if reading my mind, she raised her eyebrows for emphasis
and continued, "Of course, the military was all segregated
back in the early 1940s. But Daddy was a smart man. He was
among the first Tuskegee Airmen in the U.S. Army Air Corps,
a group of Negro fighter pilots during the War. He flew lots of

bomber combat missions over Europe. None was shot down by the enemy."

"What a hero." I swallowed hard at this new information about Winnie. She had shared few details about her personal life with me.

In a softer tone, she continued, "Daddy's squadron was awarded a Presidential Unit Citation. He also was one of the few who was honored with the Distinguished Flying Cross award. I saw him receive it when I was a little girl." My friend smiled wistfully before sharing the final comments about her father. "Daddy died of pneumonia in 1947, just two years after he returned to the U.S. from Italy. Segregation in the military ended in 1948. Sadly, he didn't live to see it." She lowered her gaze.

I expressed my condolences, and we both paused respectfully at the mention of his passing. With such a sorrowful admission, I resisted asking about the underground sisterhood.

Winnie patted my leg. "By the way, I must tell you about Jackson."

"Indeed. How is he getting along?" I welcomed the change in topic, especially if it was an update about Jackson.

"He's at his auntie's farm for the summer. Helping with the crops and chickens. It's a wholesome and good place," said Winnie, reassuring me that all was well.

"Good to know that." I was relieved. "Also, I hear there is a day camp of some sort at one the churches in town. Don't know much about it, but it sounds like something that Jackson might like."

Winnie suddenly clasped my hands between both of hers, while her violet eyes centered on mine. "Claire, I think it's time you learned about some important developments going on in town." She scuttled forward to the edge of the wooden bench and revealed the same story my Zeta sisters had already shared. Before I could tell her that I knew this information, she asked for my help.

CHAPTER 35

"You would be ideal for the youth camp project," said Winnie. "We need young, energetic, enthusiastic women — especially good teachers, to lead this important work. Yes, good women, smart women, black and white women of courage to turn this culture around." She spoke as if she were addressing an audience and I wondered how many times she had delivered this message.

With a sigh, I looked down at our intertwined hands—black and white. Raising my head and meeting her gaze, I told her what my Zeta sisters shared.

"Ruby Miller and Belinda Bailey are dauntless and are risking a great deal by fighting against the status quo in Selma," I said. The intensity in Winnie's eyes paralleled the passion in my voice.

Rubbing my temples, I tried to make sense of what had happened. "Two weeks ago, Mamiza told me she joined my class to learn how to sign her name. She wanted to register to vote and sign her social security checks when the time came. Her sister, Mariah Jesse Willis, would never get that chance. Mrs. Willis had signed her name with an X. Mamiza's niece, Delberta has been used and abused and deals with visual disability every day." My head throbbed.

"But Jackson is making up for it all," said Winnie as she reached to touch my shoulder.

"Jackson's love of reading and good grades made his grandmother so proud," I said.

Winnie looked heavenward. "I bet she's beaming from above."

Closing her eyes, she paused before continuing, "My dear,

you are here for a reason. God knows, your energy and spirit serve a purpose. Every effort for Jackson and your other students has touched their lives."

Winnie lifted herself up and off the bench with both hands. I stood and hugged her one more time and breathed in the floral fragrance I came to know and love. "Thank you for being my friend, Winnie, and for helping me to be a better teacher. I'll think about helping out at the youth camp." I wondered how Bruce would react to Winnie's suggestion, although I had already made up my mind.

"Bless you, girl. We surely will get Jackson to camp next summer. You have my word." She turned to walk away, but after a few footsteps, pivoted back towards me with a pointed finger in the air. "And I will talk with my cousin."

"Wonderful," I said, grinning and wiping my brow while trying to absorb all the information Winnie had shared.

~

The sticky heat of the approaching summer afternoon sluiced upon me. The walk from Rohns a couple of hours earlier had been pleasant. Now, at mid-morning, the familiar moist air oozed into every crevice of my body.

As I steadied my foot on a bench to tighten the buckle on my sandal, I heard footsteps and a familiar tapping sound against the cement. I was no longer alone.

Sylvia Bader appeared from around a bend. Two mockingbirds fluttered away as she spoke, "My lands, Claire, what are ya' doin' here this morning?"

I greeted her and considered the simple question she posed. One that I couldn't honestly answer. "This place is so peaceful. Seems like more of a blossoming public park with rows of trees and flowers, and benches that even welcome visitors."

I casually waved a hand toward a nearby seat and shrugged

off the apprehension I felt at the possibility of an earlier arrival by Mrs. Bader. She could have passed Winnie on the path.

Mrs. Bader's sudden blank stare made it hard to determine whether my comments about the cemetery had offended her or if her thoughts had shifted to her dead father. Overall, this encounter was one I didn't need. "I noticed the grave site of General William Parsin Rohns up the path," I said with proper respect.

"Yes. I try to visit both daddy and my beloved Charles every Sunday, but just didn't feel up to it yesterday." She patted her brow with a lace hanky tucked in a sleeve and fanned her too-rosy cheeks. "Can you sit over yonder with me a bit?" Without waiting for me to answer, she clumped toward the bench where Winnie and I sat earlier.

Mrs. Bader was winded and looked flushed after the walk from Rohns. I sat down, tetchy relationship aside.

"I do enjoy having you and Bruce in my home and 'preciate the way y'all take care o' the apartment. That lieutenant who lived there before you wasn't nearly as good at cleanin' as you, my dear." She laughed and raised a brow. A gleam in her eye at eighty-plus years told me he must have been a charmer.

"I even had to git Mamiza in there to dust and wash when he was working at the base," she added with a laugh.

"I'm sure he was grateful, Mrs. Bader." This woman had a knack for backhanded compliments.

"Oh, he did thank me. Brought me chocolates every week. A dear boy."

Speaking with exaggerated glee, I said, "Chocolates, my goodness."

Wistful for only a moment, she continued, "Ya' know there is a lot o' high society in Selma." She suddenly narrowed her eyes.

"What do you mean, Mrs. Bader?" Two or three more drops of sweat raced the length of my spine as she broached the crux of her seemingly friendly chat.

"Evrabody has their place here. It has been that way for a very long time."

Fearful the path of her comments was going to lead to another race discussion. I smiled and quickly turned the conversation in the direction of General Rohns.

"Traditions make everyone feel secure and safe. I bet your father fought hard for honor and tradition. What was he like, Mrs. Bader?" I asked with more than a spurious interest.

"My daddy was the pride of the Deep South." She beamed and gazed into the space to the right of my head as if viewing a newsreel of a special event. I breathed a sigh of relief. She was deterred, at least for the moment. "He even wrote a book about war tactics that was used by both sides during the War Between the States."

"That's amazing! He sounds like he was a smart and clever man."

"He surely was. He also had his beliefs, and you couldn't change his mind. He hired a prominent architect to design Rohns Manor and began building it for him and Mama just after the Civil War in 1867. They weren't married 'til the year it was finished in 1878. I came along five years after that." Seemed like a long time to build a house, but Mrs. Bader explained how many of the parts and materials were specially made and shipped from overseas.

"The original Rohns Manor had big ole Greek columns on the edge of the porch. After Daddy passed on, Charles and I moved in with Mama. We had the outside remodeled and added the columns that are there today."

"They look authentic. I thought they were the original ones. At least a hundred years old."

"Lands, no. But they're authentic a'right. We got 'em some forty years ago from the old Traveler's Home, a hotel for nigra travelers. Charles always loved the veranda and columns on that place and jumped at the chance to get the pillars, by golly."

Mrs. Bader's explanation didn't sound right to me. I had

doubts about a white man of Charles Bader's status making a purchase from a Negro business owner forty years earlier. Such an interaction wouldn't even happen today, in 1969.

"Bet it didn't cost much to buy the columns back in those days." I spoke with a forced naivete.

"Why, honey, he didn't *pay* for them." She looked at me with incredulity.

I had thought as much, but feigned ignorance. "You mean the hotel owner gave him the columns?" More witless babble.

She cleared her throat. "Let's just say they bartered an exchange. The nigra owner got to keep the land where the hotel was built and a promise of no more trouble from the posse. It was fair trade. Daddy got the columns and a few other incidentals."

I remember seeing a picture of the Traveler's Home in a Selma history book at the library, I smiled politely. "Sad to read that it burned down."

"An accident. Anyway, his establishment brought a whole lot o' nigras into our fair town. We sho' didn't miss it." She studied my face. "I know it don't sound right to you, but there is lots more to the story, child. You wouldn't understand it all. Fact, neither do I." Another chuckle as she fanned herself with the hankie to indicate how incidental it all was.

I moved my watchband to loosen the sweat as well as check the time. "Sorry, Mrs. Bader, but I need to run. It was nice to chat with you. And, you do have a beautiful home." More kowtowing, but it allowed for an easy escape. I couldn't listen to another word.

She grabbed my wrist with a concerted twist. It hurt. "Bye-bye, for now, honey. You do be careful, ya' hear? A lot of people in this town are not free thinkers." Her smile was taunting. She released her hold on my arm.

Suddenly weary and gritting my teeth, I turned to leave. Ahead of me was the cemetery exit where a white pickup was pulling away.

CHAPTER 36

"I'm pregnant and I'm scared." I must have read the sentence ten times. Lucy wrote her office phone number in the one-page letter and asked me to call her. She was finishing up a case and would be in court, but "please call on Tuesday." If this was one of her jokes, it was cruel. But even Lucy wouldn't be that mean. Would she? *How could this happen? She didn't have a steady boyfriend. She always had many.*

Today was Tuesday and I'd reconciled my guilt of being secretive with Bruce, knowing there would be more to share after my phone call. I hung up the receiver twice before finally dialing Lucy's office phone number.

The news was true. She'd had an on-and-off relationship with an Air Force captain. He was her date for our wedding. Pleasant enough but didn't say much. I was floating on a cloud back then, with intermittent nausea, and hardly remembered the reception. Fortunately, Mother was an expert at caring for the social niceties. Apparently, Lucy's captain got deployment orders for Nam. It happened the night before he left in June.

"Do you love him?" I asked.

It was good I was sitting when she responded, "More than I ever thought I could love anyone."

I listened as my sister explained that she hadn't told our parents. We both knew they had expected her to marry one of the eligible lawyers or doctors she always dated. The father of Lucy's child was a career military man. This was not the man Mother would have selected.

"We're going to be married when he's home on furlough, Claire. Likely late November or early December. Will you be..." She hesitated.

"I will be there, Lucy," I said, swallowing hard as I felt the depth of her request. I also knew that Bruce likely could not go. We had planned to visit at Christmas.

"I haven't been the best sister," said Lucy. Her voice cracked as she continued, "But I need you, Claire."

Blinking back moisture in my eyes, I thought of the time Lucy carried me home when the ice pond in a nearby open field cracked. I fell in, hip-deep, and was soaked with frigid water. Special moments with Lucy were rare, but this one stayed with me. She tugged at both of my arms as if she feared I was going to drown.

"And will you be my *matron* of honor? My *only* one. Please."

I sobbed into the phone thinking about the fuss she and Mother made when I told them Sandy was to stand in honor *with* her at our wedding. I could barely answer. "Yes, of course." I wiped at my face. "I will. It would love to be your matron of honor."

Lucy was crying and couldn't answer. I pulled at a tissue and blew my nose.

"I love you, Claire," said Lucy.

"Love you, too. Talk soon." We hung up with promises to connect over the weekend. Lucy planned to tell our parents, and I wished her luck. Numb, I sat clutching the two damp tissues until the grandfather clock chimed on the half-hour.

I was eager to tell Bruce, but it would have to wait. Collecting my purse, knew I had to get to the library before it closed.

~

As I approached the library, I saw a white pickup pull into the only empty parking spot. White pickups were everywhere in Selma. But this one had a dent in the side bumper. And in the same spot as the truck I had seen following us from the high school. Curious about the driver, I slipped into a parking spot about a block away and waited.

Suddenly, a cigarette butt flew out of the open driver's window, and Belinda Bailey hopped out of the passenger side. She slammed the door and stomped around to the front of the vehicle. The balding head of Johnny sat behind the wheel. He sneered at her passing, but Belinda only picked up her pace and thrust her nose higher into the air. I wasn't the only woman who didn't want to be near Johnny.

Before she entered the library, Johnny's beefy palm slammed against the metal door. His mouth was contorted in an angry snicker as he shouted something I couldn't hear. He reminded me of a caged animal, awaiting the chance to pounce upon its prey. Belinda almost lost a white open-toe sandal as she picked up speed and grabbed the heavy library door, ties of the navy-blue apron dangling from her handbag.

Johnny sped off. I sat for a few more minutes, and then pulled into the spot he'd vacated. I back-combed my hair, trying to smooth out the too-wavy parts and dabbed at my lips with a tube of lipstick. Pleased with my image in the rearview mirror, I headed toward the library entrance.

As I entered the library foyer, Belinda was nowhere in sight. I ambled through the hallways, looking around corners. *She had to be in here somewhere.* Pushing open the door of the ladies' room, I almost collided with my red-eyed, sniffling friend.

"Hi, Belinda. Are you alright?"

"Hey, Claire. Oh, I'm fine." She forced an exaggerated, happy face. Hardly convincing. Holding my purse with two hands in front of me, I watched her visibly slump. Tears began to flow.

"What's the matter?" I put a hand on her shoulder.

Belinda blew her nose into a wad of paper towels and tossed them into the trash basket. She swallowed hard and sighed before she spoke. "Johnny and I had a little disagreement this mornin'. I'm a bit upset, but I'll be all right."

"You sure? Anything I can do?" I quickly scanned her body for any signs of bruises, cuts, or torn clothing.

"Yeah, I'm sure." Her expression morphed into one that suggested intrusion. "Johnny wouldn't hurt me." She glared and sniffled.

As if sorry for her abruptness to me, she spewed her fears. "It's just that he promised me he would stop drinkin' and drivin,' and hangin' around with that men's group. He's away a lot and might even be havin' an affair." She covered her face with both hands.

I didn't know what to say in that moment but couldn't resist putting my arms around her. "Of course, he denies it. He swears he and his friends have very important work at hand, and he and his daddy are needed in the *cause.*"

I figured *cause* meant racial issues but wanted to soothe her. "You don't know he's having an affair. But it does sound to me like he and his friends have some pretty strong opinions about integration in Selma."

Belinda took a few breaths and settled. She splashed her face with water and took out the powder compact from her purse. I thought of Bruce's design work for the Men's Alliance lodge remodel. He was in their company.

"Does he know about the camp?" I asked.

"No, I don't think he knows the specifics. He's aware that my opinions about black folks in Selma differ from his, though. And Johnny doesn't think much of my friends, either. Nothing personal, Claire."

"I think it is personal, but it doesn't bother me. I just don't want you harmed because of me." My words were direct, but not without empathy for my friend.

"I don't make a big deal 'bout the situation in this town in front of Johnny, not usually. He does have a temper, and I don't want to upset him ya' know. He can be a good man, and his family has a long history in Selma." She bit the side of her lower lip.

"Does your work at the church upset Johnny?"

"Oh, he doesn't care much 'bout the church. He goes with me on Sundays. Must keep up appearances. He's a school principal, after all." She rolled her eyes and tossed her soft curls from left to right.

"Besides, Johnny knows that Ruby and I were pretty active in the Christian Youth Education group at Mt. Hope Methodist when we were teenagers. And we kept it up during summer vacations when we were home from college. In Johnny's eyes my volunteerin' is what's expected, even if it's an extension of my teen years." The memory made her smile.

"So, what's the problem?" I asked, sitting on the sofa near the restroom entrance.

Belinda's jaw tightened as she sat down next to me and stared toward the floor.

"Remember what Ruby and I told ya' in her kitchen about the group of white women and black women, mostly our ages, who just want peace and equality between folks in this town?"

"Yes. Of course." *How could I forget?*

"Well, the director of Christian Youth at Mt. Hope has been there since we were kids. Probably fifteen years. She's a good and devoted woman who spends most of her time praying and working with the kids at the church and in the community. Since the Civil Rights Act, she's been helping white kids to understand differences and respect all people."

"How does she manage such a project in Selma society?" My blurting was impulsive, but Belinda's news was so exciting. Plus, this was the person who needed to know about Jackson.

"She's separated herself from the social scene, even though Mt. Hope is the biggest white church in town. All the doctors, lawyers, and business owners are members. The history goes back three or four generations. Everybody who's anybody belongs, honey child." Belinda flapped her lashes and bobbed her head again.

I laughed at Belinda's mimicking, easing the icy tension. *She was darn good at it!*

"Well, Ruby and I decided to help the director put together little skits for the kids to perform. I wish we were all better writers, but it was fine. I can draw a little and design sets. Ruby is good at organizing, making calls, and working with folks. The director knows who to contact and likes to work behind the scenes. 'Course we all play piano. We made a good threesome." Belinda's candor reflected who she was.

"What were the skits about?" I loved to write and had acted in several plays in high school and college. *Bruce probably wouldn't want me involved. And with a Protestant church, to boot.*

"That's where it gets a little sticky. We did a musical last week showing black kids and white kids playing and singing songs together in a church choir. The theme was set around the Gospel of John 4:7-10. Ya' know, the story about Jesus and the Samaritan woman at the well? The woman is surprised that Jesus, a Jew, is speaking to her, a Samaritan woman."

She folded her arms above her tiny waistline and emphasized the Bible message, "We want the kids to know that Jesus wasn't about judging and segregating people and neither should they be."

"I know that story. One of my favorites and usually part of the Gospel around Easter time in my church." Protestants and Catholics weren't so different. Same God. Same message from The Word.

"Okay. So, you know it's a life-giving story about accepting all people, no matter what race or religion they might be. It's also about showing kindness and compassion, which is something many traditional Selma residents don't understand when it comes to equality between white people and Negroes." She dropped her hands to her knees and stretched forward in her seat, raising her voice at the last few words of her sentence.

I hoped no one would walk into the restroom and overhear us. It was unlikely there was another safe place in the library to talk. "Bet the music was great. How did the congregation take it?"

"A few members were indignant, including my own husband." She stared at the tiled floor while turning her diamond-studded wedding band around her finger.

"Frankly, most didn't get it and reacted purely on the entertainment value of the performance. The kids did a great job in dancing, singing, and acting. Lots of talent. I just hoped it would encourage them to look to the future, to make a difference in this town."

Belinda's voice faded off. "Really wish we could do more…"

"What do you mean?" I asked.

"We would like to produce more skits, maybe send out a newsletter for teens. The schools wouldn't cooperate. At least not yet, but the churches would."

"Do you think anybody at the Catholic church would help?"

"Oh, they've already helped a lot. Father Moore, the priest at the St. Antoine Mission Church recently wrote a letter to the editor in the *Selma News* about how white folks, too, have suffered as result of the racial strife in our city. He tried to convince everyone that we all need to come together."

"I can see how racism would be a moral crisis for any religion," I said, rather surprised the newspaper ran the letter.

"Father Moore is well respected in Selma. He did a nice job of tellin' it like it is. Gotta give him credit."

"What did the priest say?"

Breathing deeply, Belinda related his message, "He wrote how living in Selma had become harder since the passage of the Civil Rights Act. He admonished the clergymen for not speaking out about the disparities they had witnessed and reminded them how they had been called to do so by their vocation. He also accused them of hiding from the truth for fear of reprisal, loss of support from their congregations, and attacks upon the businessmen who were members of their congregations."

"Wow. That took real courage." My chest swelled with hope.

"Yup. Apparently, a brave heart runs in his family," said Belinda. "The priest's brother was one of the people who marched with Reverend King across the Pettus Bridge. The guards tried to block their efforts and criticized his faith, damning these so-called *people of God* for marching without the required permit. Completely silly, because the city officials would find some reason not to issue a permit even if they tried to get one. The priest told the guards he believed in justice for all. He said a prayer blessing the marchers and walked away."

"That's pretty impressive." I wanted to meet this priest and his brother and planned to talk to Bruce about attending the St. Antoine Mission Church. However, I knew he would be worried about the message that would suggest. He liked attending Sunday Mass at the quiet conservative country church with its rotating rural clergy and white congregation. Most of the parish members were nearby plantation owners and farmers.

"Well, Johnny knows about all of this activity, and he's not impressed." Belinda shuttered.

If Johnny wasn't impressed, did that mean he'd hit her?

CHAPTER 37

Still reeling from my encounter with Belinda that morning, I stubbed a toe on a gargoyle's face. Struggling to dry a still-damp body, I swore I'd never forget the humidity of a Selma summer. Bruce had called and told me he was staying at the base to work on his architectural drawings for the Lodge. Exhausted when he came home, he barely touched any of the dinner leftovers.

"Come to bed, honey." With two floor fans and the window air conditioning unit blasting, I could hardly hear him. Our June and July electric bills were double those of late spring, and we couldn't expect them to be lower in the heat of August. The time was approaching when we'd have to shut the lights at night to save money. The crawling critters in the dark would have to be overlooked. I cringed.

Anxious to get out of the sauna-like space, I wrapped my hair in a towel and cracked the door for air to clear the steamy mirror. "Be there in a few minutes. I want to clean up the kitchen first." I walked into the bedroom and pulled on my pink pajamas. Bruce lay prone on top of the bed sheets.

With a lingering gaze in my direction, he said, "We can do the dishes in the morning."

I immediately knew what was on his mind and committed to a speedy cleanup. His enticement appealed to me. Yet, ever since my unexpected discovery of the crawling roach in the frying pan during our first week at Rohns, I couldn't bear to leave dirty dishes in the sink. Not in the light of day, let alone the dark of night.

I kissed him lightly. "It won't take long." He pulled me onto the bed. "Just a couple of minutes, promise," I repeated. I hesitated another second, but ultimately pulled away to take care of business.

"Hurry," he said seductively.

Sometimes, Bruce reminded me of a little boy pleading for an ice cream cone. I kissed him again and hopped off the bed. He rolled onto his side.

The only sounds I could hear through the glass door between our bedroom and the makeshift kitchen were the grinding and whirring air conditioner blade. Bruce said the damned thing slashed away at our hard-earned dollars.

A full moon illuminated the kitchen as I reached for the light switch. I peered out the window and saw a sudden burst of flames engulf the carriage house beyond the pecan tree in the yard. In a couple of leaps, I was at the door in time to see two hulking figures bending over our Ford. One guy held a container in his hand. I tore open the door and pushed through the thin screen.

"Stop!" I grabbed the handrail and jumped down the steps, two by two. Stumbling over the towel that fell from my head, I bolted toward the car. The men sped off on foot, dropping a kerosene can behind them.

"Bastards!" I shrieked, tearing down the pavement after them, ignoring my aching bare feet and fortified by the passion of my own loudly spoken profanity. The uneven cement on my sprint almost cost me a twisted ankle. I couldn't keep pace any longer and gave up the chase. Trembling, I watched the two figures disappear into the distance, then leaned on my knees to catch my breath.

I hobbled back toward the Manor. "Dear God!" I crossed myself, acutely aware of the fluid on the ground and the overturned can near our car.

"Bruce, Bruce, there's a fire! Wake up!" My throat hurt from the shouting.

Ignoring my aching ankle, I landed on the porch and tore through the screen, rushing into the shadows of the kitchen. The incessant rhythm of the air conditioning unit rattled in our, flame-illuminated apartment. No response came from the bedroom.

"Damn it, Bruce, wake up!" I tossed aside the thin sheet and pulled at his arms. "There's a fire in the backyard."

He stumbled out of bed and staggered toward me, knocking over the alarm clock. The glass face shattered as it hit the hardwood floor, and I could see blood trickling down his ankle.

"What on earth?" He stopped at the open door, tugged at his shorts, then ran one hand through his hair while he dabbed at the cut on his leg with the other.

He turned and grabbed my wrist. "I'm calling the fire department. Get out! Go!"

As I barreled onto the wooden porch, I screamed back, "What about Mrs. Bader and Mamiza?"

"I'll find 'em," he shouted back from inside the apartment.

Barely minutes later, Bruce ran out into the yard and snatched a shovel that lay on the ground near the rose garden. "Stay here!" He nodded in the direction of the floral shrubs, away from the flames that were stretching toward the outreaching limbs of the pecan tree. "Help is on the way!"

I stood, mouth agape, as he raced around the side of the house. I prayed that we'd get the two women out before the old place disappeared in a burning inferno. The far side of the pecan tree was ablaze. Branches, leaves, new buds, and old shells, gone. Trembling at the site, I ignored Bruce's command and ran up the grassy mound around the terrace that led to Mrs. Bader's bedroom. Even if she was a racist bigot, I couldn't stand by and watch the old woman die.

Halfway there, I stumbled upon her body lying on the ground.

"Mrs. Bader, wake up, wake up." I jostled her arms and hoped she was still alive. The blaze was a golden blur before my eyes. Mamiza was likely still in her sleeping quarters in the cellar below the house. I prayed Bruce would hurry and continued to cajole Mrs. Bader into consciousness, slapping her hand and babbling encouragement.

"Mrs. Bader, please wake up." I held her wrist and pressed four fingers against her pulse as she lay on the ground. A slight throbbing pumped against my thumb. Fire sirens blared in the distance. Mamiza was still nowhere in sight.

I continued to rub Mrs. Bader's arm and offer soothing words of comfort. At least she was away from the falling embers, and she was breathing. Realizing there was little else that could be done, I turned back to help find Mamiza before it was too late. I stood up just as Bruce appeared from the far side of the manor.

"Over here," I waved. "I found Mrs. Bader. She's safe."

He waved back and shouted, "The fire trucks are comin'!"

"I hear 'em," I said, although I doubted that he could hear me. Cupping my hands around my mouth, I yelled louder, "Where's Mamiza?"

Frantic, I ran toward him.

"I'm sorry. I searched the whole place, her quarters in the cellar, the parlor, the yard. I couldn't find her."

Bruce was now at my side and coughing. He encircled me with his arms. I buried my head into his bare chest and mumbled, "We can't lose her, Bruce."

I pulled from his grasp and barreled back toward the terrace entrance to Mrs. Bader's bedroom. The pecan tree was quickly becoming a frame of empty limbs. Flames inched their hot breath toward the back of Rohns Manor, leaving destruction and smoke in their wake. A faint hint of burnt nuts hovered in the air as a full moon illuminated the scene.

"Claire, where are you going?" Bruce was quickly on my heels.

"Back to the house to see if I can find Mamiza," I shouted over my shoulder without stopping. "And Kitty. Have you seen Mrs. Bader's cat?"

Bruce soon was at my side and grabbed my wrist.

I pulled away. "Please, Bruce."

"I'm coming with you," he said firmly.

Puffs of gray smoke entered my lungs and clouded my vision. I pulled my pajama top up around my nose and trudged on. Climbing the grassy mound, I raced toward the terrace door that led to Mrs. Bader's bedroom and rushed inside. Next to Mrs. Bader's bed, covered partially by a silk quilt, lay the motionless body of Mamiza. I knelt at her side and held her limp wrist to check her pulse. Barely a beat.

"Mamiza, Mamiza, you're going to be all right. Stay with me. Please, stay with me." My command sounded convincing, but I feared the worst. I begged again. She didn't respond.

"We've got to get out of here, Claire," Bruce yelled, pulling the quilt away as Kitty appeared. She scampered between our legs and out onto the terrace, grateful to be free.

Bruce grabbed Mamiza's ankles and began to pull her lanky frame toward the open doorway. Slipping my hands under her armpits, I used all my weight to nudge her forward. The smoke was getting thicker by the second.

"Is anyone in there?" I could hear one of the firefighters shouting from his megaphone. Other firefighters jumped down from the truck and began to uncoil their hoses. Bruce ran to tell them about the two women, both unconscious. I continued to soothe Mamiza, begging her to hang on. "You're gonna be all right. Help is here."

No sound came from her lips. I folded my hands over her heart and pleaded, "*Dear God, please save her. She has children to care for, with no one else to do the job.*"

Jackson and Delberta needed their aunt. So did their sister whom I had never met, as well as Delberta's baby, and the other little one on the way. I wondered what would become of these precious young people if Mamiza wasn't around to guide them. Maybe the aunt who lived on the outskirts of town would help, but she had a brood all her own.

Mamiza's chest moved ever so slightly, inflating hopes that my prayers would be answered. "Please stay with me, Mamiza," I said pleading and squeezing her hand.

As Bruce and one of the firefighters approached, a sense of deep gratitude enveloped me. I looked at the man with a black bag in his hand and said, "Her name is Mamiza Jesse." As soon as I spoke her name, the man stopped in his tracks.

I stared at his hesitating stance and said, "She's barely hanging on to life, sir. Please help her." Although my body trembled, my voice was commanding.

He moved closer and stood over Mamiza, as he gazed upon her face, and scanned her body. Flicking a gloved thumb toward Bruce, he said, "This gentleman told me Mrs. Bader was unconscious. Where is she? Her son, Billy Chas, and I went to school together." His comment clearly communicated his priority.

"Mrs. Bader is lying up on that berm," said Bruce.

"Thanks. Much obliged." He tipped his hat and started to leave.

"Wait a minute. What about this lady? Who'll take care of her?" Bruce shouted at him, standing like a statue, both hands splayed toward Mamiza.

"First things first, sir," he hollered over his shoulder, barely turning his head to look back at us.

Bruce had learned about cardiopulmonary resuscitation in basic training but had never had an occasion to use it. As if he were an expert medic, he pumped Mamiza's chest and blew air into her lungs.

Her head lurched forward as she struggled to let out a sputtering breath. "You're gonna be all right, Mamiza. Come on," he said. With her coal-dark eyes flickering and quivering lips, Bruce stopped pumping and collapsed onto the soft earth. Her consciousness brought a pure thread of joy to this bleak disaster.

"Bruce, she's alive. You saved her." I threw my arms about his neck.

"Missus Bader and Kitty." Mamiza coughed out words that were barely audible, her eyes wide with worry. She gasped, then coughed suddenly, turned her head to one side and closed her eyes.

In the background, a team of paramedics carried Mrs. Bader off on a gurney to a waiting ambulance. An oxygen mask clung to her nose and mouth. Billy Chas was now on the scene and was clasping her hand. Always the dapper gentleman, his clothes were now covered with soot and his hair was disheveled. If I didn't know who he was, I would not have recognized him. Slung over the side of his other arm was Kitty, Mrs. Bader's cranky Persian-Angora mix.

No one returned to help with Mamiza. I watched as Bruce tried, once again, to sustain her life. I prayed and pleaded.

Nothing worked.

CHAPTER 38

Miraculously, the Ford survived the blaze. The kerosene can that had been tossed aside by the two perpetrators was confiscated by the authorities. Two policemen, chewing something that didn't smell like spearmint gum, took a report from us. The questions the officers rattled off were routine, telling us they'd be in touch if they needed further information. Since I didn't get a good look at the culprits, however, I couldn't identify them. I did know they were either young or very athletic or both. They could outrun me.

Mamiza's funeral was scheduled for the following Saturday at Mt. Gideon Baptist Church with Reverend Mease officiating. Bruce left the newspaper on the kitchen table, circling a sparse entry about Mamiza on the obituary page, listed under *Deceased Negroes.*

The smoke and dank air hovered shroud-like over Rohns Manor. The firemen arrived just in time to save it, although several rooms sustained water damage. The mansion now sat empty, except for us. For two days following the event, I struggled with the stomach flu or a bad case of nerves. Steamy days melted into cooler nights as the onset of fall lay before us.

The *Selma News* reported the fire had been perpetrated by some random youth—a teenage prank that got out of hand. "I told the reporter that the men *looked* young. I didn't say they *were* young." I slapped the newspaper against the table. "Quite a twisted interpretation of my report and no mention about investigating arson or homicide. Not a word about a possible Klan prank or political motivation. Sounds like the authorities are all about protecting the status quo." Bruce was equally disgusted.

Mrs. Bader had suffered a minor heart attack. She was hospitalized and hooked up to oxygen. Her prognosis remained guarded, but she was tough and was expected to recover with sufficient bed rest. We needed to make a respectful visit to the hospital. I had touched the death of people close to me more in the past six months than in the previous twenty-two years of my life. It all made my stomach churn and my head throb.

When Bruce got home from the base, he devoured dinner, while I picked and nibbled at the food on my plate. "I doubt Mrs. Bader will be out of the hospital in time to attend the funeral."

"Probably not. Heart attacks are serious. Especially at her age. Let's go over and visit her, honey. Maybe Billy Chas will be there. I'm assuming he'll attend Mamiza's funeral." He folded his napkin and placed it on the table.

"Oh, he'll be at the funeral," I said. "From what I've heard, Mamiza practically raised Billy Chas. He sure looked a mess the night of the fire."

"Upset about his mama, for sure," said Bruce.

I put down my fork and said, "He didn't even ask about Mamiza. You don't think Billy Chas had something to do with that fire, do you?" I knew he was genuinely worried about his mother. Yet, there was something about his appearance that night that didn't seem right.

"No, that's a stretch. I think we should cut him a little slack, honey. Why would he be involved with a fire on his family homestead? His mother almost died. Probably had the heart attack while struggling to get out of the house." Bruce raised his eyebrows as he looked at me.

I got up and reached for the dish towel. "You're probably

right. It's just that I feel like I've lost a sister in Mamiza." *Does placing blame ever help the pain to go away?*

Bruce looked at me with warmth as he smiled and spoke softly, "You have a sister, Claire. Maybe one who isn't close, but you do have your very *own* sister. Maybe you should call her sometime."

Reminded of my conversation with Lucy, I put the towel on the counter and sat back down at the table. "Bruce, I have something to tell you about Lucy. I actually have a lot to tell you about Lucy." I retold the litany of my sister's phone call as well as the captain and father-to-be.

Amazed, Bruce looked at me with wide eyes. "Holy cow! Yeah, I remember that guy. She hardly spoke to him the whole night. Knowing your sister and her moods, I felt sorry for him."

I nodded. "Me too. But she said she is madly in love with him. Apparently, she met him working on a labor relations case with one of the automotive companies a couple of years ago before he was called back into military service."

"And your parents never knew?" asked Bruce.

"She was afraid to tell them that the relationship was serious. They had designs on a more affluent prospect for their *precious eldest.*" I spat out the last two words, more at my parents than Lucy.

Bruce looked down at the floor. "I saw she had written you a couple of weeks ago," he said looking directly into my eyes now, his brows slightly knitted.

"I should've told you sooner, Bruce. So much has been thrown at me these past few weeks." I rubbed my forehead. "And now Lucy's pregnancy and her asking me to be in her wedding. We were planning to go home for Christmas, but the ceremony will be earlier." Tears ran down my cheeks.

He wrapped his arms around me. "Honey, we'll work it out. We'll go to Lucy's wedding whenever she decides to plan it. It could mean that we won't be home for Christmas, though."

I closed my eyes and absorbed the warmth of his embrace.

"If we're going to get over to the hospital, we'd better hurry before the visiting hours end," Bruce whispered in my ear.

"Yup. We'd better go," I said, carrying the dishes to the sink filled with soapy suds. Glancing through the kitchen window, I noticed the bronze-colored ball of the setting sun as it slipped behind floating clouds. The glow highlighted the charred and barren branches of the pecan tree. As I struggled with my muddled emotions, I was distracted by the scene. The scrawny barren tree, once laden with the heavy nuts, was a tall pole, with fractured, arm-like branches, begging to be rescued. It reminded me of the *Don Quixote* book cover from one of my college lit classes. Quixote, the zany knight errant who sought a better society and rode off into the sunset to find his ideal. He didn't give up. The nuts from the pecan tree had taken blood from my fingers once, but I wasn't going to give up either.

I covered the leftovers with a second plate and placed them in the refrigerator. I knew what had to be done. Living at Rohns Manor was no longer going to work.

CHAPTER 39

The antiseptic scent of the hospital clung to my nostrils and brought back unpleasant memories of my hospital admittance after I'd lost the baby. "Be right back," I told Bruce as we entered the lobby. "I need to visit the ladies' room."

"I'll wait here." He grabbed a copy of *Esquire* that lay on a table and plopped into the chair.

It wasn't that long ago that I'd had a hospital stay for the D & C. I had never heard of the fancy French letters for scraping the uterus. Just as I splashed cold water on my face, Ruby and Belinda entered.

"Hey, Claire," Ruby stared at me. "Ya' look like you've seen a ghost. You alright?" Belinda reached out and offered a quick hug.

"Sure, I'm fine," I said attempting to assure myself as well the others. "I don't do well inside hospitals." I didn't mention the reason.

"I don't think anyone likes to be in a hospital. Just thought we should stop by and visit Mrs. Bader. Poor old dear." Ruby fluffed a brush through her hair as she spoke.

"Johnny told me that you and Bruce saved her life," Belinda said astonishingly. "That took a lot of courage, Claire."

The shock I registered on my face must have been misread as horror.

"I'm so sorry, honey," she said and squeezed me tight. She stroked my back as she continued talking, "Word is y'all pulled her out of the burning house, and none too soon."

The tradeoff that really happened that night gouged deeply. *Sounds like we were to be labeled heroes for saving Sylvia Bader's life... yet no one knew at what cost.*

"We didn't pull Mrs. Bader out of the house," I said as I stood back to face my sisters. "I found her outside Rohns Manor, near the terrace that led to her bedroom. She likely walked out by herself." Hesitating a moment, my voice choked with strain. "Did you know that Mamiza did not survive that fire?"

"I saw the obituary in the mornin' paper. I'm so sorry, Claire. She was special to you and a loyal servant to Mrs. Bader for many years." Ruby's sympathies softened my edginess.

A fleeting sensation of weakness overtook me, and I lowered myself into a chair in the sitting area of the large restroom. "I can't live in that house anymore. I just cannot bear to look at the dead pecan tree, the place where I saw the kerosene can, and the memory of the two men escaping from the scene. Someone wanted to burn that house down, or at least scare us a whole heck-of-a-lot." My lids closed and I worked on the breathing exercises I'd read in Lamaze preparation articles.

Ruby spoke immediately, "We have a carriage house out back that my grandmama lived in while I was growin' up. It needs a little cleaning up, but y'all can move into it if you like. I'll ask Bobby, o' course, but he won't care. He's been talkin' 'bout rentin' it out. Just hasn't gotten around to doin' it. This is perfect. And he won't bug ya' about teaching at the white schools, like someone else I know." She glared at Belinda.

Belinda rolled her eyes.

Ruby softened her stance.

"Y'all are both very kind," I said, "and your offer is appreciated, Ruby. I'll have to talk with Bruce." I realized I'd slipped into saying *y'all*. It felt fine—even comfy.

"Take your time. By the way, it's furnished. Not as fancy as the floral Queen Anne style of Rohns Manor, but cozy." Ruby flashed an authentic smile, revealing her perfect teeth.

The superficial bond of our Zeta sisterhood had taken on a different dimension since our chat in Ruby's kitchen a few weeks earlier. Belinda's safety was still on my mind. I hoped she wasn't being exploited by Johnny's outbursts of anger. Moving into Ruby and Bobby's carriage house did sound appealing. We could escape the scrutiny of the Baders at last.

Bruce and Bobby were both waiting for us in the lobby. "Well, hi ladies." Bobby smiled broadly at us as we walked toward the elevator.

"Aren't we missing someone?" *What would Johnny's excuse be this time?*

"If you mean Johnny, 'fraid he won't be able to make it. He had a meetin' to go to," Belinda fidgeted and tried to make light of his absence, though unconvincingly.

"Your chariot awaits." Bruce broke the sudden tension of Johnny's absence as he bent in an extravagant bow and reached out to keep the elevator from closing. The three of us squeezed into the box and the two men filed in. My anxieties eased as I felt the warmth of my friends surround me. I didn't know if Bobby Miller belonged to the Men's Alliance or not, but he was different than Johnny. Bruce winked at me. For the first time since we arrived in Selma, I felt a sense of peace among people of my own race.

When we entered Mrs. Bader's hospital room, Billy Chas sat in a chair at her bedside. As he jumped up to shake hands and extend whispered greetings, the uneasiness in my belly returned.

Mrs. Bader's eyes were closed, and the oxygen mask covered most of her thin face. Her pale demeanor melded with the white sheets and pale cotton blanket. Ruby placed a vase of flowers on a nearby table and all walked outside her room.

Billy Chas motioned toward a sitting area up the hallway. Bruce asked about Mrs. Bader's condition. He said she was improving but was still very tired. Doctors hoped to release her soon.

He took out a handkerchief and blew his nose. The usual demeanor of shielded steel seemed to melt as he spoke. "Bruce and Claire, thank you for what you did for my mama. If it wasn't for you..."

He hesitated, then continued in a lowered tone, while scanning our group with a set of soft eyes I'd never seen from him before, "...Mama would no longer be with us."

"Glad we could help. But Claire deserves the credit. She found your mother lying on the grass." Bruce meant well, but my mixed emotions about being a heroine for Mrs. Bader would never be resolved. Especially not now.

"She got out of the building on her own, honey," I spoke honestly and didn't feel comfortable taking any credit.

To my chagrin, tears ran down Billy Chas' cheeks and he tugged at the monogrammed handkerchief again. "Part of the credit for saving Mama's life goes to Mamiza. Mama told me Mamiza got her out of the house when she saw the flames in the yard from her quarters. She told Mama that Kitty was still in the house. Then Mamiza laid Mama on the ground and went back to fetch Kitty."

Billy Chas paused and sucked in a deep breath, unable to continue. The menacing man who had poked holes in my sensitivities for the past few months melted into oblivion. Intuition blared caution, but the façade had faded—at least for the moment.

He was reverently silent before he continued, "Mamiza was the lady who made me suga' cookies when I was a boy. Yeah, she even changed mah diapers." Billy Chas laughed at the disclosure and blew his nose again. He stared at the speckled linoleum floor, slowly moving his head up and down. Suddenly reminded he was not alone, he cleared his throat and gazed into the empathetic faces that surrounded him.

"I'll be at her funeral on Saturday. Doubt Mama will be home in time, though. See y'all there, I expect. I'll tell Mama y'all stopped by to visit. Thank y'all."

With eyes downcast, he turned and headed back towards Sylvia Bader's room.

CHAPTER 40

"Y'all are heroes," said Winnie Holmes. The cadence of her drawl across the phone line resonated gently as she spoke.

"If you're talking about the fire, Mamiza was the hero. Furthermore, she could have been saved." This was the first time I'd said the words that *she could have been saved* aloud. A sense of relief underscored the weight of hearing myself speak this truth, even though my heart was racing.

On the couch, in the comforting embrace of the cushions, I hugged the phone cord close. "Guess it's no surprise that the fireman was more concerned about Mrs. Bader than Mamiza. But he had no right to play God." I dug my nails into my palms to keep my voice from giving me away.

How can one person feel so helpless, yet so responsible at the same time? The twisted phone cord was turning my finger reddish blue.

"There was nothing else you could have done, Claire. Mamiza had high blood pressure. She took heavy doses of medication to keep it under control. I'm sure the excitement of the fire was way too much for her. Will sure miss that girl. Don't blame yourself, my dear." Before I could respond, she added, "Remember this, you and your husband stopped those damn thugs, those killers, from winnin' another battle. You stood up to them!"

Winnie's message was clear, but I couldn't erase the image of Mamiza's lifeless body. "If only we could have saved her," I said. "Bruce breathed air into her lungs for ten minutes, but it didn't bring her back to life." Even with fingernail marks in my hand, my voice was breaking.

"Not a bit surprised about it all," she said after a few minutes. "Vigilante men use fire as a warning and a threat."

"But Rohns Manor? It just doesn't make sense."

"My guess is that it was meant to scare you, Claire, and it just got out of hand."

Although the combination of temperature and humidity reached beyond a hundred degrees, a biting chill nipped at me. But only for a second. "I don't scare that easily," I said. Regardless, we had to get away from Rohns Manor.

"On another note, Winnie, one reason I called was to ask for your help in contacting my students. With all that's happened, we won't be meeting for class tomorrow evening. We'll tack on the missing class on at the end of the session."

"Opie and I will take care of it."

I wondered if Opie was still angry. "Sure that's okay?"

"Don't worry, we'll get the word out about the class being cancelled. Everybody will understand. Will I see you at the funeral?"

"Definitely. I wouldn't miss paying my respects to Mamiza."

After ending our call, I dialed Bruce at the base. The phone rang several times with no answer. I hung up and redialed. This time another airman answered his line and said Bruce wasn't there. He had left for the day.

I lay on the comforter for a few minutes, drifting off and not awakening until 4:00 p.m. After the three-hour nap, I rummaged through the cupboards and freezer. We would feast on a special meal and then I'd tell Bruce about Ruby's offer to rent their carriage house to us. Although I'd never set foot inside the cottage, I was charmed at what I saw through Ruby's kitchen window. It looked like a dollhouse, complete with white lace curtains and a small front porch. Gardenia shrubs, filled with unopened buds, wrapped around the perimeter. The flowers would likely be in full bloom now.

Drenched with renewed warmth, a sense of peaceful wholeness filled me. I couldn't wait to tell Bruce. By 5:30, dinner was ready, complete with candles in the silver candlesticks on the massive dining table. The golden flame of the candles cast an inviting glow, unlike the intense blaze of a few days past.

When Bruce hadn't arrived by six, I blew the candles out, lowered the oven temperature, and sat on the front porch with a magazine. On the other side of the street, two young boys climbed onto the limbs of a pecan tree, much like the one that once stood on the Rohns grounds. Soon I wouldn't have to bear the painful sight of the empty limbs outside the kitchen window. I wondered what would become of Mrs. Bader without Mamiza to take care of her. Strangely enough, the two women did love each other.

By the time nannies called the few kids in this spacious neighborhood indoors, my anxious thoughts about Bruce's tardiness had morphed into anger. I stomped into the house, turned off the oven, and put the casserole into the refrigerator. After cleaning the kitchen and tucking away the candlesticks, I wandered into the living room and flipped on the television. The clock chimed eight bells. It was beyond Bruce's bedtime, and he still hadn't arrived. With mounting fear and insatiable worry, I walked around to the window one more time. *Should I call the police?* I stared at the phone. Suddenly, the screened back door banged so loud the curtain rod on the tiny kitchen window fell.

"Bruce, is that you? Where have you been?" I walked through the long hallway almost shaking. "I've been worried sick."

Approaching the bathroom, I heard him flush the toilet, followed by a bellow, then a spit and a second flush. I pounded on the door.

"Bruce, are you alright? What's the matter?"

The door opened and my husband staggered out.

"Have you been drinking?" I said, a fist on each hip.

He wiped his face with the towel still in his hand. "Yes, I have. There is something I need to tell you." He held the doorframe for support and didn't move.

I couldn't imagine what news could be so terrible he'd need to get drunk, miss dinner, and stagger into the house so late.

He gently led me to the kitchen table and pulled out the two chrome chairs. When he took my hand in his, I sat down. Controlling my trembling knees, I looked into his watery eyes, buried in hollow sockets. His face was pale. Slumped over with half of his shirttail dangling from his trousers completed an image of my husband I had never seen before.

"Claire, I got orders today."

"Orders?" I'd wanted to think that the OTS appointment came through, but the appearance of my husband didn't suggest the likelihood of such news.

"I've been ordered to deploy," he barely spoke.

I gripped the chrome edge of the table and stuttered my next words, "You mean, you mean they're gonna send you to Vietnam? What about OTS? It was nine months, then OTS...it was a deal." A wave of nausea washed over me. I shut my eyes to stop the dizzying spiral.

He bent in close and continued, "Apparently, Uncle Sam needs me in Nam first. The officer training enrolment will come after my tour of duty. At least that's what I've been told. Sounds more solid this time."

He slipped onto his knees and buried his head, childlike, in the folds of my shift. His hands slipped to my elbows. "I know. It stinks, but we're going to get through this together. I love you."

He then called forth his best southern drawl, looked me in the eyes, and teased, "Y'all hear, hunah?" His nod was a plead.

Wiping at the tears spilling onto my cheeks, I couldn't resist a smile.

"When do you have to leave?" I pinched tight lips awaiting his response. Suddenly I noticed the glimmer of a half-crescent moon suspended in halo fashion out of the kitchen window, over the top of Bruce's head. *God, please protect my angel.*

He stood, steadied himself and walked to the sink, filling a glass with water. "Want some?"

"No." I waited, with breath baited in trepidation. "When Bruce?"

He placed the empty glass in the sink, wiped the corners of his lips with the back of his hand, and gripped the edge of the tiny countertop.

"First of all, sweetheart, this is a TDY assignment. That means temporary duty — six months and I'm back. But I leave December first."

"What! Before Christmas?"

"Yes, I'm afraid so, Claire. Before Christmas. And before Lucy's wedding." Bruce looked down at his shiny polished cordovans.

"I guess Ruby and Bobby's cottage house won't matter, " I muttered.

"What does their cottage house have to do with us?"

"I was going to tell you. Ruby and Bobby have invited us to live in the small cottage behind their home. I was so excited. I can't continue to live at Rohns...not after what's happened. I made a special dinner for us so I could surprise you with the news."

"Claire, that sounds great. However, you're going to have to go live with your parents. I'm sorry."

"Oh, no. That's not going to happen." I shoved the chair aside, calmly announcing that I had a plan.

CHAPTER 41

Amazing grace!
How sweet the sound,
That saved a wretch like me!
I once was lost, but now am found.
Was blind, but now can see.

As we entered Mt. Gilead Baptist Church, the organ harmoniously chimed the melody of the beloved hymn. Seething tear-filled eyes blurred my vision as I looked around the sanctuary. Mamiza's earthly struggles were no more. The thought didn't minimize the loss I felt. And my Bruce was being sent to Vietnam. To top off the precarious twists and turns, my practically estranged older sister would be living with me.

At least one issue had been resolved. I was not moving back in with my parents in Detroit. After my adamant announcement to Bruce, I took immediate steps to enable my living arrangements during Bruce's absence, beginning with a call to Lucy to discuss Ruby's cottage. I mentioned that Selma had lots of labor law opportunities, especially within the black community. I also touted the built-in babysitting arrangement. She agreed to move in with me, right on the spot, and to help pay the monthly rent and grocery bills. Conversations with Mother and Dad had not gone well — not a surprise. *Perhaps I'd tossed a lifeline to my sister, one I never knew she'd ever need.*

"Why are you doing this for me, little Sis?" Lucy had asked in that call. "And how can I ever repay you?"

"Just consider it payback for hauling me out of the pond when I was seven."

"Deal!" Her response a virtual explosion.

We both howled and my grin didn't fade, even after we finished talking. I couldn't remember a time we'd ever kibitzed like this.

~

"Good mornin', ma'am." I dabbed at my eyes and smiled politely at the man in a well-worn black suit. He nodded back as he handed me two cardboard fans. The name of the funeral home was boldly printed on one side. I accepted and hesitated before passing one to Bruce. The funeral fans might only be for ladies. Not a custom that was familiar.

We slipped into a pew halfway up the aisle and took our seats. I almost genuflected, but Bruce caught my elbow to keep me upright. *This was the first time I had ever been inside a church that wasn't Catholic.*

Two drinking fountains, at least four feet tall, stood in opposite altar corners. Made of shiny steel, they seemed to loom in mockery of the local status quo. Public drinking fountains in town stood in pairs as well but were built in two sizes—chest-high for whites and waist-high for coloreds.

As I prayed to the large oak crucifix at the apex of the nave, Winnie Holmes approached a small platform planted between the pine pulpit and the sanctuary. An American flag draped behind her. She maintained a teacher-director stance as choir members dressed in flowing white robes and sky-blue trim sashayed around her and onto the platform. Through the windows above the nave, billows of real clouds floated hazily in the heavens, while organ chords continued to resonate against stark white walls.

I smiled at Bruce and said, "Feels like this is a little piece of heaven."

He brushed his nose and cleared his throat without turning in my direction. "Except for the Lysol," he said.

A half-dozen floor fans generously spread the scent of cleansing products and oiled soaps but could not overpower the bountiful aroma of fresh gardenias from lush bouquets strewn about the altar.

I scooted closer to Bruce just as Belinda slipped into the pew space next to me.

"Where's Johnny?" I asked in a lowered tone. I was glad to see her and happy no one else decided to take the seat first.

Belinda immediately tensed at the mention of her husband's name. After a few seconds, she rolled her eyes, held on to her black straw hat and leaned toward me. "He had a conference to attend at the state education department and spent the night in the city. He said he didn't want to drive back to Selma in the dark. If I know Johnny, he probably had a couple of beers and some whiskey. Best he didn't drive back last evenin'."

"Uh-huh." I shook my head supportively. She squeezed my hand and held a stoic gaze toward the front of the church. Our eyes didn't need to meet for me to sense her apprehension.

Bobby and Ruby slipped into the seats next to Bruce. Ruby flitted her fingers at Belinda and me and adjusted the feathers on the side of her pert silk pillbox. Her thick hair was pulled back and draped in sleek contrast over the folds of her shawl-covered shoulders.

A simple lace mantilla covered my head. It served the same respectful purpose without a flare of fashion. A few months earlier I would have been aghast that my attire didn't command attention and turn heads.

Bruce sat in quiet reverence. As I studied his stoic profile, he centered his attention on the statue of Jesus above the altar.

Please keep him safe. I prayed every day that Jesus would watch over him in Vietnam. *What would I do without Bruce?*

I reached for a worn leather-bound hymnal, tucked into the wooden rack on the back of the pew in front of me. Flipping through the curled introductory pages, in search of information about Negro funerary practices, many titles reflected my mourning for Mamiza. *Swing Low Sweet Chariot. We Shall Overcome. This Little Light of Mine.*

Midway through the book and tucked into the binding was a neatly folded slip of paper. I opened the thin onionskin and smoothed the creases on the worn page. The title read, "Joshua Fought the Battle of Jericho."

I poked Bruce and pointed toward the hymn. "Look at this. It's a traditional spiritual, but just typed on a piece of onionskin."

He pointed toward the subtitle a few spaces down the paper, "A-Marchin' into Selma." The added words pointed toward the spirit of the times—down with segregation, the walls must fall. Other verses were about freedom, "let my people go" and "we will see Jordan." Inspired by current social problems, new lyrics had been created for the solace of the faithful who worshipped here. The future held numerous possibilities, not only for a city and a culture *but for a Yankee teacher.*

As I repeated the verses in my head, Jackson Willis walked past our pew with Delberta at his heels. Jackson wore shiny new brown oxford shoes, slightly large for his feet. Someday, he'd be able to walk into a shoe store and try shoes on for a proper fit. Unlike today, when someone had to measure his bare foot on newspaper and take it to the store for a close-to-correct size.

Peering over Delberta's shoulder cooed a beautiful taw-ny-skinned baby. His hair was blond, but coarse and curly, with eyes the same shade as the blue trim on choir members' robes.

At my side, Belinda vigorously rummaged through her purse. Bruce was looking in Delberta's direction. He likely also wondered where the baby got his fair-colored genes. Delberta nudged Jackson and glared at a tall, lanky younger sister who straggled behind, directing both toward the front row. The girl was likely the middle-school sister I had never met. She was a budding beauty with doe-shaped eyes, long thick dreadlocks and lashes, and a blossoming young figure. A dreadful thought struck me that she might get pregnant too. She had to get enrolled in the Methodist youth program. I made a mental note to talk with Winnie about her, and soon.

I squirmed and rubbed the side of Bruce's thigh. My husband had truly mastered the look of nonchalance since his military training. "Remember to conceal your strategy. Cover your game." Bruce laughed, often quoting the text of his training sergeants.

Just as the choir began a second verse of an unfamiliar spiritual, Billy Chas rolled a wheelchair up the front aisle. Sylvia Bader's frail frame sat erect. Her skin was as white as bone China and as delicate as the lacy handkerchief in her hands. They sat in the first row next to the children.

As we exchanged glances with the Baders, Bruce reached to squeeze my hand.

"There are two of your students." Bruce nodded toward Lily Mae Brown and Opie Doone as they walked up the aisle, arm in arm, heads bowed. They were followed by a group of ladies, donned in all-white dresses.

Ruby reached across Bruce and whispered, "Those ladies in white are professional mourners. They're paid to weep and wail." She raised her brows to signify their status in the Negro community.

Nodding, I whispered back, "I thought they belonged to a special women's religious auxiliary."

Ruby tipped her head in a slight nod. *Were some of these women members of the Fems for Freedom movement?*

Six pallbearers followed two funeral directors marching in synchrony and carrying the pine box that held Mamiza's body.

I recognized the youngest pallbearers, a couple of the boys working the pit at Billy Chas' barbeque party.

Winnie's arms waved as she orchestrated the choir, directing them in the first official verse of *Amazing Grace*. The professional mourners commenced their lamentations. The shouts, the music, and the wailing evoked an ethereal aura that drifted to the highest rafters.

The pallbearers lowered the casket that held Mamiza's body onto a metal stand before the crucifix and the crowd quieted. Reverend Mease mounted the pulpit, adjusted his thin, wired spectacles over each ear, and spoke to the mourning faces, "My brothers and sisters, we are blessed to hear the Word from the Good Book at this home-goin' service for our dear sister, Mamiza."

I looked out among the diverse assembly. Mamiza brought us all here—black and white, to this place, like a watershed of ecological pieces all fitting into their niche. The line that physically divided black and white Selma was Lincoln Highway and Mt. Gideon Baptist Church. Today that line was non-existent.

Reverend Mease continued, "Brothers and sisters, Psalm 30:11 tells us that the Lawd will turn our mourning into joyful dancing. Jesus heals. He heals our dear Mamiza, and he heals us all."

"Amen!" An echo of passionate voices responded in unison.

The Reverend studied our faces. "Woe to him who builds his palace by unrighteousness, making his countrymen work for nothing, not paying them for their labor."

As he finished his sentence, his eyes shifted toward Mrs. Bader and Billy Chas, and then moved throughout the church. The profiles of both Mrs. Bader and her son held blank expressions, spotlighted by the sun's rays beaming through the window. Mrs. Bader pulled out a handkerchief and dabbed at her eyes.

"The balm in Gilead of the Old Testament does not heal, but condemns and blasphemes, while the four Gospels of the New Testament shout the good news, mah brothers and sisters." In a lowered tone, he proceeded to shepherd the flock, "Remember, it is Jesus who heals. The Lawd God is our Savior." Beads of sweat glistened on his brow as he bowed his head in a deep and devoted delivery of the Word.

"Amen!" The crowd's response affirmed the triumph once again.

"Now y'all hear this." His voiced raised a couple of pitches as his long arm reached toward the church ceiling. "If our dear sister, Mamiza, could speak with us right now, she'd thank two young folks, Mr. Bruce and Missus Claire. These young people pulled her from the flames and brought her whole to her Heavenly Father."

As Reverend Mease spoke our names in the middle of his sermon, blood rushed into my cheeks. "And they be here with this congregation right now. Praise be to Jesus."

As all eyes moved in our direction, my stomach fluttered, and I reached for Bruce's hand. He clasped my fingers and smiled in humble appreciation toward the Reverend at the pulpit. Seconds later, we both bowed our heads in humble acceptance of the recognition.

"Amen!" Faithful participants didn't miss their cue.

When the service was complete, the morticians led the group of pallbearers to the hearse that would take Mamiza to her final resting place, a small cemetery nearby that was once a burial ground for slaves. The organist continued lamenting chords, while the white-robed choir chimed each note with perfect pitch, orchestrated by Winnie. The choir swayed with harmony of melody as the procession of attendees followed Mamiza and the pallbearers from the church.

Swing low, sweet chariot,
Coming for to carry me home.
Swing low, sweet chariot,
Coming for to carry me home...

CHAPTER 42

Uncertain if my overall malaise was from the painful events of the past few weeks or something else, I made the appointment to see a doctor. Bruce came and went from the base and ran his morning route. Mrs. Bader returned to Rohns with a full-time nurse. Bruce chided me about calling my parents to tell them about his deployment. Yet, I procrastinated the phone call until Lucy and I had finalized some alternatives. Finally placing the call to my mother, she expressed her concern over Bruce's deployment but was more interested to have me return home.

"You'll be moving back home, of course. We'll get your room ready, dear," she said before I could say more. I thanked her for the offer and told her to hold off, explaining we hadn't made plans that far ahead. With a quick comment about running errands and assurances about calling soon, I said goodbye.

~

"Are you okay with going to see the doctor alone, honey?" We drove down Broad Street and across the Pettus Bridge toward the base.

"Oh, sure. I'll call you as soon as the appointment is over." Efforts to sound buoyant fell flat. Nibbling a few saltines didn't dispel the persistent nausea. We wanted to be pregnant, but the timing never seemed to jive with our real life. I had skipped a cycle, and the symptoms were all too familiar — except for the low-grade temperature.

Bruce cast an affectionate look at my stomach as he got out of the car. "Don't worry, Claire. Whatever news we get today, we'll work out."

I smiled faintly and nodded as he walked away.

Stopped at a traffic light, the ripples on the surface of the Alabama River reflected the sunlight in a rainbow of colors. With time to spare, I crossed the bridge for the umpteenth time and pulled into a space across the street from Rexall Drugs. I hopped out of the car and started toward a picnic table on the lush embankment to get a closer view of the ripples at the river's edge. Stepping onto the sidewalk, familiar voices distracted me, and they weren't friendly. I immediately ducked into an entry of one of the buildings.

"Damn you, Johnny! Why the hell did you screw up like that? What were ya' thinkin,' buddy? Belinda is a gem." The booming tone was that of Billy Chas Bader.

Encountering these angry men seemed to be my destiny, only this time their squabbling intensified. From the conversation I pieced together, Belinda had finally caught her husband. Johnny had a girlfriend, a teacher, in Montgomery where he supposedly had attended regular State Board of Education meetings. When he didn't come home, Belinda became worried and called another principal. There was no conference. When Johnny walked in the door, Belinda confronted him and told him to pack and leave.

"Yeah, sure. I see how you look at her." Johnny slurred his words, and it was only 8:00 a.m.

"Ah, c'mon," said Billy Chas. "We dated a couple of times in high school, but you were the apple of her eye, and you know it. You two were meant for each other. That is until you decided to play around. Jerk."

"*Were*, is the key word. Okay, man. I have done some dumb stuff, but you ain't perfect either. You started that fire in the woods, Billy, and almost killed a bunch of those nigras."

"Shut up. You were at the ceremony. Always are," Billy Chas spat back.

"The work the Men's Alliance is what's keeping the nigras in their place in this town. Somebody's got to do something about all this liberation and integration crap."

The sound of a match scraped against a picnic table. Likely Johnny lighting a cigarette. He coughed and continued, "There is one thing I'm actually sorry about, though."

"I should never have hit that old nigra lady."

"What? You killed Mamiza's sister? Why didn't you tell me? We could have handled it. Damn it, Johnny."

"It was a fricken' accident, man. What could you have done about it? Pay for her funeral?"

"We could have smoothed it over, concocted some story." There was a pause then Billy Chas continued in a lowered tone, "Yeah, sure. I could have paid for her funeral."

"Well now, ain't you the thoughtful one, Mr. Bader," Johnny sneered. He followed with a roaring laugh that ended abruptly in a fitful cough.

He cleared his throat and continued his litany in a louder tone, "Furthermore, if it wasn't for that stupid Yankee girl and her soldier boy husband, none of this would have happened. You've been on edge since they got here, Billy boy, and ya' damn well know it."

"Well, if you'd played inside the field instead of outside the ballpark, maybe we'd have made some inroads with those two. Because of the fire, they're so scared they're moving out of Rohns. Claire would have probably looked in on Mama for me. Now I'll have to find a full-time caregiver to help her."

My muscles tensed and shivered at the mention of my name. *Showdown time.* Before I could make a move, Johnny grunted and sniffled, then spoke, "I have another confession."

"What else?" Billy Chas spat back.

"Well, I wanted to scare the Yankees a bit. I know Belinda's been poisoning Claire's mind. Trying to get her connected with female politics and all. So, I thought a little blaze might bring them down to earth. Ya' know, let them know who runs this town."

"Hey, wait a minute. Ya' started the fire at Rohns, my home? Are you insane?"

"It wasn't meant to be so big. Jis' got out of control."

"Ya' almost killed my mama, you damn drunk. Mama! I can't ever forgive you..."

A thud against the picnic tables and grunts from both. A gasp and heavy breathing. I had to get help and fast, but also stay inconspicuous. I sprinted toward the Ford like a gazelle on the hunt. Fists on flesh and a string of angry expletives continued.

Suddenly, a loud shot echoed from the direction of the two men. The ripple at the river's edge shattered into a splash. I turned to see the two struggling down on the embankment, Billy Chas trying to pull a gun from Johnny's hand.

Another shot. Billy Chas lay motionless on the ground.

Maybe I screamed. I only remember running toward the car and looking back at the scene as Johnny held the gun barrel in his mouth.

And then everything went dark.

CHAPTER 43

When I opened my eyes, white light was everywhere. Two young doctors chatted quietly with a nearby police officer. A long tube taped to a needle hung from my left arm. *Why was I in a hospital?* Bruce sat next to me, holding my free hand in both of his. "Honey, it's okay. You passed out. But you're all right." His voice was reassuring but not enough to erase the horror of the images flashing into my head of what I had seen on Broad Street.

"Dear God, Bruce. Johnny Bailey shot Billy Chas and then he shot himself. I saw them." My sobs overtook any further conversation, and I couldn't stop.

Bruce leaned over and took my face in his hands. "I'm so sorry you had to see all that, Claire. Damn it!" He placed a damp cheek against mine.

A nurse came rushing through the door. She excused herself as she injected something into the tube dangling from my arm. "This will help, darlin'," said the full-figured matron dressed in white from head to toe. "You've been through a lot, and you need to rest."

"May I just ask this lady a couple of questions first?" the officer interjected. "I promise not to be long." His charm could tame a roaring lion.

Not to be bamboozled, the nurse was curt. "Make it quick. In her condition, Mrs. Zuretski needs to rest." She gathered her tools and left. The two doctors nodded and followed.

With wide eyes, I wrapped both hands over my mouth and

whispered, "What did she mean, *in her condition?*" Her reference reminded me of the obstetrician appointment that I never kept.

"Oh, my God. The baby. Am I pregnant, Bruce?"

"I think the nurse meant you were in a state of shock. And, no, you're not pregnant. That was the first thing they checked. You've been struggling with some sort of virus. That's why you also had a temperature." Bruce's eyes were hooded, and his lips parted as if he wanted to say more. But we weren't alone. Not certain if I was relieved or not. There was so much I wanted to say to my husband at that moment but couldn't. *The on and off pregnancies...threats to my safety...Bruce's deployment.*

"Excuse me, folks. Ma'am if I could just find out a little more about what happened out there at the river's edge. Sorry, but it's important." Although patient, the officer was emphatic. He had a job to do and was obviously not leaving until he was satisfied.

Looking at the man, Bruce lowered himself back into the chair beside the bed. He reached for my hand and spoke to the officer, "Go ahead, officer. How can we help?"

I starred at the rotund policeman as he pulled out his notebook and pencil. My knees trembled under the sheets, as I posed the question, "Are Billy Chas Bader and Johnny Bailey alive?"

The officer cleared his throat and said, "Both men are dead, ma'am." I lowered my head, then listened to his explanation. "Johnny Bailey shot a bullet clear through Billy Chas Bader's skull. Then shot himself. Died instantly. Fortunately, an officer driving to Craig heard the shots and called through on his CB. Billy Chas Bader struggled to survive but didn't make it. He passed in the ambulance on the way to the hospital."

"What about Mrs. Bader? Does she know about Billy Chas? And Belinda?" I hesitated as I mentioned Belinda's name, after what Johnny had done. "Belinda is—rather, was—Johnny's wife."

"Yes, ma'am. Both ladies have been informed." He tipped his cap. "Some of the women from the Selma Ladies League are with Mrs. Bader now. She has a daughter in North Carolina who is on her way here." With a sigh, I glanced at Bruce and blinked. We didn't know Mrs. Bader had a daughter.

I painfully relayed what I had seen and heard between the two men that morning. At least as best as I could recall. I explained that Johnny sounded drunk. Billy Chas couldn't believe that he had cheated on Belinda, and they argued.

"I think it was all a big accident. Johnny and Billy Chas were friends. Johnny drank heavily, likely clouding his judgment." *Why was I making excuses?* The whole scene was so incredible. Somehow, I had to reconcile what I had witnessed.

"Was that all?" asked the officer. "Did they argue about anything else?"

Hesitating, I looked at Bruce. With a blank expression he repeated the officer's question, "What else did they argue about, Claire?"

My head ached. But my memory of the scene was vivid. Billy Chas and Johnny had admitted to many crimes. Straining to speak, I related the illicit acts I had overheard from the two men.

The officer busily took notes. When I finished, Bruce leaned forward, elbows on his knees and stared incredulously at me. He rubbed the back of his head. He looked at the officer. "Well, that sure explains a lot."

The policeman closed his notebook, thanked me, and said he'd be in touch if more was needed. I nodded with a weak grin. Bruce shook his hand, and the officer left the room. Closing my eyes and noticing the soft pillow beneath my head nudged me from the events of the moment. I faintly felt Bruce's kiss on my forehead.

CHAPTER 44

Our Selmians for Success class wasn't the same without Mamiza. The adults shared memories that stretched back to her childhood. I told everyone about Mamiza's hesitation to join the class. The story brought giggles and smiles. It was a good time to take to share a few special words about each of my students.

"You have all made such great progress these past few weeks." A gentle wave trickled inside me. Mamiza's spirit was here, among us. I stood an inch taller and released an appreciative sigh. "And I know Mamiza would want you to keep coming to class as we move into the fall session at the end of September."

With a decided nod, Lily Mae spoke up for all, "We be back, Missus Claire. Delberta be back too, don't you fret none. Her baby got a bad cold, and she is havin' a tough time with Mamiza gone and all."

Delberta hadn't returned after the funeral, and I was worried about her. "I'm so sorry her little one is ill. It's been a tough summer." My voice trailed off thinking about what also lay ahead for Bruce and me.

"Yes, she's a beauty and mighty smart too. But that poh girl was raped by one of them white mens." Opie's retort didn't hold back her vile disgust.

"What?" I sat down. "Did they find out who it was? Put him in jail?"

"Sad, sad, sad. Delberta didn't have her glasses on and couldn't tell who done it to her. Least that's what she says.

She had no case." Opie's head bowed. "And I'm afraid it done happen again."

"Outrageous!" Another twinge and my hand went to my belly. "We've got to find out who did this, Opie." I raised a fist, just as pounding resonated at the classroom door.

Before I could reach to open it, Belinda and Ruby stepped into the classroom. Strands from Belinda's loosely held ponytail fell over her ears. Her eyes were red and swollen, and she wore no makeup. Ruby had an arm around her friend's shoulder.

Belinda's perfectly round eyes didn't seduce their typical attention. They almost bulged as she glared straight ahead. The wall where her hand rested and held her upright. She shoved the hair from her face and stood near the doorway and teetered.

"I know my Johnny killed Billy Chas Bader. He didn't plan that. But he did plan to take..." tears dripped down her full cheeks, "to take his own life."

Ruby's knuckles tightened as her arm clung around Belinda's shoulders.

Unable to move, I stood in stunned silence, absorbing Belinda's pain. My adult students glared in disbelief at the two white women. I wanted to wrap my arms around my friend, but the vehement expression on her face suggested otherwise.

With a triumphant wave of a sheet of paper into the air, she curled her lips and stared at each of us before speaking, "This note was written by Johnny. It says it all...hit-and-run of Mariah Jesse Willis...and the fathering of Delberta's child, soon to be *children*." She shouted the last words of this sentence.

"Guess the cad couldn't take the birth of number two! Johnny was in cahoots with Billy Chas Bader, master perpetrator of evil deeds." Belinda paused to take a deep breath. "But that's not all. Johnny and one of his daddy's paid farm hands started the blaze at Rohns Manor. Can you believe that?"

She screamed her final question to all, repeating it a second time. "The plan was to scare the hell out of you and Bruce, Claire. But the damn deed backfired on that rotten piece of flesh. Never knew they'd kill dear Mamiza and almost killed Sylvia Bader." She reached to grip Ruby's free hand.

I walked slowly toward Belinda. Not to be consoled, she firmly held up a halting palm. "I'm so sorry, y'all, and Claire. I had to say it. Say it directly to your faces."

Ruby reached out and squeezed me tightly. She turned and followed Belinda toward the door. Soon, the only sound to be heard was the clicking of high heels as the pair walked down the empty hallway.

I perched a hip on a nearby desk and looked upon the stunned faces that sat motionless before me. Although I had been personally privy to the murder suicide of Johnny Bailey, it felt like a snug bandage was just yanked from my wound. Seeing pain drench the face of my beautiful friend hurt as much as watching her husband kill Billy Chas and take his own life. I knew healing would take time, and I admired her strength. Her relentless courage in this moment was not typical. *If I were Belinda, how would I have responded?*

As I mentally toyed with words of hope and more condolences, Reverend Mease stood. Slowly splaying both palms heavenward, he tilted his head back and raised his eyes. This was the same heavenward glance I recalled upon seeing him during our entry into Selma. All stood, folded their hands, and closed their eyes. The Reverend quoted scripture:

So shall ye say unto Joseph, Forgive, I pray thee now, the trespasses of thy brethren and their sin; for they did thee unto evil: and now we pray thee, forgive the trespasses of thy servants of the God of thy father. Genesis 50:17

When he had finished all responded with a loud and assertive, "Amen!"

"Thank you, Reverend." My words were barely audible. *Indeed, the Lord is our judge.* No need to say anymore.

Focusing on the lessons during the final hour of class was hard, but the students were accustomed to setbacks. Attending to their academic tasks was beyond reasonable expectation, but all tried. The Reverend rewrote a sermon for the third time and Lily Mae and Opie quizzed each other on the practice voter registration questions. With an upcoming election in November, I was hopeful for Lily Mae's and Opie's success.

Since Bruce struggled with a cold, I had driven by myself. Torn by a desire to seek Belinda and sit and help her, I had matters to settle at home first. I pulled into the back of Rohns near what was now a blackened old shed and went inside. Bruce was propped up in bed, a box of tissues at his side and sifting through paper files. I told him the story of Belinda's revelation.

"Those two guys were in cahoots in the worse way. Poor Belinda. What will she do?" He shook his head, and I snuggled up next to him.

"We'll take care of her." I blinked and nodded.

"Wait a minute," said Bruce. "What do you mean 'We'll take care of her?'"

I lifted my chin, swallowed hard, and continued, "Bruce, while you're overseas, I'm going to stay here, in Selma. It's only for six months."

"Claire, you're upset. Please be reasonable. Where will you live? Who will help *you*?"

"I'm going to take Ruby and Bobby up on their offer to stay in the little carriage house behind their place. I've also asked Lucy to come here and live with me."

"You're joking!" said Bruce, eyes wide as the buttons on his uniform epaulets. "Queen Lucy isn't really going to move to Selma. Do your parents know this?" He turned his head and sneezed.

"Lucy told them our plan. And I haven't returned a call, but I will—sometime soon."I'd get a lecture from my mother. The whole conversation would likely not end well.

"Since we're both going to be without our men, why not? Besides, Selma needs labor lawyers, and she can use help caring for my new niece or nephew. In fact, helping Lucy with the baby could help me learn more about how to be a mama." My eyes widened and I smiled playfully at my husband.

Bruce's face softened.

"And I can still be a part of the Fems for Freedom." I rested my case.

Bruce pulled me closer and brought his lips tenderly to mine. Gently releasing his embrace, he said, "Well, what are we waiting for?"

I looked at him blankly, uncertain what he meant.

"It's time we packed and called your parents to tell them the good news," he said.

"What good news would that be?" I posed the obvious question.

Wide eyes again, with two hands raised into the air. "That Selma is lucky to have two new lady citizens: *Welcome to Selma, Alabama!*"

Tapping an index finger to my lifted chin, I said, "Hmm. Seems as though I've seen those words somewhere." *They held a very differing meaning for me now!*

EPILOGUE

1970

Packing up materials after the Selmians for Success class one evening, I found a page of notes Reverend Mease must have forgotten. In his finely scripted manuscript, this verse spoke to me: *"For when your faith is tested, your endurance has a chance to grow."* James 1:3

Praying hard every day didn't make the time go by any faster or lessen the pain of Bruce's absence. It had only been a few months since he left, but it seemed like years. If there was any solace, it was having my sister close. I never thought I'd say that about Lucy. Never. Whoever said: *when a door is closed, a window will be opened* had a gift for optimism. I never thought of the possibility of our relationship being my window of hope.

Busyness helped too. I made curtains for the cottage and continued to try new recipes. Lucy shocked me when she signed out a gardening book from the library. Being healthy for the baby drove her toward this project and she feverishly crafted plans for what vegetables would be most productive and what planting time was best. With her belly barely showing baby growth and her vita, she had easily snagged a legal position with the Selma Interreligious Project, a Civil Rights organization dedicated to helping create economic opportunity for blacks in Selma. Lucy's support of black women in the Freedom Quilting Bee became her professional passion, while she voluntarily advised the Fems for Freedom group.

Although President Richard Nixon signed an extension of the Voting Rights Act of 1965 and the polling fees disappeared, the literacy tests prevailed. I continued teaching the adults with high expectation for all to become registered voters. They could write their names and addresses, birthdays, days of the week, months of the year and more.

With the upcoming presidential election, my students were further motivated to achieve their voter's registration card, and Reverend Mease was the first to do so. We celebrated his success with pecan pie, topped with piles of whipped cream. Delberta returned to class, even though her baby due date was close. Although too young to vote, her reading was getting stronger, and she often brought a tossed-out newspaper to class to read and share the news of the day. She was smart and announced that she was going to become a teacher someday.

If only Lily Mae and Opie could muster the same confidence.

The gubernatorial race between George Wallace and Albert Brewer proved to be a defined racial struggle. Mr. Wallace wasn't a KKK member, but his segregationist leanings were no secret. George Wallace also had strong backing from many Alabamians. His opponent and the residing Alabama governor, Albert Brewer, proposed a more moderate, middle of the line approach. He was behind education reform for *all* Selma citizens. The race between the two would likely be historically pivotal.

Literacy tests continued as a measure to assess the "right" to vote. Often this privilege was achieved by asking *certain* prospective voters to interpret abstract provisions of the U.S. Constitution. Often applications would be rejected for what officials called *errors*. With the added guidance of Winnie Holmes, my adult learners studied the Constitution and potential comprehension questions. Winnie was on top of the changing rules as well. Now would-be voter registrants were expected to be able to recite the Preamble. They also needed to be prepared to explain the meaning.

Winnie's personal story as a teacher and college-educated adult who did not initially pass the voter registration tests was intimidating. Opie had the memorization down well but continued to bring up her cousin's experience when we talked about getting her voter's registration card. It was more about Opie's self-confidence than it was about her ability to deliver. Lily Mae stammered during practice recitations and would wring her hands when she misspoke. She was making progress, only more slowly.

~

Walking out of Piggly Wiggly with Lucy one Saturday morning, I shared my empty toolbox. "I don't know what else to do about Opie and Lily Mae and neither does Winnie. I just feel that they could pass the voter's registration test. Problem is, *they* don't think so!"

Approaching the car, I positioned a sack on my hip and sighed as I shoved a hand into my pocket for the keys.

"Missus Claire, Missus Claire!" Opie and Lily Mae scurried up beside me, with boundless grins that stretched toward their ear lobes.

"Fancy running into you, this mornin'," said Opie as she tugged my grocery bag from my arms and set it on the ground.

Perplexed I knit my brows and grinned at these two girl-like women. *What were they up to?*

"Ready," said Opie as she nodded at Lily Mae.

"Never been more ready," answered Lily Mae.

Each reached inside their handbags, pulled out an envelope and tugged at the insides and held up a voter's registration card.

Lucy plopped her grocery bag on the ground and ran over to join our group hug.

"If only Mamiza could be here," I whispered.

"Oh, she is here, Missus, Claire," said Opie.

"She sho' is," echoed Lily Mae, leaning in and squeezing tighter.

AUTHOR'S NOTE

The 1960s were far from groovy. The Civil Rights Act of 1964, Voting Rights Act of 1965, the Vietnam War, and Martin Luther King's famous march from Selma to Montgomery, Alabama, all left indelible historical marks on the United States. These events still serve as a baseline for how far our country has come and how much farther we still need to go.

Beyond the Pettus Bridge was written to share a story that traverses old Southern traditions and 1960s conflicts from the perspective of a young Midwestern white woman and teacher. The story reflects what racial bias looked like in our American culture more than a half-century ago from the view of the main character, Claire Zuretski. It is a work of historical fiction grounded in facts and truths and blended with an even greater human-interest element.

I lived this story in Selma, Alabama, in 1969.

As the new bride of my college sweetheart, Frank, who was fortuitously called to serve in the military during the Vietnam crisis, and enlisted in the Air Force, I vividly recall the prejudices held by people I encountered in our move to Selma where he was stationed at Craig Air Force Base. These attitudes shocked me then and continue to do so to this day. I have been simultaneously encouraged by the progress that has emerged over the decades and the many people I have encountered along the path who have failed to allow skin color to define a person's worth. Throughout my career as a teacher at all educational levels, preschool through college, I have had the privilege and honor to see this value firsthand in my students and their families.

The Edmund Pettus Bridge, officially declared a National Historic Landmark on February 27, 2013, was the site of the brutal and bloody beatings of demonstrators marching from Selma to the Alabama state capital in Montgomery to champion voter rights in 1965. The bridge is named for Edmund Winston Pettus, a former brigadier general in the Confederate Army, a U.S. senator from Alabama, and a grand dragon of the Ku Klux Klan. As this novel goes to press, more than 100,000 people have signed a petition to rename the Pettus Bridge after John Lewis, a recently deceased U. S. representative from Georgia, who participated in the 1965 march.

The sites and landscape surrounding the city of Selma in the novel—the antebellum mansion; the Old Live Oak Cemetery; the schools, churches, and businesses; and even many of the people referenced in the novel—are authentic. Names have been changed and many individuals have also passed away. Other characters are portrayed based on an amalgamation of traits to augment, connect, and contribute to the tale.

Upon further research and a return visit with my husband to Selma in 2011, I discovered a great deal about the clandestine activities of women who tirelessly endeavored to bring about positive change in civil rights in Selma. Much of the collaborative movement of both black and white women took place underground in the 1960s. Through personal interviews with teachers, employees of civil service, and long-time Selma residents, I learned of life experiences of people my age, while also talking with younger residents who substantiated and expanded the narrative.

Citizens of both races told me about life in Selma, learning to read and write, registering to vote, and living in shanties and shotgun houses. They also talked about the restrictive social clubs, antebellum mansions, and pressure to maintain the prevailing Southern way of life. None of this magically went away with the passage of civil rights legislation.

Documentation of the underestimated contributions and changes brought about by the women of Selma was found in the context of a master's thesis written in 1989 by Elizabeth Bostick, Ph.D. I am deeply grateful for Dr. Bostick's willingness to share her thesis, books, and knowledge to help me gain a deeper appreciation of a sisterhood I did not know existed at the time we lived in Selma. Her research helped me to develop a key theme of sisterhood that prevails throughout the storyline.

Dr. Bostick is a white woman who grew up in Selma during the 1960s. She wrote about courageous females in "Women in Selma – Unfairly Forgotten." The underlying study of the Females for Freedom, my fictional name for this group in *Beyond the Pettus Bridge*, was about these educated and honorable ladies of both races who did more than "hang out their wash to dry" (*Birmingham News*, 1965). The Southern sisterhood was inspired by faith, core values, and a tireless spirit to erase the social stigma and help citizens to see how they are more alike than they are different.

Beyond the Pettus Bridge shines a spotlight on these brave women who believed in family, freedom, and faith, while they also struggled to uphold the traditional values of Southern women of the times. The culture, norms, and convictions of these educated and courageous women have helped to reshape social values and push issues of racial inequality to the forefront. The collaborative force of their efforts and the circumstances of the times and place ultimately brings my novel's protagonist, Claire Zuretski, a young white, headstrong, newlywed Yankee schoolteacher to this place and time to be a part of a change effort she never anticipated.

With much of the dissension and polarization that continues to prevail 50+ years later, I still have faith in American citizens. We have come a long way, but can always do better, work together, acknowledge our strengths and similarities, and respect our differences. In fact, today we are better as a nation than what I lived during that time.

Let's continue the journey and never give up the *dream*—nor our *hope*!

Respectfully,
Trish Ennis Dolasinski, Ed.D.

QUESTIONS FOR
BOOK CLUB DISCUSSIONS

1. Which character most powerfully stirred feelings of empathy?

2. What is the significance of the title: *Beyond the Pettus Bridge*?

3. Who was your favorite character? Why?

4. Claire and Winnie are teachers. What did you learn about the teaching profession from these two women?

5. How were Winnie and Claire alike? How were they different?

6. How did Mamiza support the female characters in the novel?

7. What did you learn about Civil Rights in Selma, Alabama, during the post-Civil Rights legislation period (late 1960s)?

8. The author lived much of this story. Why didn't she write the story as a memoir?

9. Claire is strongly urged to teach in a "white school." Why does she resist the offers from Billy Chas and Johnny?

10. The theme of racial violence is overt and covert throughout the novel. Do you think cultural norms and attitudes have changed in the past fifty years? Why or why not?

11. In what parts of the novel do you observe how adversity brings people together?

12. What was an "*ah-ha*" moment for you in this novel?

13. How did Claire change throughout the novel?

14. What role does Christianity and faith play in *Beyond the Pettus Bridge*?

15. The theme of "sisterhood" runs throughout the novel. What aspects of this theme speak the loudest for you today?

16. Is Bruce a patriotic character? Why or why not?

17. An underlying theme of *Beyond the Pettus Bridge* is the Vietnam War. How does it impact the characters?

18. At Mamiza's funeral, Claire says, "Mamiza brought us all here—black and white...this place is like a watershed with all ecological pieces fitting into their niche." How does Claire's reflection offer hope for *what is* and/or what *can be*?

9 798985 506006